D09063242

PROPERTY OF
EMMAUS PUBLIC LIBRARY
EMMAUS, PENNSYLVANIA

155.937   Donnelly, Katherine Fair
DONN   Recovering from the
          loss of a sibling.

•187331

Recovering From the Loss of a Sibling

Katherine Fair Donnelly

Dodd, Mead & Company

New York

EMMAUS PUBLIC LIBRARY

EMMAUS, PA. 18049

Copyright Acknowledgments

Grateful acknowledgment is made to the following for permission to reprint previously published material:
Journal of American Medical Association for *JAMA* article February 10, 1984–Vol. 251, No. 6 pp. 6–7 by Susan C.M. Scrimshaw, Ph.D. and Daniel M.S. March, Ph.D. entitled 'I Had a Baby Sister but She Only Lasted One Day' "Copyright 1984, American Medical Association."

"Naming a Surviving Sibling's Child"—appeared in *Thanatos* magazine and is reprinted here by permission of the authors Judith and Allen Haimes.

Copyright © 1988 by Katherine Fair Donnelly

A GAMUT BOOK

All rights reserved

No part of this book may be reproduced in any form without permission in writing from the publisher.
Published by Dodd, Mead & Company, Inc.
71 Fifth Avenue, New York, N.Y. 10003
Manufactured in the United States of America
Designed by Marilyn E. Beckford

First Edition

1   2   3   4   5   6   7   8   9   10

Library of Congress Cataloging-in-Publication Data

Donnelly, Katherine Fair.
Recovering from the loss of a sibling / Katherine Fair Donnelly.
Includes index.
ISBN 0-396-08859-7
ISBN 0-396-08875-9 {PBK}
1. Bereavement—Psychological aspects.   2. Brothers and sisters - Death—Psychological aspects.   I. Title.
BF575.G7D665 1987
155.9 37—dc19
87-26104 CIP

EMMAUS PUBLIC LIBRARY
EMMAUS, PA. 18049

Dedication

To my mother, who was a surviving sibling, and
to my father, whose sister died at age twelve.
All four of my grandparents were bereaved
parents. No one ever understood them. It is hoped
that this book will in some ways make up for it—
not only to them, but to all bereaved parents
and surviving siblings.

Acknowledgments

My grateful thanks to John H. Donnelly for his careful reading of the manuscript and whose guiding hand and heart were given many times into the wee hours in order that this work might be accomplished.

Special thanks to Angela Purpura, former chapter leader and Metropolitan regional coordinator of The Compassionate Friends. Because of her earnest desire to offer assistance to siblings of all age levels, she encouraged me to undertake this book, which would not have come to fruition without her insight and help.

My warm gratitude to Sister Jane Marie Lamb and Jeanette Colburn of the SHARE group for their wonderful guidance and support in helping to make this book one of hope and sharing.

Sincere thanks to Dr. and Mrs. Allen Haimes and their children for reading the manuscript and offering valuable suggestions to help surviving siblings and bereaved parents—and a most special thank you to Michael and Michaela.

I am especially appreciative of the many kindnesses extended by Abraham Malawski, chapter leader of The Compassionate Friends, who contributed so much in his observations and perceptions.

I am also appreciative of the many kindnesses extended by Barbara Beckman, associate editor, Dodd, Mead & Company, who was unflagging in her efforts to bring this book to completion and who went the extra mile to make it possible.

Thanks are given to Pamela Landau for her splendid editing of the manuscript and to Marilyn E. Beckford for design.

My grateful thanks to Franc Lacinski, Robin Bartlett, Mary-Angel Blount and Kay Radtke for their many courtesies.

I wish to express my deep appreciation to Jane Cullen who, because of her compassionate and caring help, will always remain in the hearts of bereaved parents and surviving siblings.

My grateful thanks to those who read all or portions of the manuscript and who made helpful suggestions: Athena Drewes, Karen Schlesier Eisen, Vivian Kessler, Ann Magid, Art and Ronnie Peterson, Marilyn Platz, and Dr. Roberta Temes.

Most of all, my warmest thanks and deep appreciation are given to the participants in this book who made it such a warm outpouring of compassion and sharing, and who have so generously permitted the use of their real names.

Contents

Dedication   iii
Acknowledgments   iv
In Memoriam   vi
Preface   vii
Introduction   1

Chapter One   A Sibling Dies   11

Chapter Two   This Isn't Real   31

Chapter Three   Anger   45

Chapter Four   Guilt Feelings   57

Chapter Five   Symptoms of Grief   65

Chapter Six   Coping with Holidays and Anniversaries   77

Chapter Seven   The Younger Ones—Part I   85

Chapter Eight   The Younger Ones—Part II   111

Chapter Nine   Other Heartbreaks   125

Chapter Ten   Parents and Other Family Members   138

Chapter Eleven   At School   157

Chapter Twelve   At the Workplace   169

Chapter Thirteen   The Haimes Family   175

Chapter Fourteen   Chuck Akerland   185

Chapter Fifteen   A Father's Thoughts on a Surviving Son   195

Chapter Sixteen   A Mother Talks of Her Surviving Son   201

Chapter Seventeen   Lynn Gardner and Her Children   209

Chapter Eighteen   Holly Shaw   216

Chapter Nineteen   Messages of Hope   226

Chapter Twenty   Helping Hands   236

Suggested Readings   256
Index   259

In Memoriam

Gustav Joseph Akerland III
Sylvia Banschick
Terry Michael Barber
Janine Anne Bellucci
Clay Morgan Bernhard
Charles Bernstein
David John Boden
Nicky Brauer
Sandra Brauer
Elizabeth Cabot
Linwood Campbell
Jesse Ray Campbell
Sherri Campbell
Trevor Campbell
Edward Scott Capriotti
Tony Carrion
Diane Randazza Channing
Sondra Rhea Chick
Kerin Suzanne Cohen
Christopher Colburn
Kevin Conroy
Russ Diak
David Dohrenwend
Wendy Famiano
Alan David Frogel
Freeda Magid Goldman
Philip Goldstein
Katherine Harley Griffith
Gregory Griswold
Michael Steven Haimes
Leslie Joy Heitner
Jessie V. Jordan
Carolyn Keats
Gilbert Kelly
Robyn Kessler
Michael Jay Kraf
Mitchell Kreindler
Simon Kreindler

Earline L. Lamb
Melvin M. Lamb
Harvey Mark Malawski
Elizabeth March
Andrew Milne
Timothy Thomas Moran
Michael Allen Nelson
Tamara Marie Netzke
Tony Peterson
John Pfister
Cassandra Purpura
George R. Pustay
Jessica Rachael Pustay
Suzanne Rebecca Pustay
Carl Leonard Radtke
Lenny Ruiz
Tracy Ralph Saulisberry
Mary Rose Schwaegler
Billy Schlesier
Randy C. Selzer
Philip Scott Spector
Dorothy Spiotto
Walter J. Stanley, Jr.
Christopher Sundland
Ronald Emil Tabatt
Dennis Sherill Tart
Brian Christopher Teague
Kathleen Toomey
Larry Toomey
Mark F. Warner
Mark Harris Wilson
Brian Witty
Rusty Witty

*For all those whose names do
not appear here, they will
always remain in our hearts.*

Preface

At last! A book that tells it like it really is—and it's tough.

As a bereaved sibling, I only wish this book had been written sooner. After reading it, I am so relieved! I'm "normal," for whatever that is! I wish that my brother, Larry, could have held on a little longer after my sister's death, and read it too.

Readers who have not suffered a loss may find themselves emotionally drained from these powerful yet painfully true stories. For these surviving siblings and bereaved parents who are searching for ways to cope, *Recovering From the Loss of a Sibling* provides a catharsis in the sharing of experiences. Part of the getting well process is going through the pain of grief.

This book offers a rare opportunity to share in the lives of many bereaved families—their pain, sorrow, struggles, and their love. It has within it the ingredients to help us to grow, to know others have experienced such hurt and still live on. To know we are not alone in itself is a source of encouragement, a source of hope.

Beyond this, the book provides others who come into contact with surviving siblings and bereaved parents (the clergy, educators, extended families, relatives and friends) with the insight and understanding they need in order to be of help.

I intend to give this book to my parents and to the parents of other siblings I know. I believe it can be used as a tool of communication to help bridge that terrible gap between grieving parents and their surviving children—the surviving sibling. It rings with truth, yet doesn't preach.

There were many times after the deaths of my sister and brother when I was overwhelmed with my own grief, but because I could see how badly my parents were suffering, I didn't want to burden them further. In this book, I was astonished to see how many siblings felt as I did. *That's one of the important messages the book conveys: siblings need to know that other siblings feel as they do.* The best way for a sibling to be helped is by talking to another sibling. That is exactly what the siblings do in this book—they tell how they feel so that other siblings can benefit.

Bereaved parents are thirsty to know how best to help their surviving children and this book provides incredible insight into the hearts and souls of siblings and the depth of their sorrow after such a loss. We learn of the problems attendant after catastrophic illness, suicide, murder, accidental death, and infant death. We hear of the pain of the parents who are desperate in their quest to help their surviving children after a loss.

I also intend to give this book to some clergy, social workers, and psychologists that I know. Perhaps they too can learn from us siblings, and some day siblings too will be understood, and their grief recognized! I believe this book will stand out as a classic because it encompasses every age level and imposes no time frames, nor is it geared to one specific group.

For me, as a young married woman, with a good husband and two wonderful sons, running a household and working full time, my grief was very complicated. Although my grief was different, it was still the same as a sibling living at home with their parents, seeing that now empty bed, an extra seat at the dinner table, or an empty crib or lonesome extra bicycle. I know that their grief must be intense, an ever present reminder—and yet, we still suffer.

Being both a sibling of a dead brother and/or sister, our guilt, our hurt, and our questions are the same: "Why them? Why not me? Was it because of a disagreement we had? Could I have kept them safe? Will mom and dad still love me?" The questions are endless, although only God knows the answers. As siblings, we ask the same questions in our hearts forever. There is no easy way through the pain of grief, but being able to share with the other sisters and brothers in this book helps me to understand myself a little better.

I remember growing up as the oldest, and always taking care of Larry and Kathleen. I took them everywhere I went, sometimes resenting it. I thought, "Well, soon they will be old enough to take care of themselves and I'll have my play-time, my fun-time, to myself." But because of their untimely deaths (Kathleen's because of a drunk driver and Larry's suicide), I will always be taking care and preserving their memories.

Fortunately for me, I can find purpose and life after their deaths by working with MADD (Mothers Against Drunk Drivers), an organization that began with a single mother, but which has expanded to other family members as well as friends. I have been able to use my grief constructively to help others in the name of Larry and Kathleen, and to help prevent the murders on our highways.

This book gives me strength to carry on. And, after other siblings read it, they too will see how they can and will survive.

Madeleine Toomey Pflaumbaum,

Surviving Sibling

President, MADD (Mothers Against Drunk Drivers),
Long Island chapter

Member of The Compassionate Friends Siblings Group

Introduction

"Forgotten grievers" is the name often given to children who experience the loss of a brother or sister. Perhaps they could also be called "lonely mourners."

If confronted by problems of a different kind, those grievers, lonely or forgotten, could have turned for consolation to parents, but those two adults, having lost a child, are too overwhelmed by their own devastating pain. One grief-stricken parent confided, "Being a parent is never easy. When a child has died, it is more difficult being parents to the children who survive. To be faced with an acting-out adolescent, a distant child, or one who is more dependent than before is more than a bereaved parent can cope with."

To add to the "forgotten grievers'" burden of loneliness and grief, it is possible that they had a love-hate relationship with the one who has died. The love is natural, as is shown in a scene in the film, *Boys Town*, in which a teenager is seen carrying a small boy on his back. A priest asks the older boy, "Isn't he too heavy?" The lad replies, "He's not heavy, Father, he's my brother." We'd like to think that all siblings behave in such loving ways, but competitive human nature deems otherwise. It's not unusual to hear brothers and sisters address one another in such less-than-loving ways as, "Go jump in the lake and take a rock with you." Or, "You're wearing my blouse. Take it off and don't you dare touch anything of mine again." Or, "How would you like a punch in the nose?"

The many verbal and physical punches thrown in childhood may continue to be thrown in adulthood—and for as long as pecking orders persist within family units. Yet, after the death of a sibling, brothers and sisters tend to remember those hostile events rather than the loving ones, and they think, "How could I have done that?" Or, "Why was I so angry?"

A sibling who is mourning the loss of a brother or sister should remember that he or she is not the only one who has ever taken part in a domestic upset, not the only one who has ever shouted at a sister or who ever wanted to hit a brother over the head. In childhood, it's natural for siblings to argue, to blame one another. It's part of the desire to learn to deal with human relationships, to excel, to win our parents' approval. It's part of growing, just as when young puppies fight and tumble in the grass. We practice on our sisters or brothers, but we gradually learn that hitting one another or getting angry doesn't always bring good results.

But none of those experiences prepares us for the loss of a sister or brother. After a death, whether we are young children or now adults, rather than remembering all the good things we shared or did together, we often hark back to the times we shouted angrily, slapped, or punched, thus creating heavy burdens of guilt for ourselves.

The range of problems and needs the surviving siblings encounter is almost limitless. And the ages of those brothers and sisters vary as much as the ages of the children who died. However, both younger and older siblings have many common concerns: "Will this soon happen to me?" "Are my parents going to die next?" "It should have been me. Why wasn't it?" "My sister was my parents' favorite, and they don't care about me." "God must have punished me for being mean to my brother." "I'm all alone now. I've lost my parents too because they talk about nothing but the one who died."

It is hard to think a child should die before its parents, but in the United States alone over 400,000 children *under the age of twenty-five* will die this year from catastrophic illness, infant diseases, suicide, murder, and accidents.

Large numbers of those children will be survived by siblings numbering in the millions—children who are yearning to understand and to be understood, children who are in pain after the loss of a brother or sister. Those millions become tens of millions, with each year also bringing the deaths of adult children *over twenty-five* who die before their parents.

Enough of figures, for this book is not meant to be a cold statistical survey. Rather, it is a warmth of sharing. The wisdom in it is an outpouring of intimate human emotions of siblings of all age levels. No matter if the surviving sibling is six, sixteen, twenty-six, forty-six, or sixty-six, the emotions experienced by siblings after the death of a sister or brother are rooted in early childhood relationships. The impact of that death may reactivate guilts, fears, resentments, rivalry in vying for parental affections, in addition to love, hate, jealousy, anger, and other emotions.

Often, reality does not set in immediately after the death of a sibling. A young child may not accept that a brother or sister is really dead, but rather may fantasize that he or she is absent on an extended trip. This may be particularly true for those age twelve and under. If a child is told, "Your brother is in Heaven because he was so good, God wanted him back," younger children may be afraid that if they are good, God will take them away too—and the subsequent formation of poor sleep habits or behavior problems may continue for a long time. With older siblings, problems may be encountered months or years later, when the finality of the death is actually faced.

In some instances, bereaved parents assume that children cannot cope with the death and will try to protect them by leaving them out of the discussions or accompanying rituals. "Let's not discuss this in front of him." "This will only upset her, so don't say anything." "He's too young to go to a funeral." "Let's talk later after they are asleep." Experts say it is best for parents to be frank with surviving siblings about the death. Children want to participate and share, but often are confused by being left alone, without answers to their questions, at a time when they are anxiously seeking the warmth and love they need. They do not understand the extreme change in grief-stricken parents who, because of their own intense sorrow, may not understand or may overlook or neglect the surviving children.

School can present problems for surviving children at all age levels, from kindergarten through college. Teachers and classmates may either give too much sympathy or avoid the sibling entirely. In some cases the problems encountered by younger children come in the form of relentless teasing from schoolmates. A ten-year-old surviving sibling told of taunts from boys on her school bus. "Your sister's dead, your sister's dead." Older siblings may develop problems of short attention span or inability to concentrate. Teachers may become impatient when children prefer to keep to themselves or are reluctant to participate. Often a surviving child may not wish to speak up in class or may show a decrease in activity. One sibling recalled a teacher who asked, "Don't you think it's about time you were over this?" Surviving siblings may only be asking for time to recuperate from the shock and to make needed adjustments in their lives.

Bereaved parents may tend to eulogize the dead child, often glorifying his or her "goodness," "cleverness," and so on, rather than remembering the "real" person who had faults as well. Surviving children, hearing repeated references to the wonderful attributes of the child who has died, may feel they are neither loved as much as, nor able to compete "alive" with an enshrined "dead" idol. This inability to live up to the glorified and untrue portrait of a sibling may cause surviving children to harbor ill thoughts toward the dead brother or sister and ultimately can lead to guilt feelings.

Children need to be assured that nothing they said, thought, or did caused the death of the sibling. Often they fear that because they were jealous or angry after a quarrel or had a bad thought about their sibling, that action was the cause of the death. This issue is of deep concern to surviving siblings. Their anxiety compounds the feeling that they are unworthy and that the dead child must indeed have been the "best" one.

Surviving children react to the way their parents behave after the death of a son or daughter. If parents display honest emotions, children will become aware that it is permissible to cry, to laugh, to be sad or angry. Because remaining siblings are often confused by the distress seen in their parents after the death, they may suppress their own feelings. Some may return to behavior previously outgrown, such as bedwetting, thumb-sucking, or clinging to parents' coattails. But whether children are expressing or suppressing their feelings, *they do grieve*—and often deeply.

Even very small children are aware that the behavior of their parents has changed after a death. It is also true that many parents do not credit children with having an under-standing of the strain caused by that death. One bereaved mother could not cope with the daily activities of two surviving toddlers, ages three and five. They ran wild, climbing over the furniture, wreaking havoc in the closets. One day, some months later, the mother looked at her watch and suddenly yelled out to the children: "Look at the time! Just what do you think you are doing up at this hour? You march right upstairs to bed." The five-year-old replied, "Now we know you are getting better, Mommy. You are hollering at us again."

Painful and frightening thoughts can assail surviving chil-dren. A sibling who is suddenly left as an only child may suffer the fear that he will be left all alone if his parents should also die. Children who are approaching the same age as the brother or sister who died often wonder if the same thing will happen to them. "Will I die, too, when I get to be eight, 'cause he was eight when he died'?" This foreboding holds true for surviving children no matter what the age level. The fear of a premature death is just as real for a twenty-eight-year-old as it is for an eight-year-old.

It is not unusual for surviving children to assume the role of the parent, wanting to soothe their parents' pain and anguish. It may help if siblings talk to someone other than their par-ents—someone they can converse with comfortably. Often siblings are reluctant to speak even the dead child's name—especially in the presence of their parents. The thought that mentioning their dead brother or sister's name may create pain for their parents causes such surviving siblings to suppress many other emotions. A nineteen-year-old sister refuses to acknowledge holidays by not returning home from college on those occasions. Her reasoning was that it made her parents uncomfortable and "my mother would go out to the backyard and cry." The young woman goes home to visit the week *after* holidays. In another family, when a surviving son would not utter his dead brother's name, his father said to him, "If you're afraid that you will hurt us by mentioning his name, please understand it would hurt us more if you did not say it."

Parents may not learn of problems endured by siblings until a much later date. One son confronted his father a year afterward and told of his deep resentment that his parents had devoted so much time and attention to his dying sister. The son felt his own needs were ignored and was angry at both his parents. The father was concerned about his son's unhappiness and replied, "I'm grateful that you've opened up the line of communication by telling me your thoughts. But, I have to be honest with you. If I had to do it again, I don't think I could do it any other way. Try to imagine that you had been the sick one. Your sister was dying. You and your brothers were healthy, living. With whom, then, should we have been with? Your sister needed every moment of our attention, every hour of our concern." The son did not agree. However, with this initial discussion, the parents and their son were able to share emotions long suppressed, and it was insightful for both parents and sibling alike.

In some instances, after the death of a child, parents tend to overprotect the survivor, afraid to let the siblings resume "normal" activities. Although coming home from a date at eleven P.M. had been perfectly acceptable *before* their child's death, that same 11 P.M. curfew now evokes deep fears about the safety of surviving children. Parents worry that a surviving child or children may suffer a premature death or the same fate as the one who had died. Thus the siblings are sent off with a barrage of warnings: "How late will you be?" "Be sure to call us when you get there." "Don't forget to call if you are going to be late." As one sibling said, "Mom, you can't hold me on a short leash for the rest of my life because Michael was killed in a car." In this case, the parents relented and the surviving daughter was permitted to get her own car.

Conversely, surviving children are often haunted by the

fear of something untoward happening to their parents. One of the common reactions arising after the death of a sibling is the fear of being left alone. Younger children may experience difficulty in sleeping when their parents are away for even a few hours. Older surviving children also suffer anxiety about their parents' whereabouts. A twenty-four-year-old sibling tells of the time her mother was due to meet her after work. When the mother had not arrived on time, Karen was upset. Ten minutes later, she was more than concerned. After half an hour had passed, her fear was so great that she called the police. In another instance, that same sibling tried to reach her mother by telephone but received a busy signal. After several attempts, each answered by the same busy signal, she called the operator who advised her the phone was off the hook. Karen's immediate thoughts were, "My mother's been murdered! Something terrible has happened or the phone would *not* be off the hook." Karen's rationale was that if her brother could be killed in an accident, then her mother could be next.

Joshua, a young boy of nine, was called into the principal's office at school and told that his brother had died in a bicycle accident. The principal, wanting to help, told the boy it was better that his brother had died because "If he had lived, he would have been a vegetable." Stricken, the boy yelled out, "I wouldn't care if he was a cabbage or a lettuce as long as he lived." Even the most well-meaning person may not have the experience or expertise to help surviving siblings.

In some instances, a surviving child will wish to hold onto something that belonged to the dead brother or sister—a piece of jewelry, a scarf, a shirt—or will wear something that belonged to the child who died. Parents often resent seeing their living child wearing a piece of clothing worn by the dead sibling.

This same type of problem intrudes on the lives of children whose parents remind them of the dead sibling at every family event—a graduation, wedding, bar mitzvah, birthday. Such comments as, "How proud your sister would be if she were here," or "How happy your brother would have been to see you graduate" cause a surviving child to wonder, "Well, what about me? Don't you think I'm important enough to have my own day?" Surviving children should not have the happenings in their lives overshadowed by constant reminders of how their deceased sibling would feel at such an event. Survivors deserve to shine on their own. On the special occasions of living children, wise parents will mention the child who died only if the surviving child speaks of it first. But the knowledge that the lost child can never have another such occasion may cause parents to lose sight of the fact that "recovering" does not mean one has to forget their dead child. There will always be moments when parents' thoughts turn to their deceased child—but these thoughts are best left unspoken on special occasions lest the words rain on surviving children's parades.

On the other hand, there will be times when a surviving sister or brother can share with parents the memory of a deceased sibling. One surviving daughter tells of the time that a friend of the dead child came to visit the family some time after the death. "It was so nice to see my brother's friend again. It's great that he remembers Billy and continues to come and share memories with us. But it also hurts to see how he is growing while my brother is not." This reaction is one often experienced by parent and sibling alike.

It is not uncommon for physical illness to beset parents of a child who has died; this may also be true of surviving brothers and sisters. Occasionally, these siblings assume the symptoms of the illness suffered by the dead child. Some of the complaints may be loss of appetite, insomnia, headaches, heart palpitations, arthritis, minor accidents, and muscular aches and pains. One bereaved mother said she felt so physically ill that she found it very difficult to get out of bed. Although she wanted to hide under the covers, she knew she had to start living again, not only for her husband—but also for her surviving children. She felt she owed it to them to be their mother once again, and to tend to *their* needs.

Does the pain ever go away after the death of a sibling? A partial answer to this question came during a radio call-in program, in which one of the guests was a parent talking about the loss of a child. Many listeners were siblings who had comments and questions. Among them was a man in Texas who said he was now in his fifties and that he recalled when he was six years old, his four-year-old sister died of pneumonia. "In those days," he said, "people were buried from their homes, and so my sister's casket was placed in our living room. I remember going to the living-room door and looking in. Then I called out my sister's name. I have always wondered why I did that, why I kept calling her." Questions after the death of a child often go unresolved and may surface even some forty-five years later, as in the case of this brother who asked, "Why do you think I kept calling my sister's name?" The pain of surviving siblings often emerges long after the death of a sister or brother.

Another mature sibling from Illinois called to say, "I am sixty-two years old. When I was twelve, my ten-year-old brother was struck by lightning and died." The woman began to weep these fifty years later, and to say how grateful she was to the radio host for having a program dealing with this subject. "I not only lost my brother, I lost my mother, too. No one understood her grief, which grew worse and worse, until she had to be carted off to an institution." Would that the many existing self-help groups or the experienced grief counselors available now had been there to help this mother and daughter. Also, many professionals who work in the field of psychology may perhaps find that their patients will one day divulge the loss of a sister or brother and that many of the patient's problems will have stemmed from that traumatic loss.

Although bereaved parents *know* they have the affection of their surviving children after the loss of a child, this is not always the case with surviving siblings who seek affection and identification from their parents in a time of terrible turmoil. One surviving sibling described a scene in which she and her brothers and sisters sought to comfort their bereaved parent. "You still have us!" To which the parent replied, "I'd give up all of you to get her back." Siblings may find it difficult to understand that their parents' grief is so all-encompassing they may say or do things they really do not mean. Parents who are bleeding emotionally are often simply unable to help their surviving children during the first months and even years.

Secret thoughts of siblings are also kept as such by

surviving siblings for many years before any attempt to speak of them is made, if ever. "My sister and I shared many confidences that we never told our parents about. Now that she's dead, I still can't tell my parents about them and I know I never will. So, I lost my sister and I lost my confidante," said one surviving sibling. A surviving brother confided, "At the siblings group I went to, we learned that many times siblings harbor secret thoughts against their brothers or sisters. After a death, they most surely will not run up to a parent and announce they wished their sibling dead. This was a cause of many guilt feelings among the siblings there." Getting on with life may be hampered when surviving siblings seek signs of parental love and approval from their bereaved parents. The sibling rivalry that existed prior to the death—vying for parental attention or affection—is often accentuated either by guilt feelings or anger at the situation, themselves, their parents, or the dead sibling. Often, too, siblings of all ages play upon their parents' grief to gain their own ends.

Each person is unique, different from all other humans and, in each one, pain expresses itself differently. Outwardly, some surviving brothers and sisters may appear to have coped with grief successfully, but inwardly they continue to suffer. But, as with the parents, siblings learn to control their grief, in that they don't consciously think of it every minute of the day. Siblings and parents can live a good and complete life, but they can't ever expect to be the way they were before, grief experts say. It is important to understand that it is normal to remember the dead—and that remembering does not preclude getting on with life.

And so we come to the real purpose of this book—to present experiences of siblings at all age levels who tell of their struggles to live after the death of a brother or sister. The surviving siblings, whose stories you will read, express their innermost thoughts and emotions, hoping that their experiences will benefit others.

Katherine Fair Donnelly

Chapter One

A Sibling Dies

Each of the brothers and sisters who appear in this chapter, all teenagers or adults, has experienced the sorrow of the death of a sibling. (Chapters on the special problems of younger children who have suffered the loss of a sibling will appear later.) As we move on in the book, we will read about the ways they have coped with their grief. But, first, let the bereaved tell us what happened to change their lives so dramatically.

Eighteen-year-old Allison Heitner sat by herself in the office where just the day before she had started a summer job. On her first day of work, her boss' brother had been killed in a motorcycle accident. Now, all alone, with no one else in the office, Allison began to reflect on the telephone call she had received the night before from her younger sister, Leslie, who was in a hospital for treatment. "I can't wait to see you tomorrow," Leslie had said. "Tell Mommy to bring lots of pizzas when she comes. I love you, Allison. See you tomorrow."

Thinking of that phone call, Allison decided that instead of waiting until evening to wish her sister a happy birthday, she would call the hospital right now. The nurse who answered said, "Leslie is in a group therapy meeting and can't come to the phone." Allison wasn't concerned. The telephone setup in the hospital was like that of a shared phone line in a school dormitory and she had received similar replies on previous occasions.

Allison then called her mother at her place of work to

make the final arrangements for the birthday visit to Leslie, but was told her mother had to leave to go to the hospital. "That's strange," Allison thought. "We usually go there during visiting hours." Concerned, Allison called home, and when her brother answered, she asked, "Why did Mommy go to the hospital?" Her brother nervously answered, "I can't tell you, I can't tell you."

Growing more concerned, Allison called the hospital again. Here she continues with the story of what happened next: "This time a kid answered the phone. I asked, 'May I speak to Leslie Heitner, please?' And the boy said to me, 'Leslie Heitner drowned in the bathtub this morning.' Annoyed, I replied, 'What are you talking about? Please put an adult on the phone.' When Leslie had first been put in that place, I knew that some of its people were probably 'sickees.' I tried at first to be sympathetic to them and thought 'Oh, all of these kids are normal. They've just had nervous breakdowns and all have had one problem or another.' That's why when the kid who answered the phone said my sister had drowned, I tried to be tolerant, even though I was outraged at his comment and thought, 'He must really be a sickee.' So I insisted, 'Please put a nurse on the phone.' Finally, a nurse came to the phone and I asked, 'May I speak to Leslie Heitner?' Her reply was shocking: 'I'm very sorry to tell you, but Leslie Heitner was drowned in the bathtub this morning.'

"I was at work, all alone, in the middle of New York City. And all the nurse said was, 'I'm sorry. I know how you feel.' As I hung up the phone, my immediate reaction was. 'Oh, no, you do *not* know how I feel. *You most certainly do not know how I feel!*'"

Allison, thinking back on the events that led her sister to that hospital and to her death, went on: "My sister and I were only ten months apart and we were inseparable. Everyone took us for twins. She was very sociable and had a lot of friends. But in her last year of high school, she started to take up yoga as a hobby. She didn't to go yoga class; instead she started to borrow from the library a number of books on spiritual at-oneness and being one with yourself. She read every one of them. Then, suddenly, she became a different person. She went from going to parties, having fun, and visiting me at school to saying things such as, 'You know, everyone is this town is materialistic. I'm reading these books and the crucial thing is to find your spiritual self.' Then she would add, 'The most important thing really is the afterlife and not being concerned in this life with money or pretty makeup or such things.' Before that, Leslie *had* been concerned with money and the things it can buy, such as clothes and cosmetics—like a normal teenager. She began to say such things as, 'Everybody here is superficial. The world is a mess because people don't even know what real life is all about.'

"Listening to this stuff from her began to be a little monotonous after a while, and people began to say, 'Stop with the yoga.' We'd go to parties and she'd say, 'Okay, everybody, let's sit down and meditate.' When we would tell her to forget it, she would say things like, 'All you people are phonies, you and your world and your wars.' Leslie was a different person now, almost possessed it seemed. She became obsessed with her books to the point where she was saying, 'I don't even know why I'm living. I don't have to finish school; that's not important. The most important thing is that I sit and meditate and become one with myself,' and she would stare at a candle. These were the first signs of change in her."

Even though Leslie had only two months before graduation, she stopped going to school. Allison recalls, "My parents were concerned about the change in her and suggested to Leslie that she see a doctor to find out why she was so depressed. To this, Leslie agreed. She went to a psychiatrist who told my parents that what she was going through was entirely normal and advised them not to worry. But Leslie became worse. She had started with being depressed, then the world was a big mess, and then she began to say, 'I know something's going to happen to me. I have this feeling that I'm not going to reach my eighteenth birthday. I can't explain it.'"

Leslie believed that, according to the books she had been reading, she was "almost at her karma" and that something dire was about to happen. Allison remembers the response she and her parents had to Leslie's prognostications: "What are you talking about? Are you crazy? You're in perfect health. You're a beautiful girl; nothing is going to happen to you." To these reassurances, Leslie would reply, "Look, I know, I know. Don't ask me, because I can't explain it."

Allison recalls the next step in Leslie's illness. "A couple of weeks went by and she began to say, 'Somebody's going to kill me. It may be the police.' Or, 'Something is going to happen. Somebody is going to kill me.' But she couldn't explain who or what."

After a series of events, Leslie was taken to a hospital where her family hoped she would be helped and where she could be taken care of. "But," Allison says, "in that place, Leslie's fears came true. She didn't celebrate her eighteenth birthday because she was dead in a hospital tub."

On Friday the thirteenth, Elaine Kraf Altman received a telephone call from her brother's live-in friend, Gwen O'Dell. "They were away on vacation," Elaine tells us. "Gwen called me at my office to say that Michael had collapsed and had been taken to the hospital. I was so upset my co-workers rushed to get water for me. My knees felt like rubber. I couldn't stand. I had to sit down. I had told Gwen that I was on the way to my husband's office because we had been about to go away, too. She told me to go ahead with our plans and that she would call us from the hospital to give us news about my brother."

Elaine pulled herself together and took the train to her husband's office. Enroute, she prayed, but she'd had an earlier premonition. Elaine reflects: "A year ago, the four of us—my husband and I, and Gwen and Michael—were very friendly. One day my husband and I met Michael alone. Gwen couldn't be there because she was spending the day with her mother who was ill. I had not seen my brother for several months and I was shocked at his appearance. He looked older, seemingly he had aged prematurely. The change in him was so extreme and haunting that I asked him about it. He claimed that he had food poisoning but I still had an eerie feeling about him. This all came to my mind while I was sitting there and looking out the window enroute to meet my husband."

When Elaine got off the train, she walked toward the entrance to her husband's office, but was afraid to go upstairs. "I was petrified of hearing that Michael had died. I walked back and forth downstairs for what seemed an enternity. When I finally went up the stairs, my husband, Martin, shook his head and told me Gwen had called from the hospital to say that Michael was dead."

Elaine recalls her reaction: "It was closing time at my husband's place of business, and although a number of his co-workers had already left for the day, many people were still there. I was unaware of any of them. I just began to scream. 'No, no. Not my brother, not my brother.' It was the worst shock of my life."

We have read how two surviving sisters learned of the death of a sibling. We will now hear how twin brothers, Joe and Richard Sundland, reacted to the death of their younger brother, Chris.

On the evening of February twenty-fourth, in a small town in Illinois, the twins and some of their friends were watching the January twenty-eighth movies of their thirteenth birthday party. Chris, their mother Sherry, and their father Tom, were also there. As usual, Chris wanted a front-row seat, which so annoyed the twins that they teased him and called him by the pet name they used when he got on their nerves—"Punkie."

The following day, Thursday, February twenty-fifth, the twins had wrestling practice after school. Chris was out playing on the creek behind their house with Heather, the girl who lived next door. The creek was frozen solid except for one small spot, into which, somehow, Chris and Heather both fell. Heather was able to get out and run home.

Sherry, the boy's mother, tells of the events that followed: "The police, divers, and rescue squad were here within eight minutes of the call at 4:20 P.M. When Joe and Rich got home at about 5:00 P.M. and saw the police, someone told them that

Chris had drowned. They came running into the house and Joe yelled, 'Is it true that Christopher was drowned?' I told him that it was true, and he threw his books across the table and yelled, 'No! No! It can't be true.' Then he ran into his bedroom. Rich just walked around seeming to be in shock, as we all were.

"It was chaos with the phone ringing and people out on the ice," Sherry continued. "The twins said they were thinking of how they had called Chris 'Punkie' the night before and of the other times they had called him names and told him to get lost. The guilt and hurt hadn't really started to settle in yet. Tom and I thought it might be better for the boys to stay overnight at the home of their friends who lived about a block away. In this way, they wouldn't be able to see the rescue operations. Meanwhile, we explained to them that the drowning was an accident and that no one was at fault. Their friends cried with them on and off all that evening. When darkness fell, the search for the body was suspended, to be resumed at dawn.

"I asked the boys if they'd like to go to school the next day, for staying home and watching the divers would help no one, but it was up to them. They decided to go. At school, the principal told Joe and Rich they could walk out of a class whenever they chose. But they did so only when some of the other boys and girls began to cry. After class, their friends, not being sure of what to say, put their arms around Joe and Rich in silent sympathy. Other children asked what had happened."

The twins' mother reflects on their decision to go to school that day: "Joe and Rich feel as my husband and I do, that by returning to school they were with their friends and were able to share their grief more satisfactorily than if they had waited to return to school after the funeral. The kids at school talked to them, cried with them, and were there for support, as were the teachers. Joe and Rich think that if they had not seen their classmates till days later, the other boys and girls might not have known what to say or how to act, and might have avoided them.

"In another kind gesture, the classmates asked the principal if they could take the late bus home for that was the bus which Chris and Heather had used. The kids did this because some of the others were calling Heather a murderer, and the boys wanted to show their loyalty to her. They wanted to protect her from hurtful taunts. Heather had been only five, but Chris had turned six just ten days before he died."

The twins stayed at their friends' home again on Friday night as the search for their brother continued. Both felt anger at seeing the TV crews and the crowds of onlookers. On Saturday, the search went on, with many more people gawking in what had become a carnival-like atmosphere. "All four of us," Sherry, the twins' mother, remembers, "felt angry that people could create a spectacle out of something so tragic. Breaking up the ice to find Chris had taken many hours of manpower, and to see people who had no business to be there out on the ice walking around really incensed the boys and us. One TV channel from Chicago had Chris' picture on the news report and gave Richard's name. That added hurt to the boys' already building emotions, but Rich said it made him feel good to see so many hundreds of volunteers helping to find Chris."

The two days of horror were over on Saturday at 3 P.M., when Chris was found. The boys' mother tells of the family's prior apprehensions: "All that any of us felt was relief, for if he hadn't been found by Sunday, the rescue workers said they would have to wait until the ice on all the lakes thawed and hope that his body would then surface."

In the preceding poignant story, days passed before the body of the twins' brother was discovered. It was only then that the reality of the drowning hit them. In the following brief account, telling of his brother's death in an accident, seventeen-year-old Billy Pfister recalls the sudden impact that woke him out of a sound sleep.

"About four o'clock in the morning, I woke up suddenly. My mother was screaming! She was screaming so hysterically that I thought somebody was trying to break in. She didn't sound like herself. So I jumped up and ran downstairs to see what was going on. My mother and father were in the kitchen, and the police were at the door. I was too surprised to move. The police officers had told my parents that my brother John, twenty-two, had been in a motorcycle accident and had died from his injuries. My mother kept screaming and saying that it was a mistake. I was so thunderstruck I didn't say anything. I just stood there."

Before the following incident occurred, Susan Keats had just moved to New York from Chicago, where her family lived. One morning, she was almost out the door on her way to work when the phone rang. Susan continues the story: "the long-distance call was from my mother. She asked if my friend Pete was here. I said, 'no,' and told her he had gone to Florida the day before. I knew something was wrong, but I pretended I had no idea why she was calling. I sensed her news was going to be bad because, first of all, why would she ask me if Pete were here? But I just tried to stay cheerful and wait for her to go on. Then it came: My sister Carolyn had been killed in a car accident."

Susan remembers asking "Why?" Why did it have to result in death, she wondered. "Carolyn was driving home with friends. She was a careful driver, but the roads were quite icy. Suddenly, she hit a bad spot in the road and the car skidded out of control. Carolyn hit a tree sideways and was thrown out onto the road, although she was wearing a seat belt. All precautions had been taken, but they just didn't work." Susan, twenty-four, questioned why someone so young, who had done all the right things, was killed.

"Why not some sort of injury? It doesn't seem fair, but is life really fair anyway? Other people want to know if there wasn't some other element present. The question they immediately ask is, 'Was she drinking?' But she wasn't. My sister never drank. I guess they figure, 'If she was drunk, that was the reason for the accident, and so it won't happen to me.' Or, 'If she was on drugs, it won't happen to me.' Or, 'If she didn't wear her seat belt, then it won't happen to me.' I suppose it's natural for people to ask those questions to assure themselves that there had to be a reason, not shared by them, that caused Carolyn's death. It's frightening to realize that here was a person who wasn't doing any of the wrong things, who was a careful driver, was wearing her seat belt, didn't drink, and yet she, a twenty-seven-year-old beautiful girl, died doing all the right things!"

In the above story, we have read how a bereaved sibling learned of her sister's death by a phone call from her mother. The following is an account of how the parents of Ellen Spector learned of the tragic death of their twenty-year-old son Philip through a phone call from the Binghamton police.

Ellen's mother and father had driven her to Albany where she was to enter the freshman class at the State University. At seventeen, Ellen was excited by the prospect of becoming a college student. "But," she tells us, "I hadn't been there twenty-four hours when my cousin called to say that he was visiting for the day and would like to come and see me. After a few minutes of chit-chat, he announced that my brother had been in a car accident and that I should go home to see him. As we drove along, I could see that my cousin was upset—a feeling that soon infected me, too. When I reached home, the number of family members and friends in our home told me at once that my brother was dead."

Ellen learned later that after her parents' long drive home from Albany, they received a phone call from out-of-town police. "My mother and father had been home only about a half hour after leaving me off at school, when they received a phone call telling them about my brother's death. It was terrible for them. They were exhausted to begin with and then to get news like that! The police had reported that Philip was with school friends after a party where they had been using nitrous oxide in balloons, I think. Supposedly, he was using a plastic bag because they didn't have any more balloons, and he died accidentally as the result of inhaling the nitrous oxide."

Russell Randazza was twenty-six when his sister Diane Channing died as a result of a brain tumor. About a year after Diane's marriage, she became subject to severe headaches. She went to several doctors to learn the cause of them and got a variety of answers. Finally, the headaches became so severe that she went to the hospital for a CAT scan, and a tumor was found.

"From what I remember," said Russell, "the tumor was so located that the surgeons could not reach all parts of it. Over several years, the surgeons performed three major brain operations. Most of this time I was in Putnam County, New York, trying to become an electrician, and I finally moved up there. So, except for my vacation time, I could see Diane only on weekends. I didn't realize the magnitude of her tumor until later on. You always think, 'She's going to go through an operation and, after a period of therapy and recovery, then she'll be fine.' It took a long time for me to realize that was never going to happen.

"There were five years between us, my sister being five years older than I and my brother was five years younger than I. When Diane died, I was at work. I was very busy and edgy because I wanted to get to the hospital. So I left work to go there. When I arrived, I walked into the room, but all the lights were out. She had already died. It felt strange to be there all alone and to know she was dead. The nurse who was there told me my family had left. So I went straight to my grandparents' home and found complete chaos there with everybody obviously upset."

At a little past midnight on a Labor Day Monday, Dan Saulisberry had just hung up the phone, having heard scattered details regarding his brother's accident. Dan was twenty-three, married, with three small children. He and his family had moved from Carson City, Nevada, to Sioux City, Iowa, where he had begun work at a new job.

Dan describes his reaction to the phone call: "I didn't think the accident was a life-threatening one when I first heard about it. I had been given only sketchy details, but later that same morning, I learned how serious it was. Tracy, seventeen, was in a coma. In the next few days, the situation became more serious and we all flew back home.

"We were there by his side for three weeks, but during that time, there was no change. Tracy remained in a comatose state. My wife and I decided to move back to Carson City permanently, so we flew to Sioux City to close up shop. But while we were there getting ready to move, I received a phone call from my dad that my brother had gone into cardiac arrest and was dead."

Dan's mother, Jo, describes happier events prior to Tracy's death: "That summer, I had been asked to help with Bible School, but, because I was working on a year-round school schedule, I was unable to do so. Since Tracy didn't have a job, I suggested he might enjoy helping, for he was quite musical and often played the piano and organ in church. Tracy was delighted and did a great job. He then was selected to go to Yosemite with a group of campers as a counselor for younger boys. In July I had gone to the National Education Association convention in Detroit as a representative of our local teachers group. Before returning home, I was able to visit Dan and his family in Sioux City for a few days.

"When I got back, I noticed that a big change had come over Tracy—he was a much more mature person. This pleased me, for he and I were very close. His father traveled a lot so that Tracy and I did many things together. He was very proud of his Italian heritage from my family and was more like me than the other children. In school, he was always getting into trouble; he was bright but was not kept busy enough. His teachers and I had many talks concerning his conduct grades. On my return, I saw that Tracy now seemed to have a goal for success in life and I was proud of him. We planned a good senior year together.

"It was a family custom that when you were a senior that was your special time," Jo tells us. "We were a family committed to enjoying everything with its members. In August Tracy got a job as a bag boy at a local grocery store. However, he wasn't going to work during the school year for we wanted him to enjoy going to school and being a senior student. He campaigned hard and was elected president of the Carson City School Band. I worked that month of August, complaining that in such fine weather, I should be enjoying the sun at Lake Tahoe. Tracy always encouraged me by leaving little messages on the kitchen table—sometimes just an 'I love you, Mom.' One day, it was a note citing Ecclesiastes 3:1—reminding us that there is 'a time for every matter under heaven.' Another day, he wrote that he knew we were all 'Lambs of God.' One of the big changes that had taken place in his life that summer was that I could see Christ living within him. His sister also noticed this."

On Labor Day weekend, Jo and her husband Chuck helped move their daughter Kathy to Reno for her senior year in nursing school. Jo remembers a conversation with Kathy in which she expressed concern about her youngest son. "Tracy helped us by driving his car," Jo recalls, "with some furniture and his big black dog sitting beside him, the convertible top down, and seemingly very carefree. I remember saying to Kathy beside me, 'I wish he would be more careful. He doesn't think anything will ever happen to him.'"

On Monday of that holiday weekend, Tracy worked only half of the day. Jo describes his jubilant mood: "He was so happy that it was his last day of work and that school would be starting the next day. We all did chores around the house. Tracy polished his car. His school friends had planned to meet and have their pictures taken in their cars for the yearbook. One of the girls in the group was the editor; another boy was president of the high school class. They were all very excited about beginning the school year.

"After dinner," Jo continues, "I was doing the dishes. Tracy announced that he was going over to his friend Mike's for the picture taking, and that he wouldn't be gone for long, and off he went. I was feeling so good. All was well. We'd had a great summer and were looking forward to a great year. Then the phone rang. Mike's mother was on the line, trying to keep her voice calm, telling me there had been an accident and that Tracy had been hurt. I gave her permission to call an ambulance, then I called out to Chuck and we jumped in his truck and rushed to Mike's house. The street was filled with people, fire trucks, and an ambulance. I had a sinking feeling that things were not going to be all right.

"I asked someone what had happened and they told me

that Tracy had been electrocuted while climbing a tree in his friend's backyard. Someone pushed me into the ambulance and then they pushed me back out. We got into the truck and rushed to the hospital emergency area where we saw a very frantic scene. A nurse put us into an X-ray room alone. We were there for what seemed like an eternity. Tracy's friends came in, together with their parents and our minister. A few doctors reported on what they were doing. They did revive him and got his heart beating again, but he was in a coma. Then they put him in an intensive care unit and we were able to see him. This beautiful child just lay there, still living with the help of a respirator. But we were not going to let him die. God would not do this to us. He had so much going for him and we had such great plans for his future. He had always loved to climb to the heights and that is what he did that day when he climbed a tree and received 12,000 volts of electricity."

Dan believes he initially denied the seriousness of the situation because he didn't want to accept it. "I was assuring myself that Tracy would be all right in a few days. But then something happened that brought the reality home. I picked up the family Bible from the coffee table. It seemed to part by itself in the middle and my eyes fell upon these words from Psalm 65: 'Blessed is the man whom thou choosest and causest to approach unto thee that he may dwell in thy courts; we shall be satisfied with the goodness of thy house.' To this day I believe God spoke to me through those words. It was as if He was telling me Tracy was gone but that he was okay. I felt both sorrow and relief simultaneously, and throughout the three weeks that he was comatose I never doubted for a minute that Tracy was enjoying the splendor of Heaven while his body lay wasting away in that hospital bed."

Florence Campbell was twenty-nine when her brother Jesse Ray, thirty-nine, first went into the hospital to be treated for a lung illness. Florence remembers what happened when her brother returned home. "He stayed with us for a period of time because there were no available rooms at the hospital. He was very weak and it was as if he were a baby learning to

walk again. One evening when I went to give him his medication, he started to urinate on himself. He could feed himself
pretty well, but he had to have help getting up from the bed to
a chair.

"One day, when I helped him onto his walker, I noticed
that he had what appeared to be a bedsore on his leg. I
watched my mother apply cornstarch to dry it up. But it got no
better. The cornstarch would dry the sore up for a while, but in
the morning it would have opened again. The sore got bigger
and bigger. At first it was the size of a nickel—like a little sore.
But it kept growing. Eventually it got round and almost like the
bottom of a cup or a saucer. The scab would come off, but my
mother continued putting the starch on it. When the scab
would come off, you could see tissue inside. It really didn't look
good. I had read somewhere before that one of the seven
signs of cancer is a sore that doesn't heal. And that's when I
started thinking that Jesse Ray might be seriously ill."

Florence didn't mention this to her mother because "she
always had this worried look on her face, and I didn't want to
push her to tell me about anything she didn't want to discuss.
But when we took Jesse Ray back to the hospital for the last
time, I got the feeling that he would be in there for a long while.
He had lost a great deal of weight, and he was getting weaker
and weaker. Then, his conversation began to be distorted. He
might talk about something that happened maybe fifteen
years ago, or about somebody in the family who had died long
before."

Fighting the acceptance of her brother's illness kept
Florence from admitting to herself that he was dying. During
the last weeks, when she visited him in the hospital, Florence
wouldn't face what was happening to her brother. "But then it
got to the point where he was lying all balled up, and he'd
often sleep like that—in a ball. He wouldn't talk, kept his eyes
closed. His mouth was tight-lipped, and he kept his fists
clenched. All balled up like that, he looked like a scared child
in the corner afraid to come out. And I would say to him, 'Why
don't you talk to me, Jessy Ray?'

"It scared me to see him because I remembered a woman next door to us who had gone to the hospital, and that's the way her eyes were when they took her out on the stretcher. Later on, it came to me that that was the way Jesse Ray's eyes were looking when we saw him that Sunday. And, a few days later he passed on," Florence remembers.

In a later chapter, this bereaved sibling tells of the guilt she felt for not knowing that her brother was dying.

In the above account, we have read about a bereaved sister who could not accept events that were happening. But experiences differ. Here's a story, emotionally the same, but quite different in details.

When his alarm went off on the morning of June ninth, Jay Goldstein awakened his younger brother, Philip, who delivered newspapers on weekday mornings. Because Philip was a heavy sleeper, Jay had to prod him into getting up. This action was to bother Jay for months to come because on that morning Philip, wheeling along on his bike, was hit by a car. The next day, June tenth, he died in the hospital without regaining consciousness.

Afterward, Jay recalled a dream he'd had on the morning of Philip's accident, but which he dismissed as just being strange. In the dream, he heard sirens after which his brother was carried away on a stretcher to an ambulance. Later, in talking about the dream, Jay came to realize that we sometimes have experiences, such as dreams, that we don't understand, and that those experiences may buffer the impact of a shock by hinting at it beforehand.

Marie Teague believes her mother may also have had a premonition of the death of her son Lenny, Marie's brother. "I heard Mom answer the phone, but she said the oddest thing before the sergeant had a chance to deliver the news— something like, 'I don't know why you're bothering me' and hung up on him. He called back and my dad picked up the phone. I heard those words, 'Oh, no' and my heart broke right there on the spot. After they talked for a moment, my father hung up the phone. I knew my parents would be coming to my room to say the words. I wanted to run.

"At his high school graduation, Lenny wanted to join the Army, but he was only sixteen," Marie recollects. "However, my parents did sign for him when he turned seventeen. Later he married a girl he'd met overseas on his first hitch and they made their home in southern California. Len became a police officer, then a corrections officer, then hung all that up and rejoined the Army to make it his career. During this time, my brother and my father seemed like ships in the night, passing each other, but never really dropping anchor side by side or long enough to get to know one another. So when a war took Len even farther away, I reckon my dad experienced a longing for a relationship that would never be. His boy was grown up and in danger, but each day was perceived as a step closer to a joyful reunion. Yet ours was a house of fear.

"Lenny was a helicopter pilot in the heat of the action in the Vietnamese War, and we all knew what that could mean. When he did die, all chances for a solid, sharing father-son relationship were gone. That hurt dad deeply, I know. Lenny has been dead seventeen years—more than half of my life, but it still strikes me as almost 'otherworldly' to think back to that terrible day when I, a teenager in Orange County, California, looked up from my homework to hear my parents say that my brother was dead. No one will ever know what depression I felt; it was so deep that it made me wish I could die."

Hearing of a loved one's death via a telephone call is a heart-wrenching experience, but sometimes the insensitivity of the caller can make it an even more brutal experience. Such was the case with Betty Tucker when a voice on the telephone said, "Hello. Your brother is dead."

"I will never, never forget that phone call," Betty states. "I was completely shattered, and totally overcome by the way that it was told. I was crushed. I had lost a father, I had lost grandparents, I had lost my other brother, Simon. But to hear about my brother Mitchell's death in such a cold, uncaring way, was too much. I wanted to say, 'Enough. Enough already.' "

Betty reflects on the earlier loss of her brother Simon. "He was retarded, but he lived with us for many, many years until the responsibility for him began to take its toll on the family. I remember when I was younger I used to sleep with my bed across the door in an effort to prevent him from running out. He had a serious weight problem, but couldn't control his eating. People used to tell my mother to put locks on the refrigerator. After a good deal of soul-searching, my mother's doctor told us he had to be put in a place where he could be properly cared for. So he was taken to a spot in the Nyack–West Point area, a beautiful, beautiful place. We used to go visit him frequently.

"Simon was there for many years. Then one day, we got a letter notifying us, 'Your son has been transferred to Willow Brook.' My husband Lenny and I went there every weekend. It was a horrible place. You may have heard about this big home for retarded people on Staten Island. The news reporter, Geraldo Rivera, did an exposé of it. My mother had remarried and moved down to Florida. But everytime she came up, we would visit Simon.

"Simon was a very good kind of person. He would have an occasional temper tantrum, but he would never get violent, or hurt anybody. He loved Lenny and he used to write us letters. I think he had the mentality of a nine-year-old. He was short, blond, with blue eyes, He had a lovely face. Sometimes when you looked at him, you didn't think he was retarded, but he really was. And, although I was two years younger than Simon, I always felt that he was a younger brother."

Betty remembers the phone call that conveyed the news that her brother Simon had died. "It was very sad, but it was a bit of a relief because I knew a tremendous burden had been lifted from my mother's shoulders. I felt good for her sake, but she was sad about it. I just remember feeling that Simon was at peace. But there was a serious problem with his burial. When he died, he was so obese they couldn't find a coffin big enough to hold his body. This was very upsetting to my mother.

Then we were told the funeral would be at 9:30. We arrived at the cemetery at 9, but it wasn't until 2 in the afternoon that a coffin could be found. The three of us—my mother, my aunt, and I—just stood there waiting for the body to be brought for burial. Simon was thirty-three when he passed away, and it seemed ironic that even in death he had to have this terrible thing about the coffin."

Betty contrasts the deaths of her two brothers: "My brother Mitchell was only twenty-seven when he died, and he had so much going for him. Mitchell and I were very close and my children adored him. He had been an extremely gifted child, so different from Simon. He was a talented musician and used to write and arrange music.

"Mitchell had developed hepatitis, but his death was caused by a drug overdose. He must have known that people who have hepatitis should not take any other drug but the ones the doctors prescribe. But Mitchell apparently had difficulty sleeping and he somehow got hold of sleeping pills, took them, and that was it. He didn't wake up the next morning."

Another sister who suffered the loss of two siblings was Madeleine Toomey Pflaumbaum. After her sister Kathleen, age twenty-three, was killed in a car crash caused by a drunken driver, Madeleine stopped going to church. She was angry at God and kept asking, "Why? Why my sister?" She thought the answer to the "Why?" was that God had let her down. Madeleine learned of Kathleen's death when her mother telephoned her early one morning. The young woman became hysterical and her screams awakened her ten-year-old son, Erik. Because her husband had already gone to work, Madeleine forced herself to be calm for Erik's sake. Sitting down, she explained to him that his Aunt Kathy had been killed in an automobile accident.

Now that several years have passed, Madeleine tells how she learned of her brother's death. "I was in the hosptial awaiting surgery and Father Cullen had just given me Communion. He and I discussed all kinds of things—the soccer season that was coming up and all the projects I was involved in. The talk was good and took my mind off the upcoming surgery, for I had just had my pre-op. Now the nurses came into the room and gave me my shot. A few minutes later a chill came into the atmosphere when Father Cullen and several nurses took places around my bed. My husband, wearing a look of deep distress, came to me and said he had bad news. He paused before he went on—my brother Larry had shot himself. Father Cullen looked at me and then turned away. I asked, 'Is Larry dead?' Father Cullen just shook his head and had to leave. Probably because we were friends, he had become very upset.

"I remember trying to jump out of the bed and being overly excited, and the nurses pinning me down. I also remember the surgeon telling me that I could go home because it was better that I not have surgery at that time. A nurse tried to 'sober me up' with tea and toast because I had just had my pre-op injection," Madeleine recalls. Subsequently Madeleine learned the details of her brother's death. She tells of the events that led to the tragedy. "Larry had gone to see my parents the night before he died. In their house my parents had an oil painting of my sister, Kathleen, which my father's boss had given to them. Larry came over that night and sat down in front of the picture. He didn't say a word to my parents, just went on staring at Kathleen's portrait. Later, my mother said she had felt uneasy about him, but he had come several times before to look at the picture and on that night she thought he was merely studying it. Since the portrait had been in the house for quite a while, my mother felt perhaps he was just getting a new perspective on it and the way it had been painted. Then he said, 'Good-bye, I'll see you,' and left. My parents' lasting remembrance is his concentration on the picture all the time he was in the house. Although they spoke to him a few times, he continued his wordless study of the picture. It's almost as if he were trying to convey a message to it through eye contact.

"My brother was interested in sports and liked to go duck hunting with his friends. One of those men had given my brother a damaged rifle before he went into the service. Now, my brother won't be going duck hunting anymore—he used the rifle on himself. I keep thinking back to the week before Larry's death. I had seen him at a christening in the family. He looked horrible. His skin was very pale. His hair wasn't combed right, and it hadn't been styled. He looked sallow and I had remarked to my mother that something was wrong with him. When she called him during the week, he said he was having kidney trouble, but nothing of that came out in the autopsy report.

"My brother left a note saying that he was sorry for what he was doing, but he felt everybody would be better off without him, that he missed my sister Kathleen and that he didn't want to go on without her. The note was addressed to his wife and, strangely, he didn't mention me, my mother and father, or my other brothers and sisters. His body was discovered by his wife who then called the police.

"Until my brother's death, I had tried to find comfort from the loss of my sister with other siblings who had suffered similar losses. Then, when Larry died, I thought to myself, 'Now, I have two siblings who are dead.'"

Chapter Two

This Isn't Real

- All of a sudden my whole world caved in. I heard my mother crying and screaming. The funeral was planned for the next day. My sister was going to be buried in the ground. It was as if part of me were gone. She was only twelve. This just can't be real.
- It's Christmas. I can't believe my brother died on Christmas. That's not what happens on holidays when you're happy and the family is celebrating together. No one dies on Christmas.
- I saw my father crying for the first time. He and my sister had been very close. I went to him and said, "You still have me." I know he was grief-stricken, but his reply stunned me: "God only takes the good ones." It was unreal to me—first to lose my sister and now really to lose my father as well.
- My brother was run over by a car in front of our house. We kids never saw him again. An ambulance rushed him away and the last time we laid eyes on him he was all bloody, but he was alive. Now they say he is dead. It's all like make-believe, like the movies. Or maybe it's just a bad dream and I'll wake up and find it isn't so; it didn't happen.

Siblings can experience terrifying and confusing thoughts during the early period of grief. They often feel alone, especially young siblings who have difficulty communicating their need to have someone to talk to. Children seldom see their own parents cry, and may become frightened and anxious when this happens. With parents so wrapped up in their anguishing problems—funeral, casket, clergy, notifying relatives—they may be unable to respond to the immediate needs of surviving children. Shock and denial are often the early impact on siblings. One sibling who had these reactions was

Karen Schlesier Eisen. Here she tells about her initial responses after the death of her brother Billy who was killed in a car accident at age nineteen.

"He was alone in the car and there weren't any other cars involved. He just hit a pole. There's a long stretch of road just before the spot where the accident happened. It was like a speedway and you went a long time without a light and then all of a sudden, there was a light. Billy hit the pole right before the light. It wasn't raining or misty, so we really don't know what happened.

"I had been married only a short time before the night of the accident and wasn't living at home. We got a phone call at about three in the morning from my mother, telling us to come to the hospital. I didn't know how serious it was. When we got there, we learned that the doctor had no hope for my brother's recovery.

"About a half hour later we were led to a little private room where nurses were waiting for me. 'Oh,' said one of them, 'You're Karen, Billy's sister.' I knew their waiting there for me meant trouble. As soon as I walked through the door, I saw my mother and thought, 'Oh my God, it's really true.' She said, 'I don't know how to tell this to you,' to which I replied, 'Then don't. I know what you mean.'

"My mother was mildly hysterical, and my father was pounding on the wall. I remember that I didn't feel part of the group. I felt that my mother and father had suffered a loss, but that I was on the outside, looking in. They didn't make me feel that way; I just detached myself from the situation because I couldn't deal with it.

"My mother said to me, 'You may go in and see him if you wish, but you don't have to—whatever you want to do is fine. But, he's a mess, horrible. There are machines all over him, and you probably wouldn't recognize him. So if you don't want that to be the last image you have of your brother, don't go.' I didn't.

"When I went to the funeral parlor, I expected this horrible sight. I hadn't seen my brother in about four months, for I hadn't kept in close touch with my family at that point. I had last talked to my brother on the phone two days before he died. I had not been feeling well on that day and had planned to tell my mother I couldn't keep an engagement we had. So I said to Billy impatiently, 'Look, I have no time to talk to you now; just put Mother on the phone.' That was my last communication with him. And here I was now at his funeral, looking at him in the coffin. But, instead of the image I had anticipated of him, he looked wonderful when I saw him in the funeral parlor. He looked like he shouldn't be dead. The funeral directors did a terrific job; I don't know what they did, but he looked great. His neck was a bit swollen, but his face looked fine. His beard had been shaved off and he just had his mustache.

"I just couldn't get over the way he looked—I thought seeing him dead would make me believe it. But when I saw him dead, I believed it even less because he didn't appear to be dead. So I went to my mother and said, 'I want to read the autopsy report. I think they messed up. It doesn't look to me as if he's dead.'"

The reaction of the preceding surviving sister—that it was not true—is one often experienced by a sibling. In the following story we learn from Bill Pfister how he, too, thought it was a mistake.

"Although I heard the policemen at the door telling my parents that my brother had died in a motorcycle accident, I was in shock and just didn't believe it. My mind kept screaming, 'It's a mistake,' but I didn't say anything because I kept thinking they'd explain that it was all a misunderstanding. Then, of course, the more they went on with details, the more I realized that it wasn't a mistake, that it had really happened. At first, I didn't know how to react. My parents were crying and my eldest brother was too. I'm the youngest. But, I didn't react at all. I just sat there and watched. I didn't know what to do. I think I was so stunned by the whole thing that I didn't know how to act. I didn't cry right away and I didn't get angry. I was nowhere at that point—totally lost for words or thought.

"After the police left, the immediate commotion toned down a bit. Then I had a chance to think about it and I thought, 'Well, that's it. I'm not going to see him anymore.' That was the hardest part—what it really meant. I began to think, 'This is really real, and I'm never going to see him again. This was my brother and it's all gone, that whole relationship.' Then I became very depressed.

"At the funeral home, I wanted to see him alone and asked my parents if I could go in first. When I entered that room, I lost my grip on everything. I just looked at him lying there. I was alone with him, and it was as if I were hoping he could hear my thoughts. It's a crazy kind of thing, to think somebody can hear what you're thinking. My first thought was, 'My God, how did you get here? What did you do?' My mind was filled with such questions as, 'What am I going to do now without you? How could you do this? We were getting on so well, why did you do it?' It wasn't that he had actually done anything, but the questions in my mind were more like, 'How did this happen? How did you get into a thing like this? How did you get into such a stupid situation?' Not in an angry way, just a grieving way, wondering, 'How did you ever end up like this?' I was half talking and half thinking, and at the same time shaking my head in disbelief."

After Allison Heitner heard of her sister's death, she didn't know what to do. "I was in the office all alone and almost in shock. I began running around the office, for I didn't know what to do. I wasn't crying because I didn't yet believe that she had died. A couple of minutes later, my mother called me at work, sounding like a zombie and saying, 'Can you come home right now?' And I said, 'Mom, are you all right?' She said, 'Just come home.'

"On the way home, I know I was in a state of shock because I saw a friend at the station and I said, 'Somebody just talked to me on the phone and told me my sister has died, but I don't believe it. I think they're lying.' I continued my rationalization, 'They said my sister drowned in a bathtub, but she wasn't supposed to be allowed to take a bath because of the medication she was taking. Also, she was supposed to be checked every fifteen minutes.' So, I was convinced a mistake had been made, and continued on my way.

"When I got home, my parents told me they had seen her and she was dead, but I still did not believe it. In order for me to believe it, I had to see her myself. I had not been permitted to visit her for two weeks and we had never gone that long in our whole lives without seeing each other.

"When I went to see her, she looked as if she were sleeping, and I said to her, 'Wake up now!' Then I became hysterical. I kept insisting, "Wake up! Wake up! Wake up now! When she didn't, the truth really hit me. But it was hard to believe, because just the night before I had been talking to her and she was in a really good mood—and she did vary up and down. But she wasn't talking about dying or death or anything like that. She kept saying, 'I can't wait till tomorrow to see you', and things like that. I think she must have fallen asleep from the medication. But the hospital wouldn't say that. Nor would they say there had been foul play."

Later, the circumstances of her sister's death continued to plague Allison. "I sent away for her death certificate because I wanted to see for myself. The certificate says, 'Immediate cause—asphyxiated by drowning due to or consequences of circumstances undetermined pending police investigation.' Also on the certificate was: 'Social Security Number—None.' But Leslie did have a Social Security number.

Now, pending police investigation, they found no foul play, we were told. Maybe they thought one of the patients got in and attacked her or drowned her. Or, maybe it said 'Asphyxiated by drowning' because the hospital would not admit that they let her take a bath while on drugs. I don't know what their excuse was. It appears to be negligence. But whatever it may have been, I think it was because the medication she was on makes you like a zombie and you can fall asleep. Also, the time of death is undetermined because a patient found her in the bathroom. Not even an aide! And this hospital is supposed to be a very good outfit, with dozens of aides on the ward. Furthermore, they knew she was inclined to be suicidal. They knew that because a few times she had been able to get hold of medication from a tray or a drug cabinet. At that point, she was so paranoid she was afraid of the people in the hospital because some of them did get wild now and then and attack each other. I know that one kid did commit suicide there. But they don't know how long Leslie was in the bathroom before she was found. But their estimate was twenty minutes. My big problem is that I don't know what happened. At first I couldn't believe she was dead and now this—how did she die?"

Elaine Altman, who had been very close to her sibling, suffered the torment of wondering how and why her brother died. "Dozens of calls were going back and forth about the funeral preparations. My brother's live-in girlfriend, Gwen, was upset because she had no legal status and it was my parents who took over. My brother had evidently talked to Gwen about his death and said if he died, he didn't want his parents to get hold of him.

"Both Gwen and I wanted to know why he had died. I was tormented with the question of what was wrong with him. My parents hadn't allowed an autopsy. They wanted to get his body home and buried. They took control of everything. They didn't even want Gwen at the funeral, but I insisted. I said that I wouldn't go if she couldn't.

"I was in such shock, I felt too weak to walk. I practiced walking the day before the funeral because I was so shaky and knew that if I was going to get through the funeral and give the eulogy, I'd have to get on my feet. My husband Martin helped by going out with me and walking and walking so I would become steadier. But, I kept getting shocks, for I couldn't believe this had happened. I'd suddenly realize he was dead and I'd get a physical shock like a blow, and then begin shaking.

"I called my close friend Millicent. My husband and I were going to attend a Bar Mitzvah and we were going to stay at her house. When I called to tell her my brother had died, she told me her husband had died the same day! It was such a double shock!"

The next story tells of a sister who was thousands of miles away in a foreign country when she learned of her brother's death in a car accident.

"I heard about my brother's death in a horrendous way," Leslie Boden recalls. "I had gone to Europe and my trip prompted my mother to do the same thing. For years she had wanted to travel but never did so because my father wasn't available to go with her. After long discussion, it finally got to a point where both my parents were able to say, 'Let's stop talking about it; let's just do it.' So my mother and I were in Europe at the same time and my father was to follow later. Mom and I spent a week together and then went our separate ways. I was due to return home on October twenty-ninth. My mother's plan was to be in Paris on the twenty-fifth of that month to meet my father there, and they would spend his vacation of one week in that city.

"I was traveling much differently—carrying a backpack and staying at cheap places. Although I was no longer a student, I was traveling in student fashion. My mother had told me where she and my father would be staying in Paris, and I planned my return home to include a stop there. On the morning of the twenty-fourth I left Athens to go to Crete, and on the way I spent several days in a little village on the south side. So, I was not reachable.

"My mother, in the interim, had apparently called home on the twenty-fourth and learned of David's accident from my father. She flew back to the States on the twenty-fifth, but David died while she was in the air. I had moved on to the town of Iráklion and called their hotel in Paris to make plans to meet my parents there. The man at the hotel said my parents had left, and advised me to call the Embassy or my cousin in New York. I called my cousin who told me to get in touch with my parents at home.

"At that point, I was terrified, thinking something had happened to my mother while she was traveling. That fear was allayed when I learned that both of my parents were at home. Then, I thought perhaps my grandmother was ill. But my father said, "David was in a—" As soon as he said, 'David,' I began to cry, 'No, no, no.' When he spoke the words, 'David was in a terrible accident,' I knew.

"This was now the thirtieth and David had died on the twenty-fifth. My other brother Scott, had been in school at the time of the accident. My father had been home alone and had received a phone call from the hospital, saying that David was there. He had gone with some friends to the concert after which they started out for Syracuse to attend another concert. They drove all night, and the boy at the wheel fell asleep. There were four other young people in the car and not one of them was hurt. When Scott learned of the accident, he rushed to my father's side. For three days, David was in a coma and my father and Scott went through all that together, talking to David, and allowing each other to cry and to give vent to grief in whatever way they felt. But for me, it was all unreal. I was far away, hiking and enjoying a vacation while my brother was lying in a coma in a hospital."

As we learned in the previous chapter, Susan Keats was also away from home, living in a different city, when her mother called to relay the news of her sister's death. Susan tells of her reaction: "I felt horrible. I was stunned and didn't believe it. I hung up the phone and went to watch "Family Ties" on the television and laughed at it—a temporary relief from my terrible morning. The only way to deal with the news was to be distracted for a short time before I could begin to let it sink in. Finally, I was able to cry and to moan 'No, no.' I said my sister's name again and again, and tried to make myself realize that she was really dead.

"A short time later my brother, who was at college in Iowa, called me. After that I had to make plans to fly to Chicago. Whenever something unpleasant happens, I react by keeping busy and that is what I proceeded to do. First I got on with the business of calling people to tell the sad news. Then I just needed to talk to someone, and so I called my boyfriend, Pete, who was in Florida. I also called a friend who was supposed to visit over the weekend. I think I also wanted to hear what their reactions would be to the news of my sister's death. Talking to them made it a bit more real for me. Still, it was too confusing—none of it made sense.

"I flew back to Chicago. Sometime after I got home, my brother and I were in the basement playing with a kitten that my sister had been fond of. My mother came down and said the funeral directors had suggested we have an open-casket viewing just for the family. At first she was against it, but she also knew from her psychology background that sometimes it's helpful because it makes everything seem final. This frightened me, for I didn't think I wanted to do that. At the same time, I really did, because it just didn't seem real. Intellectually I could believe it, but otherwise it was unreal.

"On the day of the funeral, we did have an open viewing, and it was very hard at first. But when finally I did walk up to the coffin with my brother, it wasn't as bad as I had thought. The first thing that struck me when I looked at her was, 'This is just an empty body. All the energy was gone. Carolyn was gone. This is not Carolyn.' That's why it wasn't hard to look at the body, but then I thought, 'Carolyn has to be somewhere, but she certainly isn't in this empty body.' All I could see was this emptiness and I couldn't get the thought from mind: 'Carolyn is somewhere. Carolyn has not dissipated into the universe. Her energy has not dissipated. Carolyn's person is still some-where.' And that's been comforting to me."

After the funeral, Susan found herself having different thoughts. "I would just sit and picture the accident and try to imagine her emotions at that moment. There must have been some point when she knew that something was wrong. I'm sure it all happened quickly, for they said she was killed instantly. But, I couldn't stop wondering what she thought or felt at that last moment of her life. I cried my eyes out for the first couple of weeks."

Another sister who tried to imagine how her brother felt was Madeleine Toomey Pflaumbaum. "I went to my parents' house, and as I looked at my father and mother, I said, 'This just can't be true.' No matter what my mother or father had been to us as parents, no mother or father should ever have to go through this twice, I thought. First my sister Kathleen, and now Larry. As we went through the motions, made the funeral arrangements, and so forth, I just could not believe it.

"When I walked into the funeral home the first night of the

wake, I couldn't wait to enter the room where the body was because I was certain that somehow this had to be a dream. I was convinced I was in the throes of the anesthesia of my operation and thought to myself, 'I'm going to wake up in the recovery room and everything's going to be over and this is all going to be some horrible dream.' And then I saw him lying in the coffin, and I knew it was true.

"But somehow, I understand how Larry felt and don't hold anything against him. I just feel hurt that he wasn't able to hold on for a little more time because I know how bad you can feel and I know a lot of how he felt. Maybe this route was easier for him because he had a gun."

We meet in the following story another sister who was faced with the loss of a second sibling. Betty Tucker, about whom we read in chapter 1, relates a bizarre story of an incident that took place at the second funeral.

"While we were waiting for the funeral services to start, a young woman who had been a good friend of my brother came in with her boyfriend. She introduced the young man and said to my mother, 'I would like you to meet my boyfriend, Simon.' That was the name of my brother who had died several years before. I thought, how many people name their kids Simon? Yet here was a young man by that name sitting at my brother Mitchell's funeral. My mother nodded, but she couldn't look at them. To hear the name 'Simon' was a terrible shock for my mother and I felt great sympathy for her. The whole thing was so unreal to begin with—her losing two sons, my losing two brothers, and then our hearing Simon's name while sitting at the services for my brother Mitchell."

Many surviving siblings, in experiencing the initial shock, shift gears and move into believing that the traumatic event is a dream. In the following story, we hear from fifteen-year-old Cindy Tart of her fantasy that the death of her brother was just a dream. In a later chapter, Cindy's sister, Cathy, age ten, recounts the details of the tragedy.

"My brother Dennis died on Wednesday," Cindy remembers. "My Aunt Bebe took some days off from work to stay with us Thursday, Friday, Saturday, and Sunday. I talked to my Aunt Bebe a lot. I call her Bebe, but her name is Bernice. I would hug her and cry. An old friend of mine came over to be with me. And I hugged her, too. As I talked with my aunt and my friend, I was thinking, 'It's all a dream. I'm in a dream. I'm going to wake up soon, and Dennis is going to come into this room.' I kept thinking tomorrow will be Saturday and Dennis will come here as he usually does on Saturdays and jump on my bed early to wake me up. I said to myself, 'I'll be mad at him, as usual, for waking me up so early.' Then, I thought, 'That's when I'll wake up and discover it was all a bad dream.' But then, at the funeral, when we were hugging friends and family, I found my Aunt Bebe and my knees began to give out under me. I looked at Bebe and said, " 'This is not a dream. It's a nightmare.' "

While Cindy Tart had to shake off the idea that her brother's death was a dream, Karen Kaner had to face the stark reality of her brother's suicide. He had jumped off the roof of the building where they both worked, and every day upon her return to the office she enters that same building. The reality is all too close to pretend it isn't true, although that is what Karen often wishes.

Alan David Frogel had a good job and many friends. He owned his own cooperative apartment and a car; he went out with a number of girls, yet he wasn't happy. His sister, Karen, learned from her parents that he had gone to a therapist when he returned from a vacation in a deep depression. "He came back very unhappy," says Karen. "He had gone to California to visit friends and when he came back he told his family, 'They're all very successful out there—doing well in their jobs and careers. Why don't I have a life like that?' He couldn't see that he did have a life just like that of his West Coast friends. He wasn't aware that people envied him and said literally the same thing: 'Look at that kid! Only twenty-six, and he's got a career and a job and a car.'

"When I found out that Alan had started therapy," his sister Karen recalls, "I called him and said, 'I know you're unhappy. If you want me to listen, I'll be happy to hear whatever you want to talk about. It really hurts me that you're so unhappy.' But he didn't want to talk to me. He didn't want to discuss his problems. As I look back, I realize that my offer to him was the healthiest thing I could have done for myself. I offered to listen and he didn't take me up on it, but I had still offered," Karen says. She continues:

"The Tuesday evening before he died, he was supposed to play tennis with a friend, but he broke the engagement, saying he was too tired and too depressed. He added, 'I'm going to go home and get right into bed.' But instead of that, he called his therapist at home and said, 'I'm in trouble. I need help, I'm in trouble. Talk to me. Talk to me.' But he was so worked up and uncomfortable that the therapist suggested, 'If you still feel this way in the morning, sign yourself into St. Francis Hospital. You can sign in as an outpatient and get medication for your depression. The doctors there will tell you what to do.'

"The next morning at 7:30 A.M., Alan called the therapist but he had already left for his office. However, the doctor's wife, a psychologist, spoke to him. She could tell from his voice that he was in a bad state and she said, 'Don't go to work. Go straight to the hospital. I'll have my husband call ahead and tell them to give you a sedative. Just go to the hospital and they'll know what to do for you when you get there.' Instead of going to the hospital, he went up to the roof of our office building and jumped."

Her brother's body landed on the porch of tenants on the sixteenth floor of the building. Hearing the thud, they called the superintendent who got in touch with the police. On the roof the police found Alan's briefcase, and from items in it, they learned his identity. "The super then told them that I also worked in the building," Karen says. "It was ironic that I had not gone to work that day, one of the few times I had ever stayed home because of illness. You see, I own a business and because I love my work, I rarely take a day off. The strange thing is that I don't know why I was home that day, but I just didn't feel right. However, the superintendent and a policeman went to my office and, because I wasn't there, spoke to my partner, who is also a close friend. He came to my home at once with the horrible news. I'll always love him for that, because I didn't hear it from the police and I didn't hear it from a stranger—I heard it from a close friend. But I still couldn't believe it."

Russell Randazza also found it difficult to believe his sister had died. "It really didn't hit me until later. A month or so after Diane's death, I would come home every night and just go to pieces. I had spent time with her for about four months before she expired, and tried to help her with her meals, but it upset me that she even had trouble eating dinner. My sister knew she was going to die. She wrote a note to all of us, which my mother has, that said things like, 'I love all of you. Keep me in your heart.' Finally, she could no longer write, and she lost all her motor skills. Toward the end, I hated to see her in that condition, and now I feel that it was better that she did not live for she would have been a vegetable."

After her son Chris' body was found, Sherry Sundland tells what happened next. "The two days of horror were over and now the plans for the wake and the funeral had to be made. Joe and Rich, our twins, were told everything we planned to do and what Chris would wear. During the wake they more or less stayed with their friends. We were all still numb until the day Chris was buried. At times the boys didn't want us to hold them, but at other moments they did want to be held. Coming home from the funeral is when the reality set in."

Sherry describes the reactions of her surviving sons in the weeks that followed: "The next weekend was the district wrestling matches for state placement, and we went. Neither Tom nor I wanted to go on; if only we could go to sleep and never wake up to the terrible pain. But we knew we had to go on for the twins and ourselves. The twins needed us now more than ever. Joe wrestled his way to first place and after the match he came up to the bleachers and said, 'I won that for Chris.' Both of us were crying and hugging each other. Although it broke my heart, it made me happy to see how a thirteen-year-old could put his all into it in memory of his little brother and come shining through.

"We all wanted to get away from the whole scene and decided to go to Florida. Up to that point, I really hadn't cried for Chris, for I was in such a state of shock. But in Florida, I was finally able to cry and cry I did. At one point, Rich told us to stop, for Tom was crying with me in the motel room one night. It hurt Rich to see us in such pain. Knowing he couldn't do anything to help us, he said we were keeping him awake as an excuse to block his hurt from us. The trip did all of us good. Tom and I tried to get ourselves back together again and put the memories of the ice and snow and Chris out of our mind for a while. Joe and Rich were able to do about the same thing and be typical thirteen-year-olds for a while, and swim and be carefree. To be able to laugh at the antics of a seagull eased the hurt we all felt. I think being in a totally different place and climate from that in which Chris died helped us not to dwell on his death. It gave us a change, kept us busy doing things we couldn't do at home while we all were together as a family. The twins talked with us about Chris and how he loved the ocean and the things he did the last time we were in Florida. It was a start in the grieving process after the shock and the unreal feeling wore off and a start in the steps to living again."

Chapter Three

Anger

Dan Saulisberry found himself becoming increasingly aware of his brother's absence. "The lyrics of an old Joni Mitchell song became more real to me: 'Don't it always seem to go that you don't know what you've got till it's gone?' Since Tracy was just getting to the age where I felt we could really relate to each other, I became angry that I was going to miss out on all those experiences. To this day, eight years later, I still mourn that relationship. When you're looking forward to something that is a natural event in life, such as sharing with your kid brother, and then that event is taken from you forever, you feel cheated. And you feel that way for the rest of your life because there are constant reminders of what might have been.

"I suppose I have long since accepted his death and forgiven anyone who might have been remotely responsible for it. But deep inside there's an anger and a bitterness toward the circumstances of life that brought about his death. Occasionally it surfaces when I hear of another senseless tragedy somewhere in the world. It just reminds me of the uncertainty of this life and the importance of living each day to the fullest.

"Most of it is behind me now, but there are always situations where you look around and wonder what it would be like if Tracy were here," Dan muses.

Although it was many years since her twenty-six-year-old brother Charles had died in a car accident, Froma Lippmann became very angry at him after her father's death. She was furious that her brother had abandoned her and caused her to become the sole surviving member of their family. While Froma was surrounded by a loving family of her own—her husband, their daughter and son, now grown to adulthood—she became enraged at Charles, particularly one spring Saturday. Frantically, she raced around the house searching for memorabilia of him, because a photograph or memento could "restore" Charles to her, could remind her that once, long ago, she'd had an intact family.

Froma tells what it was like in January 1951—over thirty-five years ago—when her brother died. Six months pregnant with her first child, Froma was "not allowed" to attend the burial. She later came to realize that this left her with no sense of finality to Charles' life. Her well-meaning mother-in-law cautioned Froma not to cry—"at least not in public"—because her mother wasn't crying. Again Froma denied herself the chance to grieve. That denial hurt her for longer than anyone could realize at the time.

Today, it is difficult for Froma to imagine what her brother would be like in middle age, the age of Froma and her husband. "Any mental images of Charles at sixty are quickly erased by the photographs we have of him as an energetic, effervescent young man with a new wife, a brand new home, and the beginnings of a promising career," Froma states.

The sudden death of Froma's brother in a car accident came as a shock to everyone in the family, and each person sought relief from the pain in his or her own way. Froma recalls: "My father aged visibly in the forty-eight hours between Charles' accident and his death—and he sobbed often, then and thereafter. My mother remained stoic, helping others cope with the tragedy, acknowledging her own shattered feelings only when alone, and only in the stillness of many dark nights."

Froma's brother was the first child, born nearly five years after his parents had given up any hope of having offspring. "I think I grew up feeling that Charles was the favorite child, not only older, but smarter and far more outgoing than I could ever hope to be," says Froma. These feelings were intensified after her brother's death. Froma felt she had to become perfect for the sake of her parents, never arguing, never rebelling, never going against their wishes in any way, as if she could thus compensate for the loss they had suffered. Because Froma's husband and her brother had been high school friends, and because her brother's wedding followed so closely upon her own, his death had an understandable, but often disquieting, effect. Her husband, John, became a "son" very soon after he had become a son-in-law. "My parents transferred to him all the strong feelings for a favorite child that they had given to Charles through my growing-up years. Although John fought for years against this transference of feelings, I would ask my parents, 'Who is the child born to you?'" To this day, Froma feels as if "I'd been an afterthought, and that's not easy either."

Froma had difficulty accepting gifts from her parents because her brother's death was always a part of the gift-giving. "When my parents wanted to buy us a dining room rug that was more costly than our budget would allow, my mother began to cry and said, 'If Charles were alive, I'd have two of you to buy for, so let me do this.' And so I did. It was the same when she thought we needed a clothes dryer we were unprepared to buy, and again, when we received our first TV as a gift from my parents. All these gifts were related—directly and verbally—to my brother's death, and to his ever-present absence in our lives. It is never easy to accept gifts with strings attached."

After her brother's death, Elaine Altman encountered parental callousness toward her. "On the day of the funeral, my father said, 'You may give the eulogy, but don't cry.' My parents cut everything short—like sitting Shiva (a Jewish mourning period) for only one day. When I went to see them, and wanted to talk about Michael, my father screamed at me, 'You're supposed to cheer *us* up. You're not supposed to talk about the deceased.'"

Conversely, Elaine felt rage against her parents. "There were many months when I wouldn't see them at all because of things they had said about my brother, both before and after his death. I was outraged at the way they had treated him during his life, and for a while I thought I would stop seeing them. But from ethical teachings I'd garnered, I felt perhaps it wasn't my place to judge them, that I should see them and be as nice as possible. But one thing I will not do is to refrain from talking about Michael. They could never appreciate all the beauty, sensitivity, and caring for people that Michael had. He cared very much about my parents and their feelings. It's too bad they couldn't care about his. They weren't proud of him in life or death."

Susan Keats encountered people who patted her arm and said, "I understand how you must feel." She reflects, "I remember when my boyfriend's father died, I didn't know how to console him, and I recall thinking that I couldn't possibly know how he felt. For that reason, I said to him, 'I don't understand how you feel because I have never lost a parent, but I hurt for you and I am here if you need me.'"

Susan wishes that others had the sensitivity to say the words she needed to hear. "But I have found that in the first weeks you don't want people to say: 'Well, these things happen.' This 'thing' that happened is the death of my sister. These 'things' happen to dogs crossing the street. It's the kind of 'thing' that only happens to other families until it strikes you. Then it opens up a new way of looking at your own life as well.

"So when people say, 'I understand how you feel,' you resent it, although you know they mean well. But when your wound is so fresh, it is hard. All you really want to hear from people is that they're there for you, and you can call them anytime. You really need your friends."

Cindy Tart, like Susan Keats, reacted strongly to people who commented, "I know how you feel." She recalls how such statements affected her: "What would get me really wild was people coming up to me at the funeral home and saying, 'I'm sorry. I understand what you're going through.' How can they sit there or stand there and say that honestly if they have never had the same experience! Others would say, 'Cindy, I'm really sorry about your loss. I know what you're going through because I lost my grandfather,' or they would mention some other relative. It would infuriate me that people could say, 'I know how you feel,' when they *didn't* know at all how I was feeling."

Another anger that Cindy experienced was "Why?" She thought, "Why couldn't it be someone else? Why couldn't it be some kid whose parents had abused or neglected it, some malnourished kid in another country. But my brother Dennis had no misery to get out of. It was unfair. Why wasn't it someone else, not my Dennis?"

Allison Heitner was a surviving sister who also heard "I know how you feel" and became annoyed with the people who said it. "I couldn't deal with people coming over to me and saying, 'I know how you feel.' I didn't want to see anybody after that because I didn't want to get violent and say, "You *DON'T* know how I feel. Believe me, you don't know how I feel. I also thought that my parents didn't know how I felt. I said to my mother, 'You and Daddy have each other to comfort each other, but Leslie was part of me, my closest friend, and I have no one to comfort me, no one who knows what I feel.'"

After the funeral, Allison did not want to see anyone. "I kept going up to my room and I told my parents, 'I don't want anyone to come up to see me, I don't care who it is.' I knew I was upsetting my parents, but I really didn't want to see anyone." There was only one person whom Allison permitted to come to her room. "This was a woman for whom I baby-sat. Her name was Donna. A week before Leslie died, her youngest sister, twenty-nine years old, had died of cancer. So when Donna came upstairs and said, 'Allison, I know how you feel,' I knew she really *did* know how I felt."

Allison was bitter about the help that she and her sister had sought but failed to receive from psychologists. "As far as I was concerned, psychologists were full of it. They didn't know what they were doing because they couldn't even help my sister. I used to have nightmares about the doctors who thought they knew everything, the ones who kept me away from my sister for the last two weeks of her life, who told us it was better if she didn't see me or my parents."

Allison tells of the experiences, subsequent to her sister's death, that she and her parents had with psychologists. "They would say such things to my parents as, 'Well, maybe it would have been worse because you would have been with her until the end, and then you would feel guilty.' As if it was better to have happened in the hospital than at home—how would *they* feel then? Those doctors were a joke, especially one psychologist who really took the cake. I had been gaining weight at an alarming rate, and I asked him to hypnotize me to make me lose weight. So, the doctor said, 'Okay, I'll hypnotize you.' Now, he knew that my sister died from drowning. So listen to what he said to me: 'Picture yourself in water. Close your eyes. Now picture the water going up and up and over your face until you're completely immersed!' Can you imagine him saying that to me, knowing that my sister died of drowning? And that's how he was hypnotizing me? I had no respect for them. Just anger."

Cautioning bereaved siblings and parents alike, Dr. Lawrence LeShan, noted psychologist and author of *How to Meditate*, and *How You Can Fight for Your Life*, agrees that counseling or therapy is not always the answer for the surviving siblings. "When a young plant receives a shock, it reverberates but can still stand strong against the elements. Often, so it is with surviving children." Dr. LeShan, a surviving brother, believes a good route for siblings is to talk to other siblings and to maintain warm communication with their family and friends.

Dr. LeShan urges that careful scrutiny should be given to psychologists being considered. "It is best to have an interview with the psychologist, see if you like the person and if they have a firm grip on the realities of grief. If a doctor has an instant blueprint for you after twenty minutes, run, don't walk, to the nearest exit."

While Dr. LeShan recognizes there are many fine psychotherapists, including psychiatrists, psychologists, social work-ers and ministers, he also believes there are too many "others." In his viewpoint, "You have to shop around for a good psychotherapist more than you would for a used car, because there are at least as many lemons today in the field of psychotherapy as there are in used cars."

Russell Randazza wanted his parents to understand his feelings and became annoyed when they could not. "I tried to be a son to my parents," Russell says, "but at the same time try to tell them that life had to go on. They didn't want to hear about it. So I just let them go at their own pace for a while. But then, when it got out of hand, I had several arguments with them. They turned around from being very loving parents to being quick-tempered, cutting, sharp, and short with me and my brother. I tried very hard to express to them that they had two other children, not that it wasn't fair to us, but that we're here, to help you, to love you, and whatever you feel let's bring it out; don't hold it inside yourself. It took a couple of years for that to happen. Although my father tries, he will never be the same."

On another occasion, Russell became irritated with his mother. "My parents had some 8 mm film taken when we three kids were very young. I had the film transposed onto a video cassette and I showed it to my mom for the first time. Her response was, 'Oh, Diane, where are you?' 'Where are you?' She said it twice. I stopped the movie and I said, 'You know where she is. Why do you keep on asking yourself?' I don't know, maybe she's looking for a sign or something that will put all her feelings to bed. But to this day, she will say that. My mother says that talking about Diane helps her. Sometimes she just says Diane's name out loud as part of her everyday activities. She talks to Diane as if she is able to hear her. Expressions like, 'Oh, Di, remember that?' Or, 'Well, Di, what do you think of that?' My mother says she doesn't say Diane's name as though it were a moan, but it will just pop out as it did when Diane had been here, just in a matter-of-fact way. She becomes upset when others urge her not to talk about her daughter. Diane existed and I guess it's my mother's way of remembering her. Who am I to judge her?"

Karen Kaner experienced the resentment and anger at having to take care of everything after the death of her brother. "In November and December, we thought my brother had finally grown up, but in January he killed himself. All of a sudden, I'm back to being the responsible one who takes care of everybody. I had to go to the morgue and identify my brother's body. I figured, 'If I can go to the morgue and see his body, read the autopsy report and get involved in that horror, then I can do anything.' But, what's happened since then is that I'm expected to do everything. 'Karen will take care of this. Karen will take care of that. Karen will see to it.' And I'm tired of it. I need to be taken care of."

Adding to Karen's resentment is the feeling that she has to be careful of what she says or does in her parents' presence, because they are easily upset. "I just don't have the strength anymore to watch what I say or what I do. And everything goes right back to Alan. My mother has little consideration for anyone else's feelings. Everything revolves around, 'Look at me, look at me, see what I have had to deal with.' And every time she gets upset, my reaction is, 'Look at me, he was my brother also. It hurts me, too. You just can't tear me apart like this.'"

"My cousin gave birth to a baby with a cleft palate. My mother's reaction, instead of being one of sympathy for the parents in having to cope with this child's need for an operation if it is to have a chance in life, and then speech therapy, and so on, my mother's response was, 'You should only know what I've been living through. A cleft palate isn't so bad. You can fix that. But look at what I'm going through.' It's as if her grief has taken away her ability to have any understanding of another person's pain. Right now, I have a lot of medical problems of my own, and I'm no longer able to take care of everybody else."

Karen Schlesier Eisen, another sister who resented being taken for granted, was angry that her pain was not recognized as being as great as that of her parents. "At the funeral, people said to me, 'You have to be strong for your parents' sake.' What a horrible thing to say to me! It was as if I didn't count because I am only a sister. A scene that I shall never forget took place at the funeral parlor where my brother was lying in the coffin and my parents were holding hands and crying over him. Never will I get over that. Nor will I ever forget the insensitivity of the people who added to my pain by implying that I should overlook my own grief and be strong for my parents."

Karen attempted to explain her feelings to her parents. "I said to them, 'You lost a child, but you still have one, you have me. You've lost a very important part of your life, but you have not lost the relationship. I have no other brother. You have another child. I have lost the relationship with my brother that I will never have again. I tried to tell my mother that while she suffered a terrible loss, she did not also lose a relationship. I tell her that, not because I want to hurt her, but so that she knows how much it hurts me. And not to make her feel guilty that she didn't have any more children—although she does feel guilty about that now. When a sibling is left as an only surviving child, there is a completely different kind of feeling. My parents have each other. I feel I have no one. And, this is a feeling expressed by many of the kids who came to the siblings group I facilitated at The Compassionate Friends' meetings.

"The only way you get through these issues," Karen continues, "is by talking about them. However, I don't think you can force anyone to talk. I think it just has to happen. There are moments when I don't want to talk about my brother's death. There are times when I see my mother is so upset that I want no part of it. Perhaps I'm having a good day and it's not something I want to think about then. I think about it often enough. I have pictures of my brother all over my apartment. I even have several right next to my bed. Every night when I shut out the light, he's there for me to see. Even if I've gone all day without thinking about him, he's the last thing I see every night before I go to sleep. Most of the things I think about him are good, but at other times I feel, 'This is not fair.' Then I'm really angry and unhappy because I miss him so much."

Several years after Billy's death, Karen was able to talk very honestly and share some personal thoughts with friends. "Grief is so personal, I don't get into it with everyone. But I'm at a point now where I no longer make him into a saint and make it seem as if I don't have any bad thoughts about his death. There are times when I hate my brother. A couple of weeks ago, I had a conversation with a friend. We were in Atlantic City and, during a discussion about Billy's death, I said, 'Yes, I hate my brother. I hate that he did this to me and I blame him for a lot of unhappiness in my life.'"

"I think it's honest to be able to say it's okay to hate this person who has changed and altered your life so drastically. It's never going to be the same. It's not what I had in mind for myself. There are so many things in the future that I won't have and that's his fault. I will never have a sister-in-law who is married to him. I'll never be an aunt except through marriage. But it will not be a personal relationship. I will bury my parents alone. I will go to the cemetery and look at the three of them alone. Our kids will not play together. There will be no cousins. And that's definitely not what I had in mind. I resent him for that. I don't know how the accident happened. He was careless and I'm very angry with him for not thinking a little bit more about the people who would be affected by his carelessness, especially himself."

Betty Tucker found herself puzzled that a rabbi would not know what to say at her brother's funeral. "My mother asked if I would discuss with the rabbi what I wanted said at the funeral. The rabbi whom I originally asked for couldn't come, so he sent a friend, a man who had known my brother. They had been to parties together. He was a young Reform rabbi— just starting out. After he asked me, 'What should I say?' he added, 'Your brother was my friend and this is the first funeral at which I'm officiating.' He paused and then added, 'What does a person say?' It then fell to me to make suggestions for his talk. I was drained at that point, but I said to him, 'Say what's in your heart. Make it short and sweet.' I remember it as if it were yesterday. It was such a strange happening, for what do *you* say when the person officiating at a funeral has to ask you what to say? I was overcome. It was difficult for me to say anything to him."

Anger at the clergy is an issue that arises in the lives of many surviving siblings. The unique position in the community and in the lives of their congregations makes the clergy extremely important as a source of support and comfort. When people hear from a man of God that we cannot understand the ways of God, this can be of great solace, bereaved families tell us. The message that comes best from the clergy, most surviving siblings say, is to lend an ear and provide the means of sharing pain. Sharing someone's pain is a tremendous undertaking, at best, and requires putting yourself in his or her shoes to some degree. The effect on the listener takes a toll; this may in part be the reason why some would rather avoid working with grief-stricken families.

Bereaved siblings often complain that their clergyman justified the death as God's will when asked to explain "Why?" Much anger may be directed at men of God, as it is to members of the medical profession. This anger, according to grief experts, is an initial reaction among those in the early stages of grief, and usually is a cover for their real anger—the reality of the death.

There is also a division of feelings about God among bereaved siblings. Some feel closer to God, believing there is an afterworld and that they will see their brother or sister again. Others cease to be on talking terms with God—angry that God in some way did not prevent the tragedy. As one sibling's parent said: "But God doesn't take away. God doesn't make things happen. It just happens."

One surviving sibling, Madeleine Toomey Pflaumbaum, addressed this issue. "After my brother died, it was as if it were the second time around, experiencing again all the grief that followed my sister Kathleen's death. I thought to myself, 'I wish there were someone from the clergy who could have said to me, 'You know, this is God's plan.' " Maybe I would have felt a little more comfortable with that. Instead, I had to seek that out on my own. The clergy were no better at helping me with Larry than they were with Kathleen. You know, people are with you the first few days of the funeral and then they go on with their lives, but you can't. I wish I could go back to the way I was before all this happened. But instead of hearing some words of wisdom, some sensitive statement of comfort, the clergyman said to me, 'When it rains, it pours.' I had expected some kind of consolation and that was the answer I got. So I realized that the clergy are human like the rest of us and that I had to find the answers within myself. I had to rely on my own resources. But it has left me with a bitter taste for men of the cloth who have nothing more comforting to say to a bereaved person."

Another form of resentment Madeleine had to cope with was the anger her son felt at his uncle for killing himself. "Erik is very angry. Everything that Larry had given him as a gift is now out of his room. Both of my sons are really angry at their uncle. My son Jeffrey said to me just the other day in the car, 'If you could bring anybody back from the dead and trade it in with a candy bar or something, who would you want to bring back?' When I replied, 'Who would you want to bring back?' he said, 'Well, I'd want to bring back Aunt Kathy, and Martin Luther King, and John Kennedy.' I asked, 'What about Uncle Larry?' and he replied, 'Uncle Larry was a bad person. He put himself where he is!' That from a ten-year-old! It saddens me that the clergy have so little to say to me that I might in turn comfort my children and counsel them."

Chapter Four

Guilt Feelings

After Florence Campbell's brother died, he was constantly in her thoughts. She wondered why she hadn't been aware of the seriousness of his illness. "I understand clearly now that my parents knew he was going to pass on. They must have come to accept it. But I didn't know, and I feel guilty because there were times when I was very short with him. If I'd known he had only a short while left, I would not have acted that way. I keep remembering that I said to him, 'Jesse Ray, you're not trying to do anything for yourself.'

"I was very sad for a long time after he passed, because I had never lost anyone in our immediate family. My parents had experienced the loss of a small son, but that was before I was born. This child, named Linwood, lived to the age of two. But since I never knew him, I didn't have any memories. On the other hand, I have a great many memories of Jesse Ray, and many guilt feelings, too, as the result of those thoughts. It took me some time to come to terms with those feelings. I kept thinking that I could have spent more time with him. If I had known he was so sick or that he wasn't going to get better, I wouldn't have yelled at him. I didn't abuse him or anything like that, you know, but I would get short with him.

"After my brother died, I felt that perhaps I was trying to justify my behavior, because I also had thoughts that if I had known how sick he was, I probably would have waited on him hand and foot. I probably would have shown him by my actions that something was seriously wrong. A friend said to me, 'If you had known and treated him with kid gloves, you might have conveyed that you knew he was very sick. Maybe he would have been frightened by that kind of attention from you and might have made his passing harder. If you had acted other than your normal way with him, it might have embarrassed him, because he was a proud and independent man. But this way, whether he did or didn't know how sick he was, it was probably best for him that you acted as natural as you always did. If you had babied him, he most likely wouldn't have liked being treated like a vegetable or as if he were dying.'"

Florence recalls a day when her brother was sitting in the wheelchair in the backyard. "He looked so very pitiful, and that really got to me. A friend of his came by, and as I walked away to let them have some privacy, I could have sworn I heard him tell his friend that there was nothing they could do for him. Afterward, I dismissed it. Maybe my mind couldn't accept what I thought he had said. I really can't say. All I know is that when my brother died, I did not believe I had known he was going to die. Maybe I had a mental block about accepting it. Maybe that's why I was short with him. Maybe I wanted him to do something to make it different, to change things for the better.

"I think I began to put it together when he came home for a period of time because there were no rooms at the hospital. Soon after that, he got to the point where he couldn't walk anymore, and so I knew something was very wrong. But, somehow, I didn't think in terms of him dying. Even though I realize now that all the signs were there, I just wasn't capable of accepting that he was dying. My friend, trying to comfort me and relieve my guilt, said, 'You weren't mean to your brother. You just didn't want him to be so sick, and so when you were short with him, you wanted him to do something to get better.'"

When Florence and her parents went to South Carolina to visit relatives there, they talked about her brother. "My parents and I went to see my sister, who is living down there, and other family members. One day, my sister and I were on the porch talking about Jesse Ray, and I told her that I had not known he was going to die. She said she knew. But I insisted I hadn't known, and asked, 'How come nobody told me?' I told her I didn't figure it out until we took him back to the hospital for the last time. Then it was too late for me to undo the way I had acted earlier."

In the preceding story, a sister wasn't told of her brother's impending death, but in the following account, a sister expresses the guilt she felt after remembering her sister's admonition concerning her belief that she would soon die.

"My sister Leslie said to me, 'Allison, you're the closest one to me. Why can't you believe that when I tell you I'm going to die, it's the truth. I don't care that no one else believes me, but why can't *you* believe me? What are you going to do when I die?' I said, 'Leslie, if you die, I will kill myself and I will be with you.' And she said, 'Okay, okay, seriously, okay.' And then she hung up.

"The next day, she called and said, 'Allison, I appreciate what you said yesterday, but I know how you feel about living, getting married, and having children. Promise me, if something happens to me, that you won't kill yourself, that you won't die.' But I didn't promise. She called me again the next day. And then I said, 'Okay, I won't kill myself.' As time went on, and after she was hospitalized, my father and I felt she was getting worse. We wanted to get her out, and Leslie wanted to get out, too. But the doctors said, 'No, no, no. She's not ready. We've still got to experiment and find out.' When nothing like this has happened in your family before, you tend to believe doctors. And that is just what we did. As much as my father and I saw that the hospitals weren't helping, we trusted them, even though she was getting worse and worse. But it would fluctuate and some days would be worse than others. Yet I will always remember her asking me why I didn't believe her when she said she was going to die."

Karen Schlesier Eisen, about whom we read in chapter 2, is another sister who felt guilty for a time. She urges surviving siblings not to nurture such feelings. "I remember the fights we had and I felt guilty about them—that I used to beat my brother and I was cruel to him, too, until he got big enough to keep me from hurting him. Also, I had paid his car insurance. I kept thinking if I hadn't done so, he wouldn't have been driving.

"All in all, there were many things that made me feel guilty. I would think, 'Why am I here and he's not?' I was older than Billy, so it would have been natural for me to die before him. Actually, my parents should be dead and he should be alive. You know, chronologically, things should work out in a certain pattern. At a group meeting for surviving siblings, I heard other siblings question whether their mother or father would have preferred it if it was they who had died. But you really can't think that a mother or a father could have made a choice, preferring that it was you who died first. Anyway, you can't feel guilty about being alive. It's not your fault. You didn't do anything wrong. You had nothing to do with the death of your brother or your sister. You're not omnipotent. Nevertheless, you really can't explain away guilt, it's such a personal thing and so many different things contribute to it. You have to work it out for yourself. I don't dwell on guilt anymore. It's not something I really think about a lot. The business about the car insurance faded away in time. As for the fights, I got over those and forgot about them. But there's some guilt still running around. I don't know that it all ever really goes away."

The one thing that Karen does wish is that things could have been different. "I think Billy knew how I felt about him, but I wish I could have told him. I wish that we could have had a big emotional scene in which I could have said, 'You're the most wonderful person I've ever met,' for that was how I felt even when he was alive, but I never told him. Nor do I recall telling him that I loved him—but I know he knew that I did. Nevertheless, I would feel better if I had been a little kinder in my last conversation with him. But I had no way of knowing what would happen and I shouldn't feel guilty about that."

Jay Goldstein kept asking himself about the "what ifs?" What if he had not shared his brother's room? What if he had not heard the alarm? What if he hadn't wakened Philip that morning? Jay himself had serviced a paper route until three months prior to Philip's death, and he and his brother used to leave together to go to work. Jay felt that if he still had his old paper route, he would have left with Philip and the accident might not have happened.

Those pangs of guilt in the first few months after the accident were diminished after Jay attended group meetings for siblings, an extension of The Compassionate Friends, a national self-help group for bereaved parents. At the siblings' meetings, Jay met other surviving children who suffered the same guilt, anger, sadness, and confusion that afflicted him. Today Jay realizes that nothing he did or did not do caused his brother's death and that the feelings he experienced were normal thoughts. Brothers and sisters who attended the siblings' gatherings told him they felt the same as he had—that it was natural to feel that way, but also important to understand that they were not responsible for their sibling's death.

When his brother died, Jay was fifteen years old. Today, twenty years old and a college student, he has different types of guilt reactions. "In having only two children as opposed to the three they had when Philip was alive, my parents' financial situation has improved dramatically over the last five years. As a result, my brother Josh and I now get quite a bit more of everything than we did before. That bothers me, and a bit of guilt exists. If Philip were here, it would not be as economically possible to give us so much, because they'd have two sons in college now rather than only one. But I don't dwell on this. I do know that, to the extent they could, my parents would always have wanted to provide the three of us with material things. However, I realize that, with Philip gone, my brother Josh and I have been given more. I think you are bound to have a reaction to that."

Being away at school relieves Jay of some guilt. "At home, when you go out for the evening, you feel guilty if you come home at all hours in the morning, knowing that your parents are worried. Being out of town at college makes it easier, because my late hours can't worry them as much as they would if I were at home and my parents were waiting for me to get back. I think parents normally have concern when their children are out late at night, but I think it is probably accentuated after they have lost a child."

Jay is grateful for the siblings group that was available to him. His parents also attended The Compassionate Friends group meetings, which helped them ease their pain through sharing with other bereaved families. In reflecting on his life today, Jay says, "I really don't think there is anything anyone can do for me right now. In fact I almost feel guilty that everything in my life is going so well. Everything's fine.

After the death of her second brother, Betty Tucker was concerned, not only about her own guilt, but about her mother's. "I remember that when my father died, my mother never cried. She just sat and looked blank, thinking, I suppose of the past, for she had been very close to him. Then, when my brother Simon died, she was also dry-eyed. But, when my brother Mitchell died, she just let loose. She cried and cried all night. It was a nightmare. I had to share a room with her and I remember feeling, 'Oh my God, the woman is racked with guilt.' And I thought, 'Maybe we all are. Maybe we didn't try to do enough for him.' "

Betty's thoughts stemmed from the times in Mitchell's life when she had tried to counsel him. "He was into so many strange things, magic for example. I don't mean magic tricks, but things more like voodooism. He approached it in a very intelligent way, as he did with everything. As you listened to him, you soon realized that he actually believed what he was talking about. He had told me about the drugs he had tried in the past and about the feelings he had after their use. I'd often say to him, 'Maybe you don't need to do this,' or 'Perhaps you're doing the wrong thing.'

"He had a roommate, a friend of his, who was in the music business. Mitchell had just taken a job as an agent for a musical group. Like many music fans, my brother's apartment had been fixed up with stereo equipment. My mother said it was really beautiful and she was happy for him because he had decided to lead an average life. She felt Mitchell was finally on the right road. He was off all the nonsense of the past, and felt he had really found himself. Then, the hepatitis set in. He claimed that he had never taken drugs, but all users lie when they're into that stuff. He died of an overdose of sleeping drugs, but who knows how he got the hepatitis in the first place. It could have been the result of taking drugs. It's hard to know. Even so, one thinks back and wonders, 'Maybe if we had done this,' or 'Maybe if we had said that,' things would have been different. But you don't know what's going on in another person's head, so you don't know what you could have done for him.''

Another sibling who was worried about a family member's guilt is Leslie Boden. "My brother Scott and I had gone to a grief workshop after David's death. He said to me, 'Tell me something. Did this help? Do you feel better now? I replied, 'Yes, in some ways I do feel better. I no longer feel so numb and I've been able to open myself to people more. Now I feel that I've been able to move a bit in my life. Yes, I think it helped me and I do feel a little better.' But, his reply concerned me. He said, 'Well, I'm not sure that I want to feel better.' "

In examining her brother's statement, Leslie came to two conclusions. "I think it's twofold. If you don't think about him and experience that pain every day, you feel guilty. You think you're betraying him, that you care less because you're thinking about him less, and so now your life can go on. There is definitely a certain amount of guilt in feeling better. The other part, I think, is that pain is the last direct link that you can have in a relationship with a person who has died—the last cause-and-effect relationship. For example, if my brother David were alive and he punched my arm, I would feel that pain. I would know it was David. To feel the extreme pain in the heart after his death, it's also his act and it hits you with as much impact as a punch, certainly. To let go of that pain is, in a way, letting go of him."

In the book, *Recovering from the Loss of a Child*, Dr. and Mrs. Allen Haimes, bereaved parents whose family we will read about in a later chapter, say, "Getting on with living doesn't mean you have to forget. You will always remember, so why not remember the good things in your child's life." Many siblings have indicated the same philosophy—to try and put the guilt and anger behind you and get on with your life, remembering the good things.

Chapter Five

Symptoms of Grief

The significance of life events, such as the death of a sibling, as contributing factors in the onset of illness, depression, and maladaptive behavior among bereaved children and adolescents is well documented, says Jeanette Colburn, pastoral associate and teacher. (More of her research on siblings appears in chapter 11.) "Siblings who have undergone such life events are at a greater risk of illness than those who have not and who receive adequate support. There is substantial evidence," Colburn states, "which correlates the availability of social support and the child's risk of illness."

Colburn's extensive research has revealed that, after stressful experiences such as grief, bereaved children are just as prone to illness as their parents. "Our body's immune system," she asserts, "which fights infection and disease, is suppressed and we are much more susceptible to illness. Siblings' symptoms may appear within forty-eight hours after the death, when the child begins to believe the loss is permanent, or at anniversaries, holidays, or other special events. They may have repeated colds, ear infections, headaches, gastrointestinal upsets, skin rashes, and heightened allergic responses. One might also notice that these children may be biting their fingernails, picking at themselves, or twiddling their hair to the point of pulling it out." She also indicates, "A review of literature in this field reveals that bereaved youths are at high risk for developing many of the same diseases as adults, particularly if they have a genetic predisposition. Some of the diseases specifically identified are juvenile rheumatoid arthritis, juvenile diabetes mellitus, peptic ulcer, childhood leukemia, bronchial asthma, and other allergies."

An important point unearthed in her research is shared with us by Colburn. "Studies indicate that when a person is not able to finish mourning in childhood, he may have to give in to his emotions so he is not completely overwhelmed by them. Otherwise, he may experience a sadness throughout his life, one for which he cannot find a satisfactory explanation." But it is never too late, as witnessed by the experience of Sister Jane Marie Lamb (see chapter 8) who was only able to grieve fully for her sister after her brother's death years later.

We will now hear from several adult children who tell of the physical and mental symptoms that plagued them after the death of their siblings.

After her sister's death, Madeleine Toomey Pflaumbaum's grief took many forms. When she went back to work, she cried constantly. On one occasion, she saw glass tubes nearby and wanted to smash them. It was then she realized that her anger had to be channeled into other areas. After considering various activities, Madeleine decided to join a soccer team and found that, by participating in the game, she was able to get a great deal of anger and frustration out of her system.

A few weeks after her sister's funeral, Madeleine broke out with acne, a skin condition from which she never before suffered. She visited a dermatologist who linked it to the emotional upheaval caused by her sister Kathleen's death. The condition soon cleared up with an antibiotic medication. Then for the first two months after the accident that killed her sister, Madeleine missed her menstrual cycle. This sent her into a panic. She doubted she was pregnant but went to see her gynecologist, who assured her she was fine and *not* pregnant. The doctor told Madeleine the stress she was under caused the change in her cycle. She later suffered from chest pains, heart palpitations, and difficulty in breathing and was given a tranquilizer to calm her. Her ability to function on all levels was impaired for months. It wasn't until six months later that Madeleine was able to add a simple column of figures. She couldn't even write a bank check during that time. It was months before Madeleine was able to sleep through the night. For a while, she was haunted by periodic dreams about her mother's telephone call announcing her sister Kathleen's death. Madeleine tried to redream that call, trying to change it to one in which the accident had not happened nor had her sister died.

Madeleine realized that her brother Larry, who was also to die prematurely, was grieving deeply for their sister. "He couldn't show his grief. He just could not let go and accept Kathleen's death. For example, he wouldn't allow any kind of mass cards in the house. He seemed to become reckless, almost defiant, as if nothing could possibly happen to him. His appearance, too, became very sloppy. Although he always worked and supported his family, it seemed that his whole life was lived on a casual plane after Kathleen's death. What had once been important to maintain in his appearance didn't seem important to him anymore. That was probably the depression that had set in."

Madeleine tells of an incident that occurred two years after her brother's death. "You don't really ever get over losing a brother or sister. Last week, for example, my son Erik hurt his head in a soccer game, and I had to take him to the hospital. Across from us sat a boy who was a hemophiliac and was getting plasma. Another kid, sitting next to us, was being treated for leukemia. But none of that disconcerted me, and I wasn't bothered or upset. But I did feel sympathy for the parents and I hoped the children would recover.

"Then, all of a sudden, they put next to us a woman whose son had just come in—a twenty-three-year-old with a gunshot wound in the stomach, from which he later died. The mother cried out for her son. All of a sudden, everything stopped and my pain started all over again. In my mind it was my mother crying out for Larry. I had thought I was doing so well and was having good days, but this one thing, hearing this mother's anguish, caused the intensity of my earlier grief to surface again."

Another surviving sister, Betty Tucker, tells of a throat condition that developed after her brother's death. "I was never sick or got colds. But after Simon died, I had a sore throat that lasted for about six weeks. Finally, I went to a doctor, not because I felt sick, but because I had this crazy thing in my throat. When I visited the doctor to have my throat tested, he said to me, 'There's nothing wrong. There's absolutely nothing wrong.' He then asked, 'Have you had a recent trauma of any kind?' Apparently my grief had manifested itself by landing in my throat as a nervous condition. But the throat thing stayed with me and hung on for weeks and weeks."

Karen Kaner was also a surviving sister who had never been ill. But two weeks after her brother's death, she developed ileitis and wound up in the hospital. "I've always been healthy. This was not only the first time I had ever been sick, but the first time I had ever been in a hospital. Since then it's been a very different life for me—constantly being ill. For a while, I had to see a doctor weekly and have had to take medication throughout this last year. The first time I ever missed work was the two weeks after Alan died and then right after that I was in the hospital. I have always been the strong one. I have always been the caretaker, but now I was the sick one. Throughout life I had been the one who bought the gifts and he the one who put his name on the cards; I would take care of something and he would get the credit. As adults, we spoke about it. I told him how unhappy I was about always being dumped on. For the first time, in November, for my mom's birthday, Alan took care of it. He bought the present, and I put my name on the card. Then in December, my dad got sick and ended up in the hospital, and Alan moved back home to be with my mom. Before I knew my father was in the hospital, Alan went home to stay with her. So now, here I am left as the only child, going back to those memories, and worrying now about the burden of my parents.

Allison Heitner shares with us the torment she endured after the loss of her younger sister. "I had the letters my sister had written me, and it was as if she knew what I would have to go through. She would write, 'You must go on living. Don't blame yourself.' My parents wanted to help me, but I didn't want anybody. It was my own suffering and I didn't want to share it. When my mother would cry—and at the beginning she was crying all the time—I would get angry at her. I never cried in front of my family. Instead, I'd go up to my room and cry. Every night I cried myself to sleep. I was in such a state that I quit my job and stayed home for the whole summer. Then I began to go through this phase of talking to her: 'Leslie, come to me.' As if she were a ghost, you know. I would think, 'Come, tell me how you're doing. I want to see you. I want to see you.'

"I read books about life after death and how people can make contact with the departed, but they would scare me too much. However, I did have two experiences in which I really felt her presence. The first took place during the summer after she died. I was alone. Nobody was home and I decided to lie down in the back yard. I had been in my room for an eternity, but it was sunny, so I decided to go outdoors. My brother had left his bicycle right behind the lounge chair where I was lying.

"I began thinking to myself as I lay there, 'I could go into the house right now, take some pills, come back and lie here and die and be with my sister.' There was no wind, no noise, only warm sun. Just as I was thinking about the pills, my brother's bicycle fell on my head. As I said, there was no wind and there was nobody there. Before I could even think, I said, 'Leslie, Leslie, Leslie . . . I'm *not* going to do it. I was only *thinking* about it.' In other words, I felt as if she were tapping me on the head, saying, 'Don't be stupid, Allison.' But nobody was there. I immediately said, 'All right. All right. I'm not going to do it.' I felt that it was a contact from her and she had made that bicycle fall on my head to stop me."

Allison tells how she reconsidered the idea of suicide after returning to school. "I was sitting alone in my dorm room and became depressed about her. That's when I came to my bright conclusion, as I look back on it now, which was, 'Let me give my sister an opportunity for me to be with her. Let's see if I try to kill myself and she wants me to be with her . . .'" You know, it was as if I were talking to her. I said, 'Leslie, this is your chance. If you miss me as much as I miss you, then I will die and be with you. If you want me to live, I will live.' So I cut my wrists slightly, just enough to start them bleeding. Then I became scared and called the infirmary. Even though I tried to justify it, saying that Leslie made me live, I really didn't try very hard to kill myself. But the infirmary said that in order for me to stay in school, I had to have counseling. That's how I came to see the doctor who was of so little help to me."

Allison explains in more detail the mood swings she experienced in those early days at school. "I would go through stages—from being self-destructive by cutting myself off from everybody to thinking constantly about dying. All I thought about was Leslie and I was consumed with the idea that Leslie needed me. We had lived in the same room for eighteen years and were never separated. That is how I developed the stupid thought, 'Let me try to kill myself. If I die, that means she needs me and I'll be very happy. If I live, that means she wanted me to live.'"

"So I went back to school, but I functioned like a zombie. I went to class and I got straight A's. But, every day over my head was this cloud, this thought of dying, that there is no reason to live. I wanted to be with my sister. Nothing mattered to me. That was the first time I thought about experimenting with drugs. Before that, I said I would never put a chemical in my body. Now, I thought, 'You live only once.' I could die tomorrow, I thought, and that would be the happiest day of my life, because I felt I would be reunited with Leslie. As I look back at it now, my desire to live was very strong. Although I am now a career person these six years later, I have, ever since I can remember, wanted to have children. Before Leslie died, I was totally against drugs. My whole thing was, 'You're messing up your body. You're not going to be able to have healthy children.' After Leslie died, I didn't care about anything. I was a virgin when I went to college, which today is pretty strange, but Leslie and I were very good girls. So, I went ahead and had my first sexual encounter. My reasoning was, 'I should do everything because I could die tomorrow.' "

When Mike Famiano was nineteen years old, his sister Wendy, seventeen, was struck and killed by an automobile. That accident was the beginning of a three-year struggle for Mike to retain his sanity. He describes his immediate reactions to the accident and tells of his desperate attempts to cope with his sister's death.

"It was a typical Friday night in April 1983. I had just returned from college at about 7:30 P.M. and was playing catch ball with my girlfriend in our backyard. My parents were on the patio talking to a neighbor when the phone rang. My folks were too busy talking so my girlfriend ran into the house and picked up the phone. She hung up the phone and yelled, 'Wendy has just been hit by a car in front of Fay's drugstore.'

"I dropped my glove and ran upstairs to my room to get my car keys. I tried to calm myself down by thinking aloud, 'It can't be bad because there is just a big parking lot in front of Fay's' and 'Maybe she only has a broken arm or leg.' Still those thoughts didn't stop me from running around the house like a maniac. Deep down, I felt it was worse than that."

Mike and his girlfriend got into his car and sped off in frantic haste. "I was driving like a crazy person. When I pulled up to the intersection near the parking plaza, it was filled with police cars. My first reaction was, 'Oh, shit!' I jammed on the brakes in someone's front lawn, almost hitting people as they watched all the commotion. I jumped out of the car and ran to the intersection, but I didn't see Wendy. I kept yelling to a police officer, 'Where is the girl who was hit here?' 'Where is she?' 'Did they take her to the hospital?' As I was saying that, I looked down on the ground and saw a puddle of blood. The sight made me even crazier. I kept asking the officer, 'Where is she? She's my sister.' But he never did answer me. He just kept asking me to calm down and be patient, or some bullshit like that. I do remember running back to the car and the officer yelled out, 'Drive slowly!' "

Mike tried to calm himself. He got into the car, slowly drove away, and turned the corner. Once out of the policeman's sight, things changed. "I drove like a maniac. My girlfriend said to me, 'Slow down, you don't want us to end up like Wendy, do you?' I didn't pay attention to her and just drove all the more faster. When we got to the hospital, I ran inside screaming, 'Where's the girl you just brought in here? She's my sister. Is she all right? Where is she?'

"The nurse at the front desk finally calmed me down. She asked me to give her some information. Then she brought me to a separate waiting room. About ten minutes later, my parents arrived and I went into a memory lapse. The only other thing I remember at the hospital was me being the only one to see Wendy when they were working on her and she didn't look good at all. Finally, two doctors came to us and said that her broken bones were all set. However, they were concerned about her head and neck. Therefore, they were transferring her to St. Ellis Hospital in Schenectady."

After Mike and his parents left the hospital, he remained in a dazed state. "I barely remember going home before we went to St. Ellis. I think a good friend of Wendy's called up, asking to speak to her. I believe I told her that Wendy had just been hit by a car and I hung up. I don't remember the ride to the hospital at all." Mike does remember some of the hurt that he experienced at the hospital. "It was a long wait at St. Ellis. When the doctor finally came down, he pushed everybody out of the private waiting room except for my parents. He insisted that I leave with the rest even though my mother pleaded with him to let me be there. *That is something I will never forget as long as I live.*

"I waited in an adjacent room for what seemed like an eternity when all of a sudden I heard my mother scream and started crying loudly. Then I knew my sister was dead and all I felt was numbness. When my parents came out of the room, my mother said, 'There is no hope. She is brain dead.' My mother says she remembers me punching the wall and putting a hole in it, but I don't remember any of that. To this day, I am very grateful that I got to see my sister before they took her off the respirator. She looked completely lifeless. Her hands were ice cold. I remember holding her hand and praying that she would squeeze it, but she never did. Somehow, I got back home and went up to my room. I began to hope for a miracle—during the night her brain scan would flicker and there would be hope. But that miracle never occurred and she died before morning."

The next few days were especially difficult for Mike because he worked near the spot where his sister was hit by the car. "One of the hardest parts of the next couple of days was going into work at the grocery store that was right across the street from where the accident happened. It's in the same parking plaza as Fay's drugstore. I had to tell all my co-workers what happened. Then, I had to go to my best friends' home and told them what happened. They refused to believe it and one threatened to punch me in the face. He thought I was bullshitting them, but when I broke down, he was like a zombie. He didn't know what to do or say."

Wendy Famiano was a very popular girl. She had many friends. Mike tells of their outpouring at the wake and the funeral. "At the wake, people lined up outside the door and some waited for two hours to get inside. The church was filled to capacity. The ride to the cemetery was real sad for me because we rode by our house so my sister could see her home for one last time. Cars were following behind us for blocks. The weirdest thing of it all was the driver of our limousine. He was the brother of the girl who hit my sister. I could see he was pretty shaken up himself. At the cemetery, it was impossible for me to say good-bye to Wendy. I didn't cry once. Something inside of me kept telling me to be strong. It was to be a long time before I could really cry."

Mike relates what happened to his life in the months following the death of his sister. "That summer, I buried myself in work. I began to restore my VW and worked overtime at the grocery store. It was very difficult for me to go home. I couldn't face the sadness of my parents, so I stayed away most of the time. When my sister died, I had just two weeks of college left to graduate, but I never finished. I have never had any desire to go back. I was going to the Hudson Valley Community College. I majored in Civil Techology and would have graduated with an A.S. degree. The following September, I had a chance to finish, but I did not feel I could. I decided I wanted a career with the Price Chopper chain. It was very hard working in that particular store because my sister had been killed on that corner. Eventually, I was transferred out to another one of their stores as a full-time dairy manager.

"That first Christmas wasn't too bad because I got engaged to my girlfriend. It took away a lot of the emphasis off Wendy's not being there. For the next two years, I had very little trouble. I was of sound mind and body and felt that I was over my grieving process. However, toward the end of that period, my physical condition began to deteriorate. I was very tired all the time and had developed tendonitis in both shoulders. In the summer of 1984, I contacted a skin ailment that was very painful and made me itch constantly. I still have bouts of this today when things bother me. My tendonitis grew progressively worse, especially in my left shoulder. I had a hard time sleeping because the pain would wake me up."

Mike tells what happened when his company transferred him back to the Plaza parking lot store. "In June of 1985, I was transferred back to the Price Chopper store where I began. By September, I fell apart. I went to the company's psychiatrist for three sessions. Soon after that, I broke off the engagement with my girlfriend. That proved very painful because she was there for me during my sister's death.

"Shortly after the breakup, I started going to The Compassionate Friends' siblings meeting in Albany. The first time I went there was very uplifting. I found out that I wasn't the only one who had these feelings. Then, for the first time in two-and-a-half years, I was able to go to my sister's grave in the cemetery. However, I still had a few problems so I didn't go too often."

The next four months proved to be difficult ones in Mike's life. "I was still having trouble sleeping and was constantly tired. Work became my arch enemy and each day was taking its toll. Because of the proximity to my sister's death spot, I took every chance that came along to get out of the store. I wasn't being treated very sympathetically by management. I felt downhearted and rejected. That was the time when my worst troubles occurred. I had become my worst enemy. I couldn't please myself at work, or with anything I did. I began to think of suicide as a way out. I just wanted to get away from all the pain. However, I never did anything like that except think about it. Fortunately, I never turned to alcohol or drugs for solace."

Just when Mike reached the depths of his despair, an event occurred that was to turn everything around. "In April of 1986, it had been three years since Wendy's death. I got progressively worse. I would come home from work and hide in my room. I felt very lonely and was afraid to ask for help. At that time, I felt if I asked for help, it would be rejected. The month of June was worse than April because my sister's birthday was June twenty-third. I became totally confused, not remembering very much. My work suffered because I couldn't concentrate on the jobs to be done. I had read about The Compassionate Friends' national conference to be held in Omaha, Nebraska, in July and was torn between going or not going. Thank God, I decided to go.

"The conference proved to be exactly what I needed. I made a lot of close friends from all over the country. I felt so secure that I was able to open up to people who were strangers, something which I couldn't do with people I knew. By the end of the conference, the siblings who attended became one big family. In the workshop called, 'What We Can Teach the World Around Us,' I came up with the idea of going on national television shows. All the other siblings were very supportive of the idea. When I came home from the meeting, I felt a tremendous letdown. However, I soon came to see everything in a new light."

Although Mike is still working through his grief, he understands the process better. "For the first time, I am able to cry and talk about my sister's death. In fact, I will talk to just about anyone who will listen. For almost three years, I thought I had lost my parents as well as my sister. Now that I can talk to them about Wendy, I feel closer to both my mother and father than ever before."

Elaine Altman began a search to determine where her brother was. "I began my search after Thanksgiving," she remembers. "My husband and I went away because I didn't feel that I could stay and spend that holiday with my parents. At the funeral, they had allowed the casket to be opened halfway for viewing by the close family. But when I saw the body, I said to myself, 'That isn't my brother. That's Michael's body, but he isn't there.' Since then, I've been involved in a passionate search to locate him.

"I started by reading everything I could find on the subject of life after death. I have a tape of Elisabeth Kübler-Ross talking on this subject, and I joined her organization. She believes that after people lose the earthly body, each one becomes a constellation of little lights. She claims she can see them, even though they're not within time and space. If my brother is in any of these forms, he would be very interested in what's going on. What has really taunted me is the feeling that he's missing out on the years that would have been so fulfilling after he tried so long to find himself. Right now, he's probably hanging on the window trying to get into life, and he's so disappointed about missing it.

"I haven't come to any conclusions about life after death; I'm still not sure. There are times when I really believe the reports of people who have had near-death experiences—and I want to believe Michael is existing in another form. When we were little, he used to scare me by imitating an ape. He would make his body and his face look like an ape, raising his arms high, and then he would walk toward me. His imitation was so convincing that I would yell. He had an identification with apes and also a sensitivity about them. I think someone once said, 'He looks like an ape.' But the other day I saw a huge ape in a toy store and I said, 'Look, Michael, look at this ape.' And I felt as if he were at my side.

Chapter Six
Coping with Holidays and Anniversaries

Many surviving brothers and sisters may do well for months or longer and then suddenly become depressed at approaching holidays or the anniversary of a sibling's death. According to those familiar with grief work, such reactions are normal.

One bereaved brother commented, "There's an edge to everything during the holidays. My parents are no longer happy people. I don't think they'll ever go back to being as they were. Christmas this year is just not going to be the same. My brother and I used to go caroling with a group from our neighborhood. I know I will not be doing that this year—especially because we all used to meet here at our house, and my mother would make hot chocolate and popcorn for us. That's no longer possible."

Another surviving brother was angry at his parents. "My mother uses one particular phrase over and over again every time the holidays roll around. No matter which holiday it is, she will say, 'These damned holidays are here again.' It makes my sister and me feel that we don't count, that holidays were only for the one who died. It's very unfair. Holidays are lousy for the ones who are still living. It makes you wonder if it's always going to be this way. I feel like telling my mother she's very selfish and unfair to the rest of us, my father included. At least he makes sure we get an envelope with cash for Christmas and on our birthdays. Once my sister and I tried to get my mother a gift to acknowledge Mother's Day. She put it aside and said Mother's Day was only celebrated by mothers who had *all* of their children."

Often when there are no other surviving brothers or sisters, a bereaved sibling will bemoan holidays. One sister said, "I hated holidays and feeling like an only child. I wanted to be part of a big family with lots of kids. I certainly didn't want to be an only child, and now with my brother gone, there is an empty chair at the table. The room looks off kilter when we sit down to eat. Thanksgiving Day was the first holiday after he died, but no one felt like it was a day for giving thanks. I certainly didn't feel thankful."

Betty Tucker, who lost both her brothers, her only siblings, had this to say about Thanksgiving: "I felt a sense of loss for a while this year because there was no family to join us, no one with whom to celebrate Thanksgiving, and that's sad, it really is. Everybody's so scattered around—my mother's in Florida, and my husband lost his mother last year. My father-in-law had made another arrangement. My younger son, Hank, is here because he lives at home. I have a lovely granddaughter, but at Thanksgiving my son Michael and my daughter-in-law Tanya took her on their vacation to be with my mother in Florida. So it was a very quiet Thanksgiving for us."

Billy Pfister recalls the feelings he experienced on the anniversary date of his brother's death. "It's been six years now. The first year I was a mess—even worse than I was on the day my brother died. The second anniversary still wasn't good. After the third, fourth, and fifth year, I was all right parts of the day and a total mess at other parts of the day. This year, perhaps because I've accomplished many things in the past few months, I handled it a lot better.

"My thoughts about my brother this year were: 'I wish you were here to see what's going on. I hope you can see how well I'm doing. I work at a radio station as a disc jockey. I don't know if you know that or not.' On his birthday, and on July ninth, the day he died, I played songs that I associated with him. I didn't say anything about my brother on the air—only I knew what I was doing. But, it made me feel good. I felt that he knows what I'm doing and that I want to share it with him. The songs all had the feeling of 'Let me do this because that's all I can or know to do.' "

Jay Goldstein found his younger brother's bar mitzvah very difficult. "My brother Josh's bar mitzvah was really tough because my other brother, Philip, never made it to his. He was killed just before his bar mitzvah. At the end of the service, the rabbis bring up the other siblings to bless them. They brought me up and mentioned the dear departed Philip. That was tough. My mother and father were crying." Jay indicates all bar mitzvahs are painful to the family, even though they were glad Josh had his day in the sun. "The month of my brother's death is also a little tough for me sometimes," he adds.

Dan Saulisberry tells how the holidays affected him: "Labor Day weekend is always marred by the memory of my brother's accident, for it happened on Labor Day. And, I always think about the anniversary date of his death because it was around my birthday. I don't think the holidays are as hard on me as they are on my parents. I felt like I had to be the strong one. I was feeling the pressure of how my mom and dad were and I felt obligated to be the strong support for them. I had to fulfill that duty, so I tried to maintain a reassuring posture. My sister Kathy was also very close to my brother, more so possibly than me because she was still living at home while I was married and had moved away."

In the above stories, we read about surviving brothers who reacted on special dates. In the following accounts, we will learn how some surviving sisters tried to cope.

Susan Keats recalls: "My birthday was just a few days after my sister died, but it was sort of overlooked. The members of my family were in a very emotional state that day because of the loss we had suffered. Celebrating a birthday at that time would have been festive and therefore inappropriate. But I wasn't upset about it. I didn't particularly want to have a birthday acknowledged either."

Another sister who had to cope with birthdays was Elaine Altman. "I now hate my birthday because it's a mark of my aging, while Michael won't get any older. But two birthdays ago, when Michael was still with us, his girlfriend Gwen and I decided to give him a surprise party. He was really surprised and very pleased. It was a small party and I have photographs of it. On the next birthday, which was shortly before he died, I was going to call him with birthday greetings but I didn't. I was angry with him because on his birthday I had given him a surprise party, but on my birthday he didn't even say 'boo.' I thought, 'Well then, I'm not going to call him this birthday.' Now I'm sorry I didn't. That's one of my regrets."

Because her sister Kathleen had been killed a few weeks before Easter, Madeleine Toomey Pflaumbaum thought something miraculous would occur on that day. "In church, I kept hearing the story of Jesus raising Lazarus, so in the back of my mind, I kept hoping that Kathleen would rise from the dead on Easter Sunday. I had such hope for this that when Easter came and went, I was terribly disappointed that nothing had happened."

Fifteen-year-old Cindy Tart was getting ready to march in the band on Halloween, but she was upset by her mother. "It was Halloween and we'd gotten into a real big argument," Cindy relates. "My mother had left the house to pick up my younger sister, Cathy, and she said she'd come back to pick me up and take me to school. I wasn't in any mood to say anything to her then, so I just wrote her a note. The note explained that I thought we were arguing because 'our little monster is not going to be here anymore.' (The year before Dennis died, he had dressed up as a monster on Halloween.) Then I said that I could see Christmas coming and the problem that was lying ahead of us. Sometimes I didn't want to be here because it was so hard to bear. It makes my stomach hurt. And then I told my mother, 'You're my best friend. I don't know if you know that.' "

Ellen Spector, also in her teens, was very unhappy about the approaching holidays. She remembers: "At Thanksgiving, the family was in a bad mood and not really celebrating. So at holidays I try to do things in other ways. At the school I attend, everyone gives Christmas cards, so I'm going to go out and buy Christmas cards to send, too. I know that my now being the only child in our family is going to make the holidays at home a little hard. We will miss my brother not being there with us."

"It was a Christmas such as I'd never spent before," Florence Campbell recalls. "We all sat around. Everything was very quiet. Nobody had any spirit and there was no feeling of excitement. We exchanged a few gifts, but mainly we were just going through the motions. After all, my brother had died on December fifth, and it was as if this was just not Christmas at all. And, just nine days after my brother's death, my nineteen-year-old nephew, Trevor, died aboard an air flight from Gander, Newfoundland. He was in the armed services and was flying home to spend Christmas with the family. I was remembering other Christmases, like the times I used to ride on my brother's back, and how he would take care of me when we were little. Later, you know, he took pretty much time with me, considering he was grown and married.

"Even now, it's approaching the first anniversary of his death with Christmas following right after it. It's weird, but I really don't look forward to it because the holiday brings back memories. I hear the kids in the neighborhood talking, saying, 'I'm writing out my Christmas list,' even though it's not past Thanksgiving. You know, as far as they're concerned, there is no Thanksgiving, only Christmas. I'll probably get gifts for my parents, but beyond that I'm not going to do much. It's not as if I want to neglect everybody. It's just not there. I know it's going to take a while because my brother was very close to me. Even though he was seven years older than I, he was the baby boy in the family and I was the baby girl."

Sherry and Tom Sundland reflect on how their teenage sons, Joe and Rich, spent holidays and anniversaries. "The first anniversary of Chris' death was very hard on us. Chris' birthday is February fifteenth, and our anniversary falls on

February twenty-third. He died on February twenty-fifth and his body was found on February twenty-seventh. It was a very long time to get through with four anniversaries in February. We all talked about his death and the memories it brought back. We did this as a family."

Sherry continues: "For the major holidays in the first year, we went to a friend's house for the day. For Christmas, which was ten months to the day Chris died, we decided to go to Michigan and learn how to ski. The boys were in on our decision and looked forward to something we've all wanted to learn for some time. I had as much holiday spirit as Scrooge, and we thought that going away would be a good thing for all of us. Three days after we got to Michigan, the weather turned unusually warm and all the snow melted, so we left. We spent Christmas eve night in a big motel in Wisconsin, where we had the whole place to ourselves and were able to enjoy the pool, sauna, and whirlpool. Christmas day we spent driving home from Wisconsin, and as it was almost fifty degrees, it wasn't as hard a trip as if it had been cold and snowy. We talked about holidays and how I feel that now there is something gone from our family. I said it was as if someone gives you a big beautiful homemade cake with a small piece missing. You appreciate the cake, the effort, and so forth, but you always wonder how it would have looked if that missing piece were put into the empty slot to make the cake whole."

Sherry urges bereaved parents to talk to their surviving children about the holidays and many other subjects. "Let them know you love them just as much as the child who died, and that there will always be holidays for them. Older children should be told the truth about everything surrounding their sibling's death. Explain to them how you feel, for they are probably feeling many of the same emotions and need to be a part of the family and not shut out. It might be months before their feelings start to show. Reading the sympathy cards that came, the boys told us was a help, because they felt the cards were not only for Tom and me, but for them also."

Rich and Joe were able to attend a siblings group meeting, and Sherry describes the effect on the twins: "One of the biggest helps for the boys has been their sibling group. It has made a big difference in their life, helping them to adjust to the death of their brother. We were fortunate to have as part of The Compassionate Friends a group for surviving siblings. However, if there is only a group for parents, mothers and fathers can gain a great deal there to help siblings survive. The first meeting is always the hardest, but in talking there to people who have learned to get through their grief and in hearing from them how they helped their children and what their children did in getting through their own grief, is a big step in the healing process. Just listening to other people talk at such a gathering is beneficial."

Sherry stresses that parents should avoid letting the child who has died overwhelm the surviving children on their special days of achievement—a birthday, wedding, graduation, or religious rite. "The hardest thing is not to be too overprotective of the surviving children, for it's always in the back of your mind that something could happen to them. However, you have to know where to draw the line. If they want to do something and your first reaction is to say, 'No,' stop and think about it for a while. Is it a reasonable request? Am I afraid to let them go because they will be out of my sight? It's hard to use common sense when our world has been torn apart and we are still grieving, but letting the surviving children get back to as much of a normal existence as possible is the best approach. Ask your children if they would like anything of their deceased siblings to keep for themselves. It might only be a book or a picture, but whatever they choose, it will have been their decision. They might put it away and take it out a day later or months later to look at or cry over, but they will have it to remember for as long as they choose.

"We were lucky to have a Compassionate Friends chapter start here in McHenry in May. Joe and Rich would ask after the meetings what was said and who was there, and they wanted to know how the other children died. More than once they mentioned how there should be a group for them, so they could talk about their loss and how they felt about holidays, and other issues. Fortunately, a sibling group from the

Arlington Heights chapter was started. Going to their first meeting, the twins were very quiet and didn't know what it would be like or what to expect.

"After the meeting, on the way home, it was as if a dam had broken loose. All Joe did was talk about what they heard and how the other teenagers felt and what they planned to do in the meetings. The group was originally to be for age sixteen and over, but I talked the leader into letting the boys go and see how they got along. Now they go to every meeting and are a big help to the new bereaved siblings."

Chapter Seven

The Younger Ones

Part I

Up to now, we have been reading about siblings who were primarily adults when their brothers and sisters died. In the next two chapters, we will become acquainted with bereaved siblings who were under thirteen at the same time of the tragedies.

Joshua Goldstein was nine years old when his brother Philip died, after having been hit by a car while riding his bicycle. Joshua had many problems after the accident. At first, he had difficulty sleeping at night if his parents were not at home. He stayed up until they returned because he was frightened that they might never come back, that something would happen to them as it had happened to Philip. Later, Joshua came to realize that what had happened to his brother was not a sign that it would happen to him or his parents. After he joined a siblings group that was part of The Compassionate Friends, he learned that such fears are not unusual. He discovered, too, that people grieve in different ways and that other children in the group had suffered from similar fears.

Joshua missed playing with his twelve-year-old brother with whom he used to wrestle. He remembered when Philip would play the trumpet and also the times he would play soccer with Josh in the school yard. When Philip died, it was the end of the school semester. The following September, Joshua brought a newspaper article about Philip's death to read to his classmates. When he said the first words, however, he began to cry and could not continue. His sympathetic and understanding teacher went on to finish reading the piece.

As the years went by, Josh, who was now fourteen, found himself encountering other problems. "After a while, I didn't want to talk about it as much. At home it was the same old story. My parents would try to bring it up, but I was uncomfortable. To me, I felt like, 'Well, it happened and you've got to go on and that's about it.' When you think about it, he was four years older than I. So he was twelve and I was nine. I had known him from the time I was four or five and it's just five years since he died—say about five years that I knew him and he's been dead for five, so it's about half and half. He's been dead almost as much as he was alive. While I will always remember I had him as a brother, I feel that I want to get on with life and not have to stop and think about the past."

Josh occasionally encounters a problem when he meets new people who ask if he has any brothers or sisters. "I say, 'Yes, one older brother,' because it would take too long to explain everything about my dead brother."

One good thing, Josh says, is that he and his older brother, Jay, are close. "He's at college, but I talk to him on the phone at least every two days and we get along fine. We talk mostly about sports, or I tell him about my father or sometimes my mom. Normal things, nothing really serious. We usually just keep up with what's happening every day."

If his brother Philip had lived, Josh believes things would have been different, with less concentration on himself from his folks. "My parents expect a lot from me now. They also ask a thousand questions about everything I do. It's a real pain in the neck. They say things like, 'You should be getting better grades in school,' and even though I tell them they expect too much, they keep it up. With Jay away at school, they have only me to focus on. I get most of their questions. Back then, when Philip died, I was still a kid and if my parents told me to do something, I did it because I was young. But now I'm older and sometimes I say 'No, I won't.' That's why we get into fights and they ask twenty questions as soon as I get in the door. Josh explains how he jokingly tries to repay their questions in kind. "Once when I came home from a bar mitzvah, they asked me 20,000 questions about it. The next night, they went out to a party.

When they came home, I bombarded *them* with questions. I wouldn't normally do that; I did it to show them the way they are."

   In talking about how siblings heal after the loss of a brother or sister, Josh believes communication and having someone to share your thoughts with are all-important factors. "Talking about it and hearing others talk is what helped, which is what I was able to do at the siblings group. After my brother died, nobody talked to me or was with me. You know, you get a lot of attention in the beginning from people you bump into. Then after a few months, there was an empty feeling until I went to the meetings where I met other siblings. The kids there told stories of how their brother or sister died and how they felt and when they did, I said the same thing happened to me. 'I know how you feel,' was what we all kept saying to each other. Even though we were all different ages, and our siblings died maybe in different ways, it didn't make any difference. We all had a good feeling being together and it helped us.

   Reed Bernhard was twelve years old when his ten-year-old brother Clay died in a freak accident in their home. Clay was playing with their dog and a rope. The dog became frisky and the boy landed on the ground. The dog ran around and around him until Clay was strangled by the rope.

   Remembering a strange occurrence the night before his brother died, Reed recalls: "We lived in this real old house and my room was right below the attic. I was hearing all kinds of stuff, so I slept with Clay that night, which was something I had never done before. That was the first time. For a while after that, I was reluctant to sleep upstairs and for the four months that we still lived there, I felt really uncomfortable sleeping being up there at night. My mom and stepdad said I could sleep downstairs on the couch, but somehow I just always trotted upstairs and went to my bed. But I never did really get used to it and we moved four months afterwards."

   At school, Reed received sympathy from his teachers. "They said, 'I'm really sorry.' I expected to hear those words, but I didn't want to, actually. It's just like shaking hands and stuff like that." As to his schoolmates, no one spoke to Reed about the tragedy. "I'm sure they wouldn't have unless I asked them to, and I didn't ask them to. A few of them just stayed clear of me. That didn't bother me any because they were kids who always used to bug me before." However, Reed did have friends to whom he talked about his brother. "There were a couple of different guys, and I had one friend who stayed for four or five days. His name was William. I asked him to come over and keep me occupied. He stayed in the same room with me and I was glad to have a friend there. When he left, my dad came and I felt fine because my dad was there."

Reed says when he thinks about his brother, he remembers the good times they had just horsing around or going skiing, and he misses that. All through his growing up years, Reed had wondered what it was like to be an only child. "I guess just out of curiosity because some of the guys I knew were only children. Then I got a baby brother who is a couple of months old now. He's funny and he doesn't cry much. But, I miss Clay in little ways. Like if I'm watching TV, I don't have anybody to tell 'Go change the channel,' or 'Turn the TV up,' and I have to get up and do that myself. Little things like that, but I remember them."

Like other younger children who think back and say, 'I didn't do this' or 'I wish I had done that' in relation to a dead brother or sister, Reed says he felt that way at first. Reed also says that, although he thinks about his brother fairly often, it's not as often as he *thinks* he should. "I figured I'd probably think about it more often than I do, but it's no big deal, I guess, that I don't. Like for his birthday, I thought about it the night before, and during that day, I kept thinking, 'Well, I'll go to church tomorrow.' But I just forgot to. I figured that's not so bad as long as I thought about it."

In the foregoing accounts, we have learned how two brothers coped with the death of a brother. We will now hear from a five-year-old whose sister died twenty-four hours after birth. Corey's poignant story is told by her parents, Dr. Daniel M. S. March and Dr. Susan C. M. Scrimshaw, in the following account written by them for *The Journal of The American Medical Association:*

'I Had a Baby Sister but She Only Lasted One Day'

"We love you, Elisabeth, we'll never forget you." Five-year-old Corey spoke these words to her sister, who had been born the night before and now lay dying because of severe congenital defects. Twenty-four hours earlier, if you had asked us if we thought a child should see a deformed, dying sibling, we would have been surprised that the question was even asked. During the sad 24 hours of Elisabeth's life, Corey taught us a great deal about our own feelings and about a child's capacity to handle illness and death.

The first indications of problems with the pregnancy came after Susan had amniocentesis. I was present for the procedure, and we both were thrilled to see our baby waving her hand on the ultrasound screen. We confidently waited to hear that everything was all right.

Everything was not all right. The geneticist had found two odd bits of extra chromosomes, something neither she nor any other geneticist she consulted had ever seen before. There was nothing on this in the medical literature either. Since the extra chromosomes were in only 8% of the cells examined, it was impossible to determine whether they were fetal in origin. Even if they were fetal cells, there was no way of knowing what phenotypic effect (if any) they would have. The finding was unsettling, but there did not seem to be sufficient evidence to justify interrupting the pregnancy. We told ourselves that at least we knew all the things that the baby did not have and hoped that everything was fine. We asked to know the baby's sex, and in late July, we told our 5-year-old daughter Corey that she would get a baby sister. Corey was not pleased: "You guys got it all wrong; I wanted a *brother.*"

Corey is a strong, independent child, and it took a while to convince her that you have to take what you get in the baby department. We spoke of the fun of having a sister, of teaching her to do things, of having party dresses that matched, of being girls together. We chose the name Elisabeth Herriott, a composite of family names. We did all the things parents do to prepare a child for a sibling, and by fall Corey was eagerly awaiting "our baby."

In September, Corey started kindergarten and Susan went to bed. Frequent mild-to-moderate contractions had developed, cervical effacement had begun, and she had polyhydramnios, all conditions that make premature labor more likely. Sonography showed that Elisabeth appeared to be developing normally, but since Susan was at only 30 weeks' gestation, the obstetrician thought it best for her to spend most of her time at bed rest. Susan is a university professor who has always worked and traveled (sometimes with Corey). Suddenly she was unable to get up to make Corey dinner or watch her climb a tree. She and Corey could read and talk and draw together, but Corey would speak longingly of the time when mother would "be normal again." At the same time, Elisabeth grew more active, and Corey delighted in feeling her sister's vigorous kicking and in singing lullabies to Susan's pregant abdomen.

One Friday in November, Susan went to the hospital to have some of the excess amniotic fluid drawn off. It showed traces of meconium, evidence that the baby was not doing well. Since it was now only three weeks before Elisabeth was due and sonography showed that she was a big baby, the decision was made to induce birth. We had chosen an obstetrical group and a community hospital that encourage family-oriented birth and allow siblings at deliveries. Corey had asked if she could be present when Elisabeth "came out." We read and talked about birth with her and arranged for her to be present near the end of labor and for the delivery if everything seemed to be going well.

The amniotic sac was ruptured in the late afternoon, and by 7 PM, labor had progressed so far that we called our friend who was looking after Corey and suggested they leave for the hospital soon. It was a fast but uneventful labor until the baby's heart began to show bradycardia, a sign of fetal distress. The heart tones deteriorated rapidly, and Susan was told to push hard, fast, and continuously. Within a few minutes, at 8:25 PM, a still, pale Elisabeth was born. I saw everything immediately— the color was wrong, she wasn't breathing, her lip and palate were cleft, her thumbs were elongated, and her ears were low set. I felt like I had suddenly hit a brick wall. Our obstetrician gently told us that the baby had a cleft lip and palate and that it was possible that there were other problems as well. Elisabeth was whisked to the neonatal intensive care unit (ICU), and we sat quietly for a few moments, trying to absorb what had happened. Elisabeth was alive, but it was uncertain how long she would survive, or in what condition.

"Mommy?" Corey's voice could be heard clearly from the hall. "Mommy?" I was still pale and shaky as I went out into the hall to intercept Corey. She was obviously afraid that something might happen to her mother. Moments later, she sat on Susan's bed as it was wheeled to another area of the room.

After a little while, she asked about her sister, and we told her that Elisabeth was very sick. "I want to see her." Corey clearly expected to be dealt with in a straightforward way. Kate, our labor and delivery nurse, made a quick assessment of Corey's needs and abilities. She suggested that we let Corey see Elisabeth through the window in the hall some 15 ft. from her bassinet so that the most obvious defects would not be too apparent. Corey looked for a moment then said: "Those wires on her look just like E.T.'s before he died. Is Elisabeth going to die?" I told her all we knew at the time: "Elisabeth is very sick and it is possible that she will die. We don't know yet how bad it is."

Before I left, Susan and I went into the neonatal ICU with Jeff, our pediatrician, and saw Elisabeth. Since my research is on seizure disorders and Susan's is on childbirth, we both knew right away how much was wrong. Jeff told us he doubted Elisabeth would survive the night. Together, we took inventory of her problems, which included an enlarged fontanelle, congenital cataracts, and cardiac and respiratory irregularities in addition to the features I had observed at delivery. Later that night, Susan had her bed wheeled into the ICU next to Elisabeth's bassinet, and the two of them shared some quiet hours.

On Saturday morning, Elisabeth was still alive and Corey insisted on seeing her. "She wasn't made right, Corey. She's going to die." "I want to see Elisabeth." "We'll see what we can arrange, Corey, but her face will look strange; it didn't come together right." Quietly, sadly, we talked about what Elisabeth looked like, why she would die, and how we felt.

That afternoon, Corey and I met Susan in the neonatal ICU. Corey was given a child-sized cover gown, and we entered the small room where Elisabeth now was the sole occupant. The nurses stayed discreetly back, just outside the door as we approached Elisabeth. Corey stood on Susan's wheelchair and looked at Elisabeth, now free of wires and tubes. "Ooo, gross!" she said as she saw her sister's face. She turned to Susan. "Can I touch her?" Susan nodded. Corey reached inside the bassinet and began to stroke Elisabeth's bare arm. "Her skin is so soft! Look, she has curly red hair! It's soft, too!" Corey turned again to Susan and said tearfully, "She's going to die." Turning back to Elisabeth, Corey began to talk to her. "Your skin is so soft, Elisabeth. I wish you didn't have to die. We love you." Elisabeth began to move her arms and legs in response to Corey's voice and touch. Corey turned around with an expression of delight on her face. "She loves me! She knows I'm here!" For a long time, Corey stroked and talked with Elisabeth, holding her hand, caressing her hair. Finally, it was time to go. Corey repeated: "We love you, Elisabeth. We'll never forget you. We'll never forget you." Behind Corey, we sat in stunned silence. Behind us, some of the nurses wiped tears from their eyes. How did Corey know to say hello, I love you, and good-bye to her dying sister?

Corey didn't want to leave. "I want to stay with Elisabeth. I want to see Elisabeth die." We were shocked. See Elisabeth die? How morbid! "No, Corey, we can't do that. For one thing, we don't know when she will die, how long it will take."

At home that night, as Susan was reading Corey a bedtime story, the telephone rang. It was Jeff. "Elisabeth died a few minutes ago, at 8:30. I'm sorry." We all cried together, numb, sad, but also relieved that Elisabeth's discomfort had ended. A few minutes later the telephone rang again. Elisabeth's pediatric nurse called to say that she had been with Elisabeth as she died, had stroked her and talked to her, and that she had let go peacefully. Suddenly, we regretted that we hadn't been there with her and said to ourselves, "Corey was right; we should have been there when she died."

On Sunday morning, the hospital asked me to come in to sign the death certificate and make arrangements for an autopsy. Corey insisted on going. "I want to see Elisabeth dead." We didn't know how to react to this but decided she could at least go with me to sign the papers. At the hospital, Corey bided her time. She waited until we were in the head nurse's office. "I want to see my sister dead."

The head nurse asked Corey a few questions, then spoke to me. "I just took a course on children and death. I think she should see Elisabeth. I'm more concerned about how you will hold up than I am with her."

The nurse made arrangements to see Elisabeth in a small room adjacent to the hosptial morgue. She told us that Elisabeth was somewhat blotchy and purple. Corey didn't seem to be affected by the description. She simply wanted to see for herself.

Elisabeth was wrapped in a blanket and set on a shelf in the small room. Corey was sad and fascinated at once. She re-viewed the physical deformities apparent to her and reminded herself that Elisabeth had other problems she couldn't see and that couldn't be fixed. She touched Elisabeth several times, repeating that she would never be forgotten, that it was very sad that she had died, and how much she loved her. After several minutes we left the room, thanked the nurse, and went home.

In the weeks that followed, we found that allowing Corey to take the lead in what she needed to do with Elisabeth was more valuable than we ever could have predicted. There were no nightmares about a deformed baby; the reality had been seen and acknowledged. The misshapen face was only one feature. Elisabeth also had features to love like her soft skin and hair and responsiveness to Corey. We did not have to conceal our grief from Corey but could share it. Each of us spoke up when we were sad, to be comforted by one of the others. At grace one day, Corey said, "God, we are grateful for Elisabeth, but we are not grateful for what happened to her."

Corey also expressed anger, a normal reaction, but sometimes distressingly sudden. We were very upset when a pregnant friend paid a condolence call, only to be greeted at the front door by a wordless Corey, who took one look at her abdomen and punched it. We talked to Corey about hurt and angry feelings that were real and important but could not be expressed through violence. It got better. A few weeks later, Corey and Susan saw a friend with a baby who had soft, curly red hair. Corey turned away quickly, and Susan asked how she felt. "I feel jealous," was the reply. Words had replaced blows. Corey also voiced feelings of guilt that perhaps a cold Susan caught from her in October had hurt Elisabeth. We tried to convey to Corey that Elisabeth's problems had developed very early and that a cold in October could not have caused them.

We will probably never know what caused the genetic anomalies. Our own tissue culture results were normal. Since Elisabeth was the first baby identified with that particular chromosome pattern, if it is seen again after amniocentesis a couple can be told what the consequences are likely to be. With enthusiastic support from Corey and excellent odds for a normal baby, we will try again. Corey has plenty of suggestions for the next baby: "How about twins? Then if something happens, we'll still have one."

A question might be raised about how much Corey really understood about the permanence of death. We have always been very straightforward with Corey. She was 2 years old when our pet cat died. She watched us bury the cat, then asked when she would come out again. When we said she wouldn't, Corey wanted to know why we couldn't take her to the doctor and get her fixed. By the time her great-grandmother died, Corey was almost 4 years old and understood that death was irrevocable.

Despite experience with more "normal" deaths, when faced with the hypothetical question of how to handle a child's involvement in the birth and death of a sibling, we probably would have given the conventional answers: a child should be told the truth gently but protected from "traumatic" sights and experiences. Corey taught us a lot about her abilities to handle death, about children's perception of life and death, about their needs, and about ourselves and our feelings. She taught us to listen to children more carefully. As she put it later: "When my baby sister was born my Daddy didn't know how to love her, but I showed him."

Susan C. M. Scrimshaw, Ph.D
Daniel M. S. March, Ph.D
Los Angeles

The author remembers a very touching telephone call from a young sibling named Linda Bellucci. At fifteen, Linda had learned of my planned book to help siblings through "THE ALERT," a newsletter distributed by the Sudden Infant Death Syndrome Foundation. She asked if she could tell me about her sister, who died of SIDS when she was six months old.

A concern of Linda's that she shared with me began when she was not quite four years old, the time of her sister's death. "We had just come from the doctor's office, and my mom and I and my sister were in the car. The doctor used to give us wooden tongs that you put down your throat to look at it. My mom had to stop at the drugstore. My sister and I remained in the car. I had the wooden tongs and my mother had told me to put them away. But when she went into the store, I decided to use the tongs to look into my sister's throat. My mother had come back and discovered this and was mad because my sister began to cry."

Linda recounted what happened one day about a month later: "We were supposed to visit my aunt and uncle at my grandparent's house. It was the Fourth of July, but, early that morning, I heard my mother screaming in my sister's room. I remember running into my parents' bedroom and getting my father up. Then my father was running into my little sister's room. My mother ran to call the police. When they came, and I saw my mother crying, I guess I knew my sister was dying, but I don't really know how I acted. I guess I cried too. I remember my mother was very upset and I saw her sitting on the floor beating against the refrigerator. Then my parents made me and my older brother, Ron, go across the street to our friends' house to go swimming in their pool."

Linda felt that her sister's death affected her in later years. "I always wanted another sister. My mother became pregnant and I was very happy because I thought I would get another sister. I went to school and they phoned to tell me that my mommy had a boy. I remember that I cried because I wanted another sister so much." Linda continued, "Sometimes I feel that perhaps it was good I never had a sister, and sometimes I like being the only girl and having three brothers; but other times I just wish I wasn't the only girl and that I had her."

Linda then began to weep, "I really always wanted a sister, and I guess I felt I didn't deserve one because my sister died after I put the wooden tongs down her throat. I thought I killed her." It was explained to Linda that she was just role modeling what the doctor or nurse had done in the doctor's office with the wooden depressants; that most curious and alert children might do the same thing; that her sister died of SIDS, and that she was *not* the cause of her sister's death. No one knows what causes SIDS. Linda's sense of relief at being told she was not responsible for her sister's dying was enormous. She understood that nothing she did was any different from what any normal child that age would have done, having been left with the toylike wooden tongue depressants. Linda also comprehended that the reason she wanted the baby sister so badly was because she wanted to be good to the sister and explain, 'You know, I didn't mean to harm you in any way.' Linda wanted to say 'I'm sorry' for something that needed no apology, except in Linda's mind.

The conversation with Linda gave her the opportunity to share her fears, her anxieties, and also her dreams—of becoming a tennis champion. In future years, Linda corresponded with me and sent news of her sports achievements. You will read more of these happy accomplishments in chapter 19, "Messages of Hope."

In the next two stories, we will read of other families who suffered the loss of a child to SIDS. Teri and Gordon Griswold share with us the startling reactions of their surviving child, Jessica, who was two and a half at the time her brother Gregory died. He was three and a half months old.

"At first, Jessica wouldn't talk to my husband for a good two months after the baby died," Teri relates. "We couldn't understand this at first, but one day I thought, 'My God, she was there. She saw the CPR (Cardiac Pulmonary Resuscitation). What does CPR look like to a two-and-a-half-year-old?' So I asked Jessica about it and she appeared frightened. Then I showed her a picture of Daddy with the baby in his arms, and explained to her. 'Daddy was trying to help the baby.' From that point on, she was much better and wasn't angry. She hasn't been acting out that anger toward him anymore."

Teri tells of pictures Jessica drew after the baby died—pictures that were quite extraordinary. "Jessica was there with me when Gregory died. She walked into the room with me to wake him up. Since I was so devastated in the days after the tragedy, I'm not quite sure what went on. But the day after he died, we all went to my mother's house. All Jessica did was draw. And she drew pictures of the baby's face with amazing accuracy. She drew a little round face, with the side of his face in black, blue, and purple colors. She did this over and over for three days. That's all she drew. She wouldn't use any yellows or oranges—all reds, blacks, browns—dark angry colors, you know. After that, she would be much better for a period of time."

Teri became pregnant and when she did, Jessica had questions to ask. "She was very nervous during the following months, asking such questions as, 'Is this baby going to die?' Jessica never assumed it was Gregory coming back, which I've heard is done by many kids that age. They think the baby's returning. But she specifically wanted to know if this baby was going to die, too. And she designated she wanted a girl, not a boy—because she didn't trust boy babies to go on living. We tried to explain and were very honest with her. 'We hope it's not going to happen again. We really don't think it will, but we can't be sure.'"

"We learned at school that she wasn't being social and was staying away from other kids. She was not acting as she had done before the death, and her teachers were a little concerned about this. But when I talked to Jessica about her lack of friendliness, she said she was afraid to get close to any of the other children, which made a lot of sense to me," Teri explains. "It appeared to me that she was all right with anybody older, but as soon as she'd come in contact with a child who looked like a baby, she shied away. Don't forget, there were still very young toddlers in her class at nursery school, and some of them were still using bottles or wearing diapers. These were things she associated with 'baby,' and any baby, she was afraid, was going to die. So, she wouldn't go near them because she'd had such a traumatic reaction after Gregory died."

Jessica became ill two days after the baby died, Teri recalls. "She had a fever, and the doctor said the cause might be meningitis. However, he wouldn't relate it to Gregory's death because he said the autopsy report hadn't come back yet. It seemed that her will was fading because it wasn't that she was really that sick. Before that, she had been much sicker with much higher fevers, but had never looked this bad. She refused to take a bottle because, you see, babies take them, and babies died. At that time, she still drank from bottles. But after Gregory's death, she refused them, so I couldn't get her fever down. Now she started to say repeatedly, 'I'm a *sister*. I'm a *sister*,' probably as a way of telling us, 'I'm *not a baby*,' or 'I'm *not a brother*, because *they* die.'

"At that point, both my husband and I were panicking because she looked as if she were on her way out, and I thought, 'Oh God, please no.' Suddenly, my husband had an idea. Going over to her, he said, 'Daddy's going to do some magic on you and you're going to be all better. You're going to get up and drink your bottle.' With that, he laid his hands on her, and within an hour she was up playing and coloring."

Two years later, Teri recalls, Jessica had a conversation with her grandmother. "She had never said anything like this before, but she asked my mother if Ashley (my newborn daughter) was older than Gregory now. Ashley was six months old and Gregory had been less than four months. So my mother said, 'Yes, she's older.' Jessica then asked, 'But is she bigger?' My mother could truthfully reply, 'Yes, she's bigger too.' Jessica whispered to her, 'Then maybe I can tell you what me and Gregory had to do together.' When my mother asked what that was, Jessica said, 'It was like pulling, pulling so that he could leave and be without a body so that I could stay and be with Mommy and Daddy. But it was pulling.' And she made a motion with her hands. My mother asked, 'What about Ashley? Is she pulling?' Jessica replied in an exasperated voice, 'Oh, Grandma, can't you see she has no pulling in her eyes? Apparently Jessica had been going through something right after Gregory's death, but exactly what that was we'll probably never know."

Barbara and Edward Capriotti also observed dramatic changes in their youngest surviving child Debbie who was not quite three when their infant son Edward Scott died of SIDS. (We will read about their oldest daughter Cathy, who was thirteen, in chapter 10, "Parents and Other Family Members.") Barbara explains the sequence of events that led to Debbie's new and extraordinary behavior patterns.

"There was a great age difference between our first and second child—a ten-year difference. When Debbie came along, it was like having a first child all over again, except that she had an older sister to spoil her, too. Later, when we had our third child, Edward Scott, I was very concerned about Debbie being jealous and, to avoid that, we really worked at making her a part of the family unit. She thought Edward Scott was her baby. I'd let her help me change him. We'd sit on the couch, and I'd let her hold him—with our help, of course.

"Debbie was in the house when I discovered the baby dead. She was in another room, so she didn't actually get to see him when I found his body, but she was aware of all the commotion and things being completely out of control. I quickly picked him up and took him outside. I wasn't really sure what I was planning to do, but I knew I had to get help quickly. Luckily, two of my neighbors were out front. One of them took the baby from me and started CPR on the front lawn while the other went in to call for help. By the time I went into the house to get Debbie, the ambulance had come, and so she didn't see the baby in that horrible way.

"Afterward, she spoke about it constantly. The talking was an aftermath. Before that, her time had been taken up with speaking to him, entertaining him, and being part of his life. It seemed that talking about him afterward was a way of filling up those empty spaces of the time that she had spent with him. She would continually ask us questions about when is he coming back, when can I see him again, why can't we go there, where is he? Initially, I told her he was in Heaven with God and that God was taking care of him."

Debbie, however, persisted in her questions. "One of my biggest mistakes," Barbara reflects, "was an answer I gave her one day when she was driving me crazy with eighteen different questions about why he had to die. I became exasperated and just couldn't handle any more of her constant talk about him. So I said, 'He was just such a good boy that God wanted him with Him!' Well, was that a big mistake, as I later discovered.

"After that, there was an enormous change in her—she began to be a real brat. I can't describe it any other way. She became a witch on wheels. This formerly sweet, adorable little girl became absolutely intolerable. She did everything she could to be annoying. If you would tell her to pick up her toys, she would stand there and tell you, 'no.' She would never have done that before. Fortunately, we had the SIDS Center available to us and I called them and said, 'I don't know how to handle her anymore. She's changed drastically. What can I do?' And, in the course of the conversation, I told what I had said to her. They pointed out to me, 'Don't you realize that she's afraid if she's too good that God will take her, too?' Then of course a bell rang and we had to try to undo what I had said to her—and that took *some* doing."

Barbara and Ed were able, after a year of long and laborious discussions with Debbie, to reassure her that it was an illness that only takes little babies and couldn't take big girls like her; she was not going to die, and God was not going to take her. Yet, there were still moments when the subject would unexpectedly be brought up by Debbie. "A perfect example," Barbara remembers, "was when we went on vacation about six months after the baby's death. By then we had started to get our act together and it was a happy occasion. We were in the car and had been riding along about an hour or so, when the sun came out and there were puffy little clouds in the sky. Debbie looked out and said, 'Oh, Mom, look. That's where Scott is. He's right up on that little cloud.' Well, it just destroyed us. My husband mumbled, 'Oh, my God,' and I could see tears streaming down his face. It was one of those things that was tough to handle. Yet, in a way, I appreciated the fact that she remembered him so much and wanted to feel that he was still a part of our lives."

In the various stories we have read, we've seen more and more how important it is for bereaved parents to talk about their dead child. Even though Debbie Capriotti's unceasing onslaught of questions was initially upsetting, her mother was still able to find an element of joy in the fact that her dead child was being remembered.

Friends and family would be well advised to make note of comments made by bereaved parents. One mother said, "We need that child to be recognized and remembered. People think that because his physical presence isn't here that you won't think about him. Or, they think that because months or years have gone by since his death, that it's not 'proper' to talk about him. But my son will be with me the rest of my life." A father recalled, "I didn't learn to grieve until many years later when I heard about a group for bereaved parents called The Compassionate Friends. When I went there, I found out what grief was all about. I still couldn't talk about it for a while, but later when I saw everyone else was supportive, I did." Another parent stressed, "My surviving children were impatient with me when I mentioned my daughter's name. They kept telling me to forget the past and live for the future. What they didn't understand was that part of that future would never be, and the only way I could resume a relatively normal life was to be able to speak my daughter's name with the same ease that I could speak their names."

A bereaved father also complained about the lack of understanding by surviving children: "We wish our surviving children could understand that we don't want to forget our child existed. The memories are all we have. Our surviving children, God willing, will have the future. And for that we are grateful. But all we can have with our dead child is the past, but the good things in that past. We don't want to talk about the death of our child. We want to talk about his life."

Another parent who could not pretend that her stillborn daughter, Katharine, never existed, was Johana Griffith. "When our daughter Katharine was stillborn in 1981, my husband and I were able to find support through books. When we moved back to Washington, D.C., we located a support group. At the time of our daughter's death, we were living on an Army base in Kansas. The hospital and Army community, while kind and caring, had no resources to offer to help parents deal with the loss of a child."

Johana tells of the lack of support for her surviving children, Maria, seven and Robbie, three and a half. "We tried very hard to help them with their loss but we were really 'winging it.' In some instances, I believe we did a good job, but in others we failed.

"In Maria's mind our baby was to be her birthday present—due a week before her birthday. In fact, Katherine was born two days before Maria's birthday. But she died during labor due to umbilical strangulation. Under the circumstances, I think most of what we did to help Maria was right. My husband came home from the hospital and talked to the children about the death. I came home the next day. We discussed with Maria what we would do. My husband and I decided to have a memorial mass said for Katharine at Fort Levenworth and then fly home to Worcester, Massachusetts, where we would have another mass with our family and friends, and then bury Katharine in Annisquam. We asked Maria if she would like to see Katharine. She said yes. So the day after I came home, we brought her to see her sister at a local funeral home."

Johana relates one of the mistakes that she and her husband made. "The one big mistake we made was at the burial. We were all so caught up in our own grief that no one thought to hug Maria. Later that day, she told us of this through her tears."

As for her son, Johana says, "Robby was much younger and was unable to tell us what he was feeling. We didn't do a good job helping him, but in retrospect, I still don't know what we could or should have done differently. We talked to him. We listened to him and loved him, but I think he felt excluded. We thought he was too young, so we didn't take him to see Katharine's body. We didn't take him to the masses as he'd never been able to sit through a whole mass before. When we came home from the mass in Worcester, a large group was with us. Robby was lying on the living room floor asleep, and he remained asleep for all the time they were there—very untypical of Robby. I believe that was his way of blocking out that sad day. Although we took him to the burial, we didn't explain it very well. Three months later when we were at Annisquam for the summer, we went back to the cemetery and Robby expressed fear of the 'little white box' which he thought would still be there."

Johana explains that what she thought at the time was an 'insane request"—taking pictures of Katharine at the funeral home—was especially helpful in making the baby "real" for Robby. "Every night at dinner, Maria and Robby join in asking God to bless her. And every year on what would have been her birthday, we plan a special family outing. The children make a little cake and we all sing Happy Birthday. This was their idea and they want to continue it. These birthdays have been special times for us. They have also brought us good memories and laughter. It also helped Robby epxress his hurt and anger over the death of his sister."

Eighteen months after her daughter's death, Johana gave birth to Annie. "She wasn't meant to replace Katharine, but she brought us the magic of new life. She gave us joy again and showed us that life could be good. Maria and Robby are just wonderful as 'big brother and sister.' Annie adores them and they her. Annie knows about Katharine and goes with us to visit her grave in the summer. I think that we have explained Katharine's death well to her. She too blesses her sister at dinner and has shown no fear about the death. Some subsequent children I've talked with have a feeling of burden. I would never want her to think she was a replacement She wasn't. Annie is her own wonderful self and she knows it."

Twelve-year-old Kim Brauer and her surviving brother, Michael, age fifteen, have suffered the loss of two siblings who had been terminally ill with an unknown disease. Her sister Sandy, who had just turned eight, died on February 14, 1984. Her brother Nicky was five when he died on January 5, 1985. Both children became ill the first year of their lives. Because they required twenty-four-hour care, they were placed in a nursing home for children in Albany, New York.

Kim's mother Patricia describes her difficult decision: "The conclusion of the doctors was an unknown brain degenerative disease. They didn't know how or from what the disease developed in each child. They took seizures. They frequently had pneumonia. Tubes had to be run down their throats to clear out the chest cavity of each child because they would become seriously congested. I made the choice to put the children in a nursing home because I had two other children who were only four and six years old at that point. Sandra was a year old when we put her in the home. She was blind and I wanted her to have the best care available and because I knew that, with my two little ones and their needs, I would not be able to give her the attention that the nursing home could give her. There were times when that first separation was very hard.

"Sandy had first come down with meningitis and encephalitis, which the doctors thought were perhaps the cause of that subsequent illness. They told me that if I had another child it would not necessarily be subject to the same disease. Two years later, I had Nicky and when he was twenty-four hours old, he started to have seizures. Initially, they said it wasn't connected to Sandy's illness, but then they said it was. They went back and forth like a yo-yo. Later, it became necessary for me also to place Nicky in St. Margaret's in Albany. We'd run up every five weeks to see them. The trip was a long one, and it was also sad because we saw Sandy and Nicky getting worse. Our visits were interspersed by phone calls from the hospital saying, 'Your daughter is very sick.'

"I don't know if Sandy and Nick recognized us although in the beginning I thought they did. They would laugh at Michael and Kim when we brought them along with us. Maybe it was only the sound they recognized. They couldn't sit, they couldn't lift their heads, and could offer only a little smile. That was it. Michael would always play with Nicky and Sandy. He seemed to respond to Sandy and could always get a laugh out of her. He used to read to her, and kiss her, and talk to her. He would just make weird sounds that she seemed to respond to, and she'd laugh at him. I could see he was extremely attached to her, perhaps more so than Nicky, but he gave both of them a lot of love and caring. At a later time, during Michael's confirmation, the pastor told the participants of the service that there was a child in the class who had said there was a time when he didn't think there was a God. It was my son who had said that. The minister had told me and asked my permission to use it in his sermon."

In talking with Kim Brauer, she expressed her sorrow at the loss of her sister and brother. "When we went to visit them, sometimes I wished it was me who was sick and not them, because they looked so helpless. When they died, I wished again that it was me instead of them. They couldn't do anything, you know. they had to be cared for as if they were babies. That made me sad. I would play with them and talk to them, and I was always sorry to have to leave them there. I wondered why they had to be so helpless and why they had to die. My parents had explained that everyone had to die sometime and it was just their time. But I still get sad when I think about Sandy and Nicky. Then I go up to my room and I wonder what it would be like if they were here and I could play with them. They were never really with us during holidays, but I wish they could have been. On my birthday, I feel good that I lived, but I also feel sad that I lived and they had to die. When they died, I was afraid that something would happen to my parents. I thought that they could die at any moment, because you never know when that moment will be."

When Gregory Schwaegler was two and a half years old, his sister Mary Rose was stillborn. His mother, Susan, tells of events: "Our daughter died in utero at thirty-seven weeks and was stillborn. No cause for her death was ever established. My husband Steve had told Greg that the baby had died. When we came home from the hospital, Greg just looked at me for a few seconds and then ran over for a hug. He seemed very anxious not to let me out of his sight. I held him a lot that day. For the next several weeks, he had bedtime problems.

"A couple of days later, I was finally able to talk to Greg about the baby. I asked him where the baby was, and he smiled as if to say, 'I know the answer to that.' He said, 'In your belly.' When I showed him that my belly wasn't big and fat anymore, I could almost see the light bulbs blink on in his head. I explained that the doctor had helped the baby come out but that the baby had died. I told him that meant she couldn't eat, breathe, or grow, and she couldn't come home with us. I told him we weren't able to take care of her because she was dead, but that God would take care of her for us. I also told him her name was Mary Rose. He listened to all I said with big eyes and didn't say anything. Later, however, he repeated the entire conversation almost word for word to my mother-in-law.

"After a while, he looked at the bassinet, which was still in my room, and asked who would sleep in that little bed. I said nobody—it was for the baby, but she was dead, so we will have to put it away. He got very angry and kicked it and said, 'No, no. We will *not* put it away.' I discussed this at a SHARE meeting (a group for bereaved parents, which is described in chapter 20 "Helping Hands") and everyone there seemed to think that was pretty healthy.

"Now at age three years, three months, he talks about her at odd moments. Last week an incident occurred which reminded me that he has adjustments to make that are as deep and difficult as mine have been. He was playing house with his dolls and little stove—feeding and burping them, all the while telling me what he was doing. His next statement startled me. He said, 'Now my babies are dying.' I was taken aback and asked, 'What did you say?' He repeated, 'My babies are dying.' And then he said, 'But at least I got to see my babies.' I replied, 'I wish you could have seen Mary Rose.' He answered, 'I will ask God if I can see her when I get to Heaven,' and he proceeded to call God on his toy telephone. He must have resolved the issue because he said to me, 'God told me to go play basketball now.'

"Just recently, I learned that I am pregnant again. I'm a little nervous for Greg. His whole experience is that babies die and make Mommy and Daddy sad. But we are a family that, I think, can get through anything."

In Fayetteville, North Carolina, ten-year-old Cathy Tart was used to her brother, Dennis, who was eight, teasing her by asking her to find his little red ball. "Dennis was always putting it in his mouth and saying, 'Now, where's the ball?' He was always playing with it. The ball would sometimes be in his mouth and then maybe under his leg. Then, one day, Cathy felt that familiar tap of Dennis' on her shoulder. She turned around expecting him to ask her where the ball was. "I looked for it, but couldn't see it on the floor, in his hands, or anywhere. But he was acting as if he were going to vomit. My instinct was, "Oh, my God, he's swallowed the ball.' So I yelled for my momma. 'Momma, Dennis has swallowed the ball.' And momma came running upstairs.

"Dennis couldn't talk and he was gasping for air. My mom did the Heimlich maneuver and then he fell to the ground while she was still doing it. I guess he went into a seizure because his hands started curling up and he started bending into a ball. My momma yelled out for us to call the ambulance and the rescue squad. We were afraid that my brother had already gone into cardiac arrest and he was so heavy, neither I nor my mom nor my sister could handle him. The rescue squad hadn't come, and I felt as if I couldn't help my mom. Then my mom said, 'The rescue squad hasn't come, so I've got to go to the rescue squad and bring them back.' She ran to the volunteer fire department and by the time she got there, one man was around. My mom said, 'Come quick, it's my little boy.' But he said, 'I can't go with you until another person, another paramedic gets here.' My mom just drove back and when she got to our house, there was an ambulance sitting there. The driver couldn't decide which side of our street to go on. So my mom just kind of blinked her lights and he headed up toward our house.

"Cindy and I were trying to shake Dennis or something to

keep him alive, but he would just open his eyes and close them. He was doing that when my momma went to the fire station, and when she got back he was still doing it. My mom and my sister got Dennis into a rocking chair, a recliner, and they brought him downstairs. The paramedics got in the house, put him on a stretcher, and tried to give him air. But the air passage thing they were using seemed to push the ball down further. They were putting something in his throat that would open the trachea so that Dennis could get some air, but that was just making a wider space for the ball to go down. They stuck this thing down his windpipe from his mouth, but the volunteers were not trained to do a tracheotomy so they took him over to the hospital.

"The ambulance stopped and motioned for my daddy, who was not more than ten feet from them, to move back. So my dad moved while they were talking to him. Meanwhile, my mom, my sister, and I were screaming. And I thought, 'Oh, Lord, they're going to tell him that there's no use in going on. He's already dead and there's no way to bring him back.' Instead, the driver got out and came up to our car and said, 'You're going to have to stop following so close or we'll take him home and you'll have to take him to the hospital your-selves.' If that driver hadn't stopped to say all that, we wonder if he would have been able to get Dennis to the hospital in time to save him."

Below is Cathy's vivid account of what happened at the hospital: "When we got there, my mom had to fill out all of these papers. Then we sat, waiting for somebody to come and tell us that he was dead, that there was no use. Then a nurse came into the lobby and asked for the Tart family. My mom and dad stood up and said, 'We're the Tart family,' and the nurse said, 'Please come into this room.' They led us to a chapel in the hospital. Then a nurse would come back every once in a while and say, 'They're still working on him.' She came in there about three times, and my mom would ask her, 'What are they doing now?' And she would say, 'They've got the ball out, but they're trying to bring him back.'

"Our relatives all started arriving: my grandfather, my

grandmother, my aunt, my uncle, my great aunt, my great uncle. The hospital people asked me and my sister to get out and go to a separate room so they could tell my mom and dad and all the relatives sitting there that Dennis was dead. At least three nurses—two had blond hair and one had dark hair—asked me if I wanted a drink of water. I didn't speak a word to them because I was so serious and so mad that they made us leave. Then they had the nerve to put my sister in a different room from where I was. That really made me mad.

"Then they let us back into the room with my parents and I ran to my dad and I said, 'Daddy, did he make it?' He said, 'No,' and I just started bawling my eyes out. My mother said she wanted to see her son. My grandmother and grandfather wanted to see Dennis, too. They went and saw him. I told them I wanted to see my brother, too. Then they let me in."

Cathy recalls her reactions at the funeral. "I was sitting in the middle of the church with my brother up there in a casket, and I kept thinking, 'This isn't really happening.' I loved the preacher who was there, Allan Bridges. I look up to him as if he were a father, but not as my father. You know, I love my father, and I'm glad my father is my father, but I love Allan Bridges too. Yet on that day, no words that any preacher could have said would have sat well with me. I was thinking, 'Oh my gosh, what is this preacher going to say? If I hear another word about anything bad pertaining to Dennis, I think I'm going to go crazy. I was glad that the preacher didn't say anything, because I was scared of what I would do if he said one wrong word. I was really that mad. I was very angry at God for taking my brother away."

Another sibling who died unexpectedly was sixteen-month-old Timothy Moran. His mother, Nadine, tells what happened: "On Sunday morning, Timothy had been 'out of sorts,' but since we all had a nasty bug that week, we assumed he was coming down with the same thing. However, by early evening I became concerned because he was very groggy and hadn't had anything to eat or drink in twenty-four hours, other than nursing for a few short minutes. I decided to take him to the outpatient clinic at the hospital for possible dehydration. In the car, he had a convulsion and stopped breathing. I did CPR as I tried to flag down a car on the highway. When we arrived at the hospital, they did eventually get his heart beating again for a few minutes. But it just wasn't enough, and Timmy died shortly thereafter.

"After an autopsy, we learned that he had been born with a diaphragmatic hernia, which had caused his stomach to rupture and pour acid over his heart, causing cardiac arrest. The pathology report indicated that Timmy also had Reye's syndrome, which complicated the hernia."

The Morans have two other children. Jennifer was four and a half and Molly was two and a half when their brother died. "The next morning," Nadine recalls, "when I heard the girls awakening, I went to crawl into bed with Jennifer, for I wanted to break the news to them as soon as possible. However, she had obviously sensed that something unpleasant had happened the night before because the first thing she said to me was, 'Mommy, did Timmy die? I realized then that we should never underestimate the emotions that our children can understand or handle."

Nadine set about the task of explaining that Timmy had been much sicker than anyone realized and that even the doctors at the hospital couldn't help make him better. "I stressed the fact that this was not the way things usually happen, and that doctors and hospitals usually help people. I added that most people die when they get very old, but that every once in a while things like this do happen and we can't explain why. I also tried to make it clear that although Timmy's body was dead, his spirit was doing just fine. We talked about what 'spirit' meant—the things that made us love him and vice versa, how funny and silly he could be sometimes. All the things we can think about in our minds and feel in our hearts that made us close to someone, even though we may not be able to see that person's body. We also talked about how it was okay to cry and to feel sad because we missed Timmy, just as we would do for them or other family members if they were to go away for a long time or forever."

It had been recommended to Nadine that she and her husband bring the girls into the hospital for blood tests the next day. "When all the tests came back negative, I think it helped to reassure all of us that doctors and hospitals are not always associated with death. Later that afternoon, the girls came back and dragged many of Timmy's toys out of the closet as well as a few articles of his clothing. Of course, this stirred up many painful feelings for my husband and me, but we were able to see that this activity was a means of their working out their grief and feeling close to their brother. It also forced communications to keep flowing among us all.

"In Molly's case, she asked several times where Timmy was, as if she expected him to return at any time. This led us to realize that at the age of two and a half her concepts of death and time were very limited. To this day, she continues to surprise us every once in a while with such comments as, 'Timmy says yuk' which seem to pop into her head out of the blue. Although grief is a never-ending path, we have come a long way. We have received a lot of support from our families and friends. My husband and I were both brought up in a positive and constructive type of home life, which I am certain has helped us through our grief. Personally, I credit a large part of the salvation of my sanity to The Compassionate Friends."

Chapter Eight

The Younger Ones

Part II

The siblings we will meet in this section are now adults, although their brothers or sisters died when these bereaved were under thirteen years of age.

Sister Jane Marie Lamb claims grief isn't completed with the funeral. Although it has been many years since her eighteen-year-old sister was drowned, she feels that the young woman's death still impacts on her own, Sister Jane Marie's, life and that of her siblings. "At the time of my sister's death, customs in the area included much support from neighbors and friends. Wakes were often held in the home, and friends and relatives kept vigil day and night until time for burial. This was the case with my sister Earline's death. As a nine-year-old, I felt the loss deeply. I cried and I participated in all of the rituals as did my eight siblings who were at home. My two eldest brothers were in service and unable to return home in those days."

Her sister's death was the first truly traumatic event in their family of twelve children. "We all felt the pain of our parents; for the younger ones it was probably more that which we saw in them rather than our own pain at our sister's death. Plans were discussed in our presence. My most vivid memory is of the sadness and helplessness to do anything while we were waiting for her body to be found, which was done twelve to fourteen hours later."

Sister Jane Marie remembers many things—seeing the

car racing to their home in the country to seek help for the tragic happening on the nearby government farm lake. "I remember seeing my sister in the casket, seeing the sailor who was with her when she drowned talking to my mom, and the two of them crying together. I remember moving furniture so that the wake could be in our front bedroom, and draping the mirror in the room where the casket would be brought. I remember the constant flow of people coming and going, not knowing what to say or do among the adults. I remember looking at Earline in the casket and thinking how puffy she was, and also thinking how pretty the rose color of her dress was. I remember, too, the huge number of flowers that were brought to our home."

Somehow all of that was not as difficult for Sister Jane Marie as was the time after the burial, although there had already been some involvement even for the nine-year-old. "I felt part of what was happening. The painful times began in those later weeks and months when no one wanted to talk about my sister. I was aware of how difficult it all was for my parents. Being an extrovert, I needed to discuss her death and I would listen if anyone talked about her. Whenever I had a chance, I would talk with them, but I never really talked about my feelings. My mom would say that it was too painful to talk about it and she would cut off the conversation. Afterwards she said she had tried to talk to friends and relatives, but found that they would not visit again if she spoke about Earline. She also told me that she could not grant the sailor's request to return for a visit after the burial. Her fear was that his coming would be too painful—a reminder of all that pain. The sailor lived in North Carolina and our family lived in Missouri. Through my efforts, though, the sailor did return—thirty-eight years after the event. It was a healing experience for both my mother and the sailor.

"Typical of some children, my response was to be protective and submissive. I did not want to cause my parents any worry or concern. I tried to behave in a way that would not add to their distress and that would somehow coerce my two younger brothers to desist from fighting, slamming doors, or behaving in the normal rowdy manner of young boys.

"Through the years, we were aware of the effects on my parents. We remembered Earline in many ways. Her pictures were always in a prominent place in our house. The cemetery was in the same area as our little mission church in the country. Each Sunday after mass we would visit Earline's grave, and in summer bring flowers from home. My family did not cry a great deal at the time of visiting the grave nor was it a morbid experience for us. Mom cried more when she went for walks on Sunday afternoon. Attending funerals and visiting graves of relatives had been one of our early life experiences."

Twenty-two years after her sister drowned, Sister Jane Marie's brother, Melvin, who was three years older than she, was killed in an explosion. "Having spent many years with him and feeling that deep attachment, his death was very painful," she remembers. "I again participated in every way I could in the rituals of farewell and family response." But once the funeral was over, she again reverted to the patterns established as a nine-year-old. Although she was away studying at the university with her sister who is thirteen months older than she, there was no sharing of feelings when their brother died. "My sister and I had talked about our feelings all of our lives, but somehow it didn't even occur to me to share the pain with her then. Every day for a year I cried privately when I thought of him. When I saw his wife and children, I cried privately again. No one knew how deeply I felt about his death. About six months down the road, I began to feel guilty that I was still grieving.

"The guilt led me to talk with a priest friend who helped me sort out my feelings and to realize that my grief was normal. I had come to feel that if I were a Christian I should not still be grieving. I tried to be logical, but that did not help. What did help was to talk with the priest and explore the experience and my feelings about it, and to allow myself to grieve. As I look back now it seems to me that following Melvin's death, I processed the anguish from Earline's death at the same time as that from his. I can agree with experts who say we don't have a choice *if* we will grieve when someone significant dies, our only choices are *when* and *how*. I am grateful that I have processed the pain and only wish that I could have done my grief work earlier. Earline and Melvin will always be very special in my life. I still cry at times when I think of them, but now there is a real difference, having worked through the grief."

In describing her present relationship with her surviving siblings, Sister Jane Marie has this to say. "All my siblings have had their own perception of what happened and how they experienced the deaths. They have their own personalities and ways of processing grief. It wasn't until our dad had a stroke that we began to share our deeper feelings and were able to come together in an open and supportive way in the months prior to his death. That was forty-one years after the death of Earline. We could have benefited from support and encouragement in expressing our feelings. Perhaps that is why I feel so committed to reaching out to others."

The work of Sister Jane Marie Lamb, O.S.F. (Order of St. Francis), is recognized throughout the world for her leadership in helping to establish the first support group at St. John's Hospital in Springfield, Illinois, for parents whose babies have died. The group is called SHARE—and that is its purpose: for young bereaved parents to be able to share their feelings. You will read more of this fine organization in chapter 20, "Helping Hands."

Another surviving sister reflects on the death of her only sibling, which took place many years before. "My sister Sandra died when I was twelve. She was murdered by her boyfriend when she was eighteen years old, on March 1, 1959. My sister was extremely beautiful with blond hair and blue eyes. She was six years older than I. At that time I was in the twelve-year-old gawky stage, dark haired and hazel eyed."

Marlene Levy goes back to that time—more than twenty-five years ago—to tell us what happened. "My sister had gotten engaged to this fellow. Then, after graduating from high school and her entrance into college, she decided she was too young to be engaged, and told this to the young man. It seems that he was an extremely depressed person, attached to one of the reserve units in Brooklyn at that time. I remember him as being quite attractive. He also had a younger brother exactly my age, and I've often wondered what happened to him and how he survived the tragedy.

In college my sister met someone else to whom she became quite attracted. Be that as it may, her former boyfriend came over to our house one day, because I think my sister had called him to say she wanted to return his engagement ring. I believe that he did not want it back. He told her he wanted to talk to her alone, out of the house. He took her a couple of blocks, parked behind a motel, and at that point shot her and then himself."

Marlene, who is a therapist today, talks about her own reactions to the tragedy. "Throughout the years, I experienced a great deal of denial, a limited amount of fact, and an inability to remember. So, although I know it's not a healthy thing to do, I have been able to deny the realities of that period of time. This is unhealthy because it leaves repercussions. Denial takes place when we are told something too horrible to deal with and can be a normal, healthy, and protective route. But if it lasts a long time, it is no longer healthy.

"Being a therapist at this point, I know what I've done in allowing the denial to continue and I know what's wrong with me, and it leaves me with the constant longing for a sister. Although Sandra was killed quite a long time ago, there is still a lot of unfinished business between me and my sister and how her death rearranged my life. It dissolved my family unit. My father left shortly thereafter and my mother was destroyed for many years. At that time, psychiatric care was more for parents than children, and those who were undergoing psychiatric care were also stigmatized. But, I was a very, very needy twelve-year-old at that time and could have used some kind of therapeutic care."

Marlene withdrew to books for solace. "I was left alone mainly because my parent who was there was so devastated herself that she couldn't think ahead. If she did, I think that at that time her concern for me was secondary. As a result, I have a great ability to intellectualize and what usually happens is that I grab a book. So, for a period of time my mother was taken care of and I was left alone. I have no specific recall as to what happened, other than I was making a constant search for an identity, because there had been a tremendous loss of identity—loss of family, loss of foundation. In that search for myself, I decided to become a therapist. I have a book taken out shortly thereafter from the library on *What Is a Psychologist?* It's a book that I have never returned to the library, so great was my need. I needed answers to the questions. There was no one to answer questions for me, no one to give me any support, so I presumed the intellectual.

"Over the years I have been able to get in touch with what I am searching for: why I am searching, the lack of reality that I've lived with for many years, and the reality of what my mother and father endured, how they suffered, and my own anger."

Although Marlene went to the funeral, she was so angry with her sister, she wasn't able to go to her grave. "There was a large age gap, but regardless of that, there was a tremendous amount of competition between my sister and myself. She was blond, she was the beauty, and I was not. I was the baby who had to prove herself. At the time she died, I truly believed that I would always be the ugly child, the ugly, unlovable child. And it took many, many years before I came out from under that cloud. I think I am a fortunate person because I am a beautiful woman, but had I not had that appearance, I would, I think, unfortunately have suffered more. That was the main competition—beautiful versus ugly, and when you're ugly, you have no support.

"While many younger sisters may feel that their older sisters are prettier, what I am saying is that a twelve-year-old is at the most gawky stage, the plump stage, the pimply faced stage. Then you have the blooming older sister. Had I been five and she been ten or eleven and not as aware of going into adolescence, it would not have affected me the same way, but I was just approaching thirteen and she was going on nineteen. She was blooming right then and I was at the really worst stage. So I think the age and time just added to the feeling that would normally not be there."

These feelings left Marlene with a lot of unanswered questions as to what the relationship would have been had they been older. "That's why I felt I had to be a psychologist—to find the answers to too many questions I didn't understand." Marlene reflects on what could have helped her in the beginning. "I needed someone to hold me when I cried. My parents were crying themselves. They were oblivious to people, unable to see, and totally denied life. If only I had some therapy, or if there had been a siblings group available to me, a group of others who had experienced similar things as I had."

Richard Spiotto was born on November 26, 1916, in West Hoboken, New Jersey. His adolescence was spent in fantasy, (of becoming a cowboy in the wild west, or joining the Foreign Legion in Morocco), but he had a real and loving relationship with his sister Dorothy, whom he cherished. His Swedish-born mother, Helma, was tight-lipped and spoke very little to her children. Although she took good care of Richard and Dorothy, making sure they had a good breakfast before going to school and caring for them in other essentials, she rarely spoke to them. The family had no vacations and rarely went anywhere. Richard did not have a good relationship with his father. "Whenever he went into tantrums," Richard recalls, "he would take it out on me. I received a lot of kicks and he beat me many times for no reason."

Richard's mother was several years older than his father and when they were married, his father was an immature eighteen years old. After his sister Dorothy died, both his parents grieved. But part of his father's grief keenly hurt Richard. "I remember hearing what my father said to my mother. 'Why couldn't it have been that bastard?'—meaning me." These remembrances still haunt Richard today, almost sixty years later.

Dorothy was eight years old when she died of leukemia. Richard was twelve. "In my day, a twelve-year-old was playing marbles; they lacked the sophistication of today's young adults. I was still wearing knickers. When my mother died soon after, I grew up very quickly." Richard's mother died in childbirth, six months after Dorothy's death. In the months that followed, Richard's life became a living hell.

The day after his mother's burial, his father disappeared. Richard did not see or hear from him for the next three years. "First, there was no one to console me when my sister died. My parents certainly didn't. After my mother died, I was shunted from one place to the other, visiting different relatives. It was Depression times, and some aunts and uncles were bunking in together in one apartment because of lack of funds. When I stayed with my grandmother, there was no bed for me, and I had to sleep under a table on the floor."

Richard remembers many months and years of shuffling between those relatives, feeling unwanted. He could not remember much about his mother in later years because of her deep silence, but he has clearer recollections of his father. "Because of the kicks and the beatings he had dealt out to me, I remembered him well." Although Richard's grandmother was very fond of the boy, she had problems with her younger son, who needed most of her attention. "He was out of a job in those Depression years and would lie on a couch and stare up at the ceiling." Richard spent one month with his grandmother, then one month with his aunt, then with another aunt, his place of residence changing constantly. "With my aunt, her husband took drugs and would make love to his wife in front of me. So those were rough times for a twelve-year-old." At age thirteen, Richard got a job on a fishing boat as a cabin boy. "I just wanted to flee. My grandmother was busy with my Uncle Teddy. My aunt couldn't control her husband. My other aunt was having marital difficulties. My father had not been heard from. Where then should I go? So I grew up fast. I took the job on the boat and worked with the cook. I peeled potatoes and carrots, and washed the pots and pans and lived in a furnished room by myself at age thirteen."

This then was the beginning of Richard's journey into his teens. He missed Dorothy and didn't have anyone to talk to about his sister's death. No one in the family had time to share his grief for his sister, it seemed. During the three years that Richard hadn't seen his father, the man had met a woman and remarried. "When I was fifteen, I met my father and his new wife by accident at my grandmother's house. My father introduced her to me. 'This is your new mother.' He was talking to me as though I was still a child, but I had already traveled all over the country during those three years. The woman was nice to me, but she was an alcoholic. She and my father stayed home after work, I learned, and got drunk every night."

Richard recalls that his sister had been very sick for six months before she died. "It was extremely draining on me, because there was no closeness with my father and my mother being the silent one." Richard remembers that his mother cried a lot when they learned that Dorothy had only months to live. "I remember her wilting away like a flower." After his sister's death, Richard went into a complete depression. He was at a loss as to what to do, because he felt that the only one who loved him had been his sister. "She loved me unconditionally. I talked with her all the time. I took her to school every day and would protect her against taunts." Richard and Dorothy had been tied together by a real big brother–little sister bond. His father showed a good deal of affection for Dorothy, but none toward Richard.

"After my sister and my mother had died, there was really no one interested in me or my activities." Richard remembers more of those days. "My Aunt Claire was always kind to me, but she was having problems with her marriage at the time. My grandmother would feed me with a store-bought cheese sandwich or some other item. But I had no education because no one thought of making me go to school. I left my classes in the seventh grade when I was twelve and never went back. I didn't even have the clothes to wear to school. The day after my mother died and my father's disappearance, one of my uncles made off with my father's brand new car. His wife came and took all our furniture, my mother's clothes and jewelry, and most of my clothes." To this day, Richard is saddened by the fact that no one in his family reached out to comfort him or give him affection. "They just took everything. I had nothing. No sister, no mother, no father, no home."

Richard also had a struggle with religion. He could not understand how his sister could be buried in Holy Name cemetery, which was Catholic, and yet his mother be refused burial there because she was a Protestant. "What was this world all about when a mother couldn't be buried beside her child?" When he went to see his mother's grave, Richard became confused by not seeing the name Spiotto on the tombstone, but instead, his mother's maiden name. He began to wonder, "Who are you and what is *your* name, Richard?" It was the beginning of his turning away from the church.

Today, Richard bemoans the fact that, because of the usurping of all his family's possessions, he has no pictures of his mother or sister. His mother died at Christmas time, and Richard remembers her being laid out in the living room on Christmas Day. All of his toys had been taken by his uncle's wife, and for years Richard didn't celebrate Christmas. It wasn't until he married and had children of his own that he could face the holidays.

A happy note to this story is that Richard made contact in his later years with a younger cousin, John, and it brought them a warm remembrance of many experiences they had shared as children and a bond was formed. Now Richard is looking forward to the holidays because there is one member of his family with whom he can sit down and talk, who remembers his sister, his mother, his father, his aunts, uncles, and grandparents. "It's a relationship I have never had with any member of my family. It helps to make up for all the hurtful and angry feelings I have held for my family from years ago. Today the past is dead and tomorrow is what counts."

Sheren Banschick's sister, Sylvia, was four years old when she died. He was ten and his brother Leonard was twelve. "She lived with us at home for about three years and then had to be institutionalized because of water on the brain and other problems. My mother could not provide the professional care she required."

After his sister's death, Sheren was startled at his father's display of emotion. "I remember that my father cried, and I had never seen him do that before. My brother was distraught and I remember his crying. As for me, I remember feeling a bit guilty because I wasn't as upset as my father and brother. I wasn't allowed to go to the funeral, but my brother went."

Sheren had other guilt feelings about his sister, however. "It wasn't in my nature to hurt anybody, but my curiosity certainly got the better of me, especially in relation to my sister. She was a little girl, and I would bring my friends over and show them her genitals. I felt guilty about that, for I knew it was wrong, but it was a way of getting attention. By showing my sister to these big boys, I became important and got their so-called respect."

Sheren tells of other problems he developed: "I used to walk in my sleep and I was an enuretic (bed wetter). At school I became the class clown and was very disruptive. I was left to my own devices at home and sexuality began to rear its head. I became involved in that from between ages nine and twelve, in the street, with whatever came along. We all experimented, not for too long. But I think it was another way to gain attention. Part of it might have been due to my being a middle child between an older brother who thought the world was his and what was mine was his too, and a younger sibling who was defective and had no growth.

"I remember, too, watching my sister and waiting for her to grow and to become a human being, but she never developed. It was so painful to see that there was no growth, no anything. In the three years she was in the house, she barely developed to a six-month-old. I walked around with a lot of guilt.

"I always felt concerned that I wasn't able to respond to my sister's death and the nature of the death itself, which my parents would not discuss at all. It was a real no-no for them, perhaps because there was a superstition about death—if you talk about it, you're liable to evoke it. My parents' reaction may also have been part of the reason I acted out in school, doing things like standing on my head and acting like a clown. I just needed and wanted attention. Meanwhile, my mother was engrossed with my sister and my father with his business matters. It wasn't so much that I was a holy terror to others as that I was one to myself."

Sheren's belief that if he'd had a sympathetic mother, one who had been more giving, his life would have been perhaps easier, is one that remains with him today. "I have to see my problems in relationship to where my mother was, too. My mother was not a giving person, but as a matter of fact she was very self-centered, so it was difficult for me to ask anything of her. Looking backward, I realize that if she had been more of a giving person, like my Aunt Fanny, who was a very caring person, it would have been a totally different family experience."

When Chris Conroy was seven years old, he and his brother Kevin, who was three, were playing at the top of the stairs in their home. Chris relates the events that followed: "My mother yelled out that she was going to a neighbor's for a few minutes and told me to take care of my brother. At that moment, Kevin started down the stairs with me right behind him. Somehow he tripped and went flying down the stairs. He rolled a couple of times. By the time he got to the bottom of the stairwell, his head was cracked wide open and I could see what I thought were his brains hanging out. I ran up the stairs and yelled out to my mother next door, 'Come home right away.' Then I ran back down, took my shirt off, wrapped it around my brother's head, and carried him up the stairs."

At that moment, the boys' mother returned. Christopher recalls her accusations: "When she saw Kevin in my arms, she began to scream at me. 'What did you do? What did you do to your brother?' My brother was rushed to the hospital and I never saw him again. It was very tough not seeing him; he didn't die right away. He was in the hosptial for three months. But I wasn't allowed to see him and I always wished I could have. My parents were young, in their twenties and inexperienced. My father was a drinker to boot. And, he blamed me for my brother's death. In retrospect, I can say that it was not intentional, but at the time I felt I was responsible and that somehow I had pushed him. I felt like the whole world hated me. But in reality, when he started to fall I reached out to grab him, but I just wasn't quick enough to catch him. It wasn't that I pushed him at all.

"My father took pictures of Kevin at the hospital with a Huckleberry Hound Dog they had bought him. Since I was so small, I wasn't allowed to visit him. Those pictures were the only way I had of seeing what my brother looked like, and I could see his head was all bandaged up." When my brother died, I was very unhappy. But today, I am grateful that he did. If he had lived, he would have been a vegetable all of his life. So in light of that, I'm glad he didn't have to live that way."

Today, Chris, at age thirty-five, laments the death of his brother and the death of a relationship they could have had. "If I think about it too much, I start to cry. I lost something—the potential of having a brother and a good friend. I felt guilty for years. While I sat and watched, my mother had a nervous breakdown. About a year after my brother died she started to talk to herself. She'd had a couple of miscarriages and she began to hallucinate and imagine she heard voices. She would think she saw people. She also thought I was some kind of a demon. This went on until finally she had to be hospitalized for a while. At first she was treated and put under a doctor's care. After a time she returned home but was on medication to calm her. To this day my mother is a very nervous woman. My father's alcoholic drinking didn't help matters. When drunk he abused both my mother and me. After my brother died, he hit me often. He would throw me against the wall so hard, it would break the plaster."

The combination of his mother's behavior and his father's beatings took a heavy toll on Chris. "Many times I wished it had been me who had died instead of my brother. I was lonely and scared at that point. When my father first told me that my brother had died, I didn't dare cry because my father told me to grow up and be a man. He said, 'Your brother's dead and he's never coming back.' Many years later my sister was born. There is a difference of ten years in our ages, so we are not very close. My father also stopped drinking. But by then my own problems began with drug abuse. By the time I was sixteen, I was shooting heroin. This went on for a couple of years. I knew I had problems. There were a lot of things that were bothering me. I didn't like myself—that was part of the reason I shot dope. But I also felt responsible for my brother's death. My parents had mistreated me so much that I was extremely insecure. I had no confidence in myself as a person. I'm sure this low picture I had of myself had been beaten into me. I finally went into treatment to help break the drug habit."

At first, Chris went to work as a mechanic and a pipefitter. He traveled for a while and eventually took up photography. He was a photographer for five years. Then he acted as an agent, but once again became involved with drugs—this time cocaine. "It got out of hand because I began to follow the same pattern of blaming myself. This time it was for the failure of my photography business. But I immediately sought help and now I'm doing fine. I didn't want to live my life like that again. The past is the past and while I can't ignore it, I can't let it control me. From time to time, I feel guilty and I think, 'Why didn't I walk in front of him?' Or, 'Why didn't I take care of him better?' But my brother wanted to walk down in front of me. He wanted to do it by himself. I made a couple of bad judgments when I let him do that. What I realized later was that no one is omnipotent. My mother made mistakes, as did my father, as did I."

Although Chris tries not to let the past interfere with his life, there is one thing he will not do. "I can't go to my brother's grave. I feel if I go there I am going to drop dead. I had a cousin whose husband was killed in an industrial accident. I went to the funeral. At the cemetery, I was within a block from where my brother's grave was, but I couldn't even look in that direction. Although I'm not a kid, I honestly feel that my mind is not strong enough to handle it. I'm afraid it will do damage to me, that maybe I would have a heart attack or something. So I stay away from things I can't handle. But that doesn't mean I don't think about him. I do. I wonder how it would be to have my brother with me, what he would be like. I think about that a lot.

"Today, I'm trying to keep my life on an even keel. I met a wonderful girl. She is the best thing that's ever happened to me. Now I want to look toward happiness and having a family of my own."

Chapter Nine

Other Heartbreaks

The following stories are of individuals who have had many heartbreaks. The two men below not only suffered the loss of a sibling, they also endured the death of a child.

When Andrew Pustay was sixteen, his brother George died of a kidney disorder at age twenty-eight. "In his early youth, George contracted an illness and was treated with sulfa drugs," Andy relates. "This was before the advent of penicillin. My parents always believed, although it was never proven, that the sulfa drugs had had a bad effect on my brother and his kidneys."

George left a widow and three small children, Mary, age two, Joe, one, and George, Jr., two months old. "It was incredibly sad," Andy recalls. "Here was this beautiful young family starting out in life and my brother's life was cut short in his prime."

When George became seriously ill, he was living in Troy, New York, and there Andy and his parents joined the sick man. Andy tells us, "He knew he was dying, but he kept his spirits high and he would always greet me with, 'Hi, how you doing?' However, I never stayed very long in the hospital with him—maybe five or ten minutes—because I could see he was in a great deal of pain. After each visit I returned to the home of a friend with whom I was staying, and it was there I got word from my parents that he had died.

"It was a numbing experience. He was my only sibling

and, although there was a wide spread in our ages, we were very close. We shared a bedroom and bed until he left to work in Schenectady. He had always been protective of me and we got along very well."

After his brother died, Andy experienced a certain attitude of overprotectiveness from his parents. It was not until many years later that Andy understood how his parents felt. "Now I can understand why," he says, "because my wife, Monica, and I have lost two children. We now have a surviving daughter, Katie, and I can understand how my parents felt. They didn't want to lose me. Our first child, Jessica, was two days old when she died of congential heart problems. Suzanne was eight years old when she died as the result of a bacterial infection, H-Croup influenza, which is not a flu we were told. The symptoms were a sore throat and a low fever.

"Katie, our surviving child, was four at the time. This past December, when Katie was going on eight—the same age at which Suzanne died—was a family milestone. Getting past it was difficult for us, just as getting past twenty-eight was a milestone for me, because that was George's age when he died. Both my parents and I breathed a sigh of relief when I got past my twenty-eighth birthday.

"When George died, although I was compassionate and caring, I did not know what my parents were going through. I was not to know that until I too had lost a child and experienced that kind of pain. I could not understand or in any way associate with their loss until I suffered the same loss. Grief should never be compared or measured. A sibling has pain. A parent has pain. But, a sibling does not know how a parent feels. To me, it was an incredibly dramatic revelation, after the death of Jessica and Suzanne, to comprehend the grief that my parents had experienced. I said to my mom and dad, 'Now I now how you feel.' We had all felt George's loss, but my grief as a sibling did not compare with what I know now was my parents' grief. But as a sibling, I had no idea of what my parents went through—nor should any sibling ever have to know what a parent feels. There was a great deal of tenderness between us. We had been a religious family. We went to church as a family and so there was a communication in that respect. But, in looking back, that wasn't enough in the way of communication. I suppose there never is enough."

For this reason Monica and Andy felt it important, after their daughter Suzanne died, to go to a bereavement counselor. "We felt communication was a top priority. Our counselor was very good, particularly in helping Katie," Andy states. "We found that playing with Katie after Suzanne' death was a very important form of therapy. It helped us to understand her needs through playing with her. For months after Suzanne died, Katie wanted to play doctor and hospital. This was an aftereffect of seeing her sister rushed out to an ambulance. She wanted to play that whole scene again. We tried to convey to this four-year-old child that, although Suzanne had died, her body remained and Suzanne went to Heaven. Whenever we play, she speaks of Suzanne in loving terms."

Art Peterson is no stranger to grief. When he was forty, his thirty-six-year-old sister, Elizabeth, took her own life by swallowing a bottle of pills. Art tells of his reactions not only to his sister's suicide, but to the death of his son, Tony: "My younger sister took her own life. My teenage son died in an auto accident. Elizabeth was a gentle, troubled, insecure adult who could not adjust to life and who died alone and in despair.

"Tony was a vibrant confident, talented young man who, as his mother commented on that long ride to the accident scene, went out on the crest of a wave. More important to my later state of mind, his death was obviously swift and painless. Not so my sister's. Can I, therefore, accept his death more easily than hers? Not necessarily. My emotions are different in each case and I can't compare one with the other. I feel guilt over my failure to help Elizabeth, and I feel anguish over the suffering she endured at the end. With Tony, my feeling is one of loneliness, not only because I loved him but because I enjoyed his company. I also feel cheated because I will never see him develop his superb talent. In a way, I suppose my grief for my sister is grief for her. When I mourn my son, I grieve for me. There is no way to compare the two."

Art believes it's probably impossible to equate any two situations, although they may appear similar. "Even if the circumstances and the relationships are alike, people react differently at different times or ages. Were you six or sixty when your mother died? Even if the relationship and your stage of life are the same, the circumstances will differ in some significant way. Did the child suffer or was the death relatively painless? On the other hand, the relationships are often not quite alike. Was your brother an older sibling who took care of you, or was he a younger one for whom you were responsible?"

Art, together with his wife, Ronnie, have been deeply involved with helping other bereaved parents and surviving siblings in their work with The Compassionate Friends, the national self-help organization dedicated to assisting bereaved families. When grieving parents gather in self-help discussion groups, Art explains, someone invariably brings up the question of the relative intensity of various kinds of grief. "Is a sudden, accidental death easier or harder on survivors than one which follows a long terminal illness? Does the death of a child cause more anguish than the death of some other family member?"

If you have experienced more than one loss through death, Art believes, or if you have been close to those who have, you eventually realize that these questions have no universal answer. "Of course," Art states, "you would be correct in saying that this response is valid, but it would not be acceptable to many suvivors, especially if they are newly bereaved. When grief is at its most intense, the sufferer believes that it can get no worse, and does not look kindly on those who question that evaluation."

As to the age level of a sibling at the time of death, Art has this to say: "I'm pretty sure that when most people discuss sibling grief, they're thinking about brothers and sisters of a young age. Still, as is the case with other parents who lose adult children, the parent-child relationship is very similar at any age. Art says the big difference is that the older survivor has already encountered some fairly substantial grief and realizes that life can be harsh. "It still hurts and probably just as much, but you aren't nearly as surprised at forty as at fourteen."

Surviving siblings may, in part, be influenced by the anguished questions of their parents about the child who died, such as "My child died in a drowning and his body was never found. *That* has to be the worst." Yet another parent may cry, "My son died suddenly and there was no chance to say good-bye, no opportunity to hold him. *That* has to be the worst." The parent of a child who suffered intensely before dying may lament, "My child had a terminal illness and I had to watch the slow disintegration and not be able to help my child's agony." When bereaved parents are lost in the throes of trying to convey their unceasing pain, they are not really making comparisons about the grief. Their need to find answers to "Why?" generates the questions about who suffers the "worst pain."

Art indicates it is therapeutic for survivors to talk about how much worse their situation is than those of others, at least during the early months of grief. "In The Compassionate Friends, we hear parents engaging in this activity with great vigor. If, however, you pay very close attention, you will also notice that as time passes, the veterans quietly drop out of these discussions to let the newly bereaved people take over. It isn't just that they recognize the futility of comparing griefs, but that they see the need for others to discover this themselves. This respect for the rights of others is one of the nicer characteristics of self-help."

Although bereaved parents may come to realize that it is not that any one person's grief is greater than another, but that the horror of it may be different, surviving siblings may be left with the initial impact made by the parents' early statement that "Ours is the worst." And, although parents may garner such comfort and insight at self-help meetings, surviving siblings may not because group discussions are not always available to them.

Art's wife, Ronnie, comments on the intensity of grief: "It isn't so much what the name of the relationship is, whether it's parent or sibling, it's what is invested in that relationship—how much dependency or identity is invested in it. It's a matter of whether you're proud of being the little sister of the captain of the football team or whether you're proud of being the doctor's mother. If that's a big thing in your life and it's wiped out, it's wiped out. There are just so many variables. But I do think there may be more variables in the sibling situation than in the parental."

On her twenty-seventy birthday, Roberta Wilson examined her feelings about her brother's death. "Mark died six years ago when he was twenty-seven, and this is the first time I have really talked about it.

"For the first two years after his death, I couldn't even say his name. My parents couldn't say it, nor could my sister. When my mother finally spoke his name, I guess I thought I could too. Now I'm able to say it, but I am so depressed all the time. I guess not having been able to talk to someone these past six years has taken its toll."

Roberta's nightly dreams are a reflection of the horror she experienced when she and her parents were asked to identify her brother's body at the morgue. "He had shot himself. At first we thought maybe he had been murdered. We just couldn't believe he would take his own life. But the police dispelled that thought when they told us my brother had telephoned them before shooting himself. However, the police did not arrive in time to save him. At the morgue, there was a glass partition we looked through to see him. There was a fly hovering around him and my mother became very upset at the fly. I dream about that fly. I dream I see my brother's face as it was in the morgue and relive that terrible day. I also dream that I am trying to find him. All of a sudden he appears and we hug each other. But then he disappears. In other dreams, I think he doesn't approve of what I am doing.

"There has been a lot of guilt. My brother and I were very close and were such good friends. I feel I should have been more aware of what was going on; he had a lot of depression. After his death, I tried going to a therapist, but the first question asked of me was 'How long do you think it will take to get over the death of your brother?' I didn't think a therapist who asked me that question was going to be of help to me."

Going to the cemetery has both a calming and a disquieting effect on Roberta. "When I go to his grave and I see the year he died, it freaks me out. I can't believe he has been gone that long, or that he has had no part in our lives for all that time. Everything that has happened to me since his death has had an edge to it. Today I think, 'At my wedding, he would have looked so good in a suit.' Or, 'He would have been such a great baby-sitter and uncle for my little boy, Michael.' I go to the cemetery about four times a year, and I feel better when I do. I feel as though he knows I've been there.

"My sister grieves in a different way. She has not been able to go to the cemetery with me. I am sure she misses him very much. She is very bitter and angry, however. She won't talk about him, as it is painful. Nor does she have any pictures of him. I don't keep them prominently displayed, but I have one or two around. They are not in spots where visitors would see them, so no questions would be invited.

"At first, I was very angry. But it doesn't pay to remain angry. However, once that leaves you, you're left with an emptiness, because the anger allowed you to think, 'How could you do something like this? How could you be so selfish? Look at what you have done to me, to my parents, to my sister.' My brother had been trying to kick a drug habit. My parents had wanted to send him to a very expensive place to get help. They were going to take all the money they had and do that for him.

"Since his death my parents have moved to Florida. They had a business in New York, but my mother couldn't remain living on the same block, with the neighbors and everything. It's been very therapeutic for them. They now have a different outlook. My father took up ceramics and other crafts."

Roberta regrets that she has had no one to talk to about her brother's death. "I haven't been able to talk to my parents. They don't want to rehash it is the feeling I get. So I've really had no one to share with or talk to about him. It was such a loss to me, doubly so because we were friends and very close. Not all sisters and brothers have that kind of relationship. I just couldn't talk to anyone, not even my husband. I got married two years after my brother died. It's very strange, but I feel that my husband has all the qualities that I had liked in my brother—his sense of humor and his way of making things better. I know I have to keep a grip on myself and go on with the rest of my life. As my father always says, 'You've got to keep your chins up.' "

Roberta wishes she could comprehend the reasons why her brother took his life in the manner he did. "When I think about the ways a person can commit suicide, like jumping off a roof, swallowing poison, or taking pills, I can rationalize those means. Of course, any way is bad, but shooting yourself is so violent. I know I will never get my brother back, but I would like to understand him, to know why he took his life in that particular way. He had been seeing a woman. Perhaps he had a disappointing love affair. That, combined with trying to overcome the drugs, was probably too much for him to handle."

Little details about her brother's everyday existence remain indelibly etched in Roberta's memory. "I still remember things like his phone number and his address. And I think, 'They are still here, but he isn't.' But I do believe that one day when I am dead—and I hope that is a long time from now—I will see him again. We just don't die and go into a casket." Roberta jokes, "But when I do see him, I'm going to kill him for what he did to all of us."

Jim Jordan was the third of three children. His brother Van was born in 1934; his sister Jo Lynn in 1931; and Jim in 1943. By the time Jim was a teenager, Jo Lynn and Van had grown up and had escaped the extreme poverty of a cabin in the Ozarks, home of Dogpatch, USA. Jim's wife Debbie describes the relationship between her husband and his only brother:

"When Jim was six, Van, with the cooperation of an aunt and a lie, joined the Air Force. He served as a jet mechanic and flight engineer for more than twenty years. Jo Lynn married about the same time, leaving Jim alone with his parents. Around that time, Jim's mother tired of her husband's alcoholic abuse and took her son to live in Idabel, Oklahoma, where she worked at odd jobs in restaurants, bakeries, and even in a hotel which her sister owned. Jim grew up in the streets of

Idabel. Although these were not the same as big-city streets, he still became wild and street smart. When Van came to visit his mother and younger brother, he took on the same role of the brutal father that Jim and his mother had fled from. So as Jim grew up his encounters with his brother were few, short, and always physically and emotionally painful.

"When Jim was thirteen, his father borrowed a rifle and shot himself in a hotel room in Kermit, Texas. Because of the harshness of his upbringing and the memories they left with Jim, he could not express any feelings over his father's suicide, although now he admits that is something he may have to face one day. At seventeen, Jim joined the Navy and spent six years in the military. This made Van proud of him for the first time in their lives. When Jim decided to leave the Navy, that decision spoiled the pride of both Van and their mother. However, Van wasn't paying too much attention to anyone before he died.

"Jim doesn't regret the circumstances of his brother's death. 'Van went with a smile on his face. He was doing exactly what he wanted to do—he was flying.' Van had been crop dusting, something his family warned him against doing. On the morning of April 1, 1985, Van finished his next-to-last passes over a field. As he turned, the sun got in his eyes and a split-second hesitation sent his plane into a power line. The momentum of the impact dragged the plane upside down along the ground. Van was rushed to the hospital where he died in less than an hour."

Debbie relates the two rituals Jim used to sort out his feelings about his brother's death. "The first was the fulfillment of a promise he and Van had made to each other. Years before, Jim and Van had promised each other that, whichever brother died first, the other would drink a beer at the graveside to say good-bye. To these two hillbillies, having a beer together was the ultimate in male bonding. After the funeral was over, Jim, true to his promise, took a beer to Van's grave and toasted his brother. It helped. Jim knew that he, at least, had been a good brother."

The second ritual was writing. Debbie explains: "Apart from being a talented wildlife painter, Jim is a wonderful storyteller, but a combination of dyslexia and bad schooling discouraged him from writing. However, that didn't stop him from using those skills. When Jim returned from burying his brother in Texarkana, he took out a notebook and penned a few of his memories of frog gigging and hunting trips. He didn't write much, just a page or two, but it helped. Even if Van paid no attention to him in life, Jim knew his brother very well. This practice has helped Jim to write other story ideas down. One day, Jim and I may write short stories or books together." (*Author's note:* Debbie Jordan, together with her colleague Mary Johnston Davis, write under the pseudonym of Rosemary Jordan. Their work is highly regarded in romantic fiction. Perhaps Jim's memories of his brother will generate a co-team of Jordans.)

"During the same year his brother died, two of Jim's best friends died. Facing these losses throughout 1985 made Jim face his own mortality. They showed Jim that he is finite. Although he's a strong man, he is just one man. Jim has always been kind and generous, but 1985 tried his reserves to the limit. If he gained nothing else from these losses, he finally realized that he must give to himself if he is to give to others. It's an important lesson many people never learn."

"Although several years have passed since their deaths, Jim says he is still grieving Van, as well as Robert and Olie. He admits that he still has some anger over the good things that never were, but he can live with that feeling. During the past two years, he has focused most of his art on waterfowl, a subject that would have pleased Van. Often, Jim imagines what Van would say if he could have seen a particular picture. When he talks about his brother, his eyes redden. That's the general extent of his public tears. But the redness is a sign of the strong emotions which Jim isn't afraid to show. He talks freely about his losses. He's one of the best examples I know of how a man can face grief openly and survive. I'm proud he has given this example to our teenaged son, Jimmy. I believe this lesson will help him face the difficulties he will meet in the real world. I hope Jimmy can teach this sensitivity to his own son when he gets older, to know that it's all right for a man to grieve."

We have read in the previous stories about various heartbreaks encountered by bereaved brothers and sisters whose sibling died in their lifetimes. In the following account, Scott Kessler tells of problems that affected him as a subsequent child.

"My parents had a child named Robyn. When the baby was a month old, she died of Sudden Infant Death Syndrome. My parents later adopted a daughter and I was born afterwards," Scott relates. "Until I was into my teens, my parents were very protective. They really watched over me and my sister Lori with an extra amount of care, because they feared losing another child."

Scott describes how he became personally involved at a very young age in the work his parents were doing for the Sudden Infant Death Syndrome Foundation. "At the time, my mom and dad were officers of the Long Island chapter of SIDS, and they used to hold parent meetings in our house. I can remember when I was nine or ten years old, I would be lying in bed and unable to fall asleep because I could hear people downstairs talking, crying, or even laughing. Once in a while, my mother would come up and ask me to come downstairs. She wanted to show these frightened parents that here was living proof that a child could survive. They could have another child without fear that the same thing (SIDS) would happen to that child. The idea that 'just because it happened once doesn't mean it's going to happen again' was stressed. I was a model of sorts to show these parents that as a subsequent child I had survived.

"I didn't mind being brought downstairs because there were always doughnuts, which I liked to eat. At first, I wanted to watch what was going on, but later I wished there wasn't so much talking and commotion. Although it did disrupt my sleep until late at night, I realized I was being a help to the people there. I remember they would look at me and the way they would smile. I sensed they felt better when they saw me."

Scott wonders whether his life would have been different if Robyn had lived. "One of the things I used to do was go to sleep wondering what she would have been like. Would she have been like me? What would she have looked like? How pretty would she have been? Who would her friends have been? Also, my parents might not have been as protective over me as they were. But, my parents were still good parents. They knew how to bring up a child and they are both warm and loving people. I think the basic thing is that I would have been more in the dark about death. And that is something I don't think anybody should be in the dark about—not even a child."

As a youngster, Scott remembers being concerned when his mom and dad would argue. "I know my parents had problems after the baby's death. I'm not really sure how long it lasted. They used to fight very often when I was a child and I used to worry that they would get divorced. That was my big concern, for then I would have two parents living apart and I wouldn't know who to stay with. Until I was about ten or eleven, that was my biggest worry. After that, I took a different view. I began to think it would be fun to have two sets of parents. I had all these strange ideas, thinking what it would be like and wanting them to get divorced. But they didn't. Now I'm glad for that. My friends always loved my parents. They got along great with them and thought they were the best parents."

Now twenty-three, Scott recalls his views on death as a child: "Because my mom and dad were so involved in the activities of the SIDS group, I was sort of thrown into it too. As long as I can remember, I recall stuffing envelopes, even when I was seven years old. There were brochures and things for the parents and other people interested in the subject. This forced me to grow up fast. Unlike most of my friends, I was faced with death. I knew what it was. I had read about it in the brochures when I was very young. In our house I heard people talking about it constantly, about babies dying and the grief they went through. So I had to come to grips with death much sooner than any of my friends did. A child in my own family had died. We used to visit the cemetery where this baby was buried. It made me think, could it happen to me? It also made me realize that life doesn't go on forever."

Scott reflects on his thoughts at an early age: "As a child, you don't think in terms that you could be the one who's hit by a car or you could be sick or ill. You don't usually think of those things when you're a child. But if you're involved with an organization such as SIDS, you have a different perspective. You realize that people do die and you don't know why. Even at that early age, I had to come to grips with the reality that life does not go on forever. For some of us just being alive and seven years old is a miracle. I think it made my life a little easier—in the sense that I wanted to live. And knowing that I could die made me want to live more."

Chapter Ten

Parents and Other Family Members

Our parents are our idols, our role models. We look up to them. They're supposed to be strong and take care of us. But after the death of a child, strong men weep and often women can no longer function well as mothers. When parents are bleeding emotionally, they are unable to be pillars of strength to surviving children.

Although some sons and daughters become angry with their parents when no parental support is available, other surviving siblings may assume the parent's mantle—wanting to be a father or mother to their parents. They want to make things better for the parents just as the parents did for the children when they were small.

Karen Schlesier Eisen tells of her desire to look after her parents' needs: "After my brother Billy died and for a long time after that—years in fact—I wanted to make everything better for my parents and compensate for their loss. I wasn't trying to replace my brother, but I wanted to protect them from the problems that I had. I didn't want to burden them with things like my divorce or anything else that might cause them pain. So I would always say, 'Everything's fine. I'm happy.' Meanwhile, life wasn't fine; life was horrible for me.

"I had gotten married six months before my brother died. But instead of my husband being supportive, we fought all the time. He resented the amount of time I spent with my parents. I was also told that he could not deal with my crying. So I didn't cry. I think I only cried once in front of him because I didn't want to upset him. I was trying to make everybody happy. I didn't want my parents to be upset and I didn't want my husband to be upset. So, I cried to and from work, hysterically, on the train. Sometimes I locked myself in the bathroom and cried so that he wouldn't know, pretending I was taking a shower."

Karen tried to explain to her husband how distraught she was because of her brother's death. "I kept telling him, 'Try to imagine how you would feel if your sister was dead.' But he couldn't do that. As a result, we never talked about Billy because he couldn't deal with death. Since he and my brother had been doing similar work, they had frequent contact with one another. But I hadn't seen my brother more than twice in the last six months because I had been so busy with my married life. So, after Billy died, I asked my husband for information: Tell me what Billy was doing; how were things with him, and so on. I needed to know something about my brother, because I had lost track of Billy's life in those months. But my husband would tell me nothing.

"On the day that my brother was dead six months, I started to cry. It was the first time I got upset in front of my husband since he had reprimanded me. I began to cry, and he said, 'I'm sick of this. It's been six months and you ought to be over this by now.' After that, I said to myself, 'Okay, that's enough. As soon as I can, I'm getting out of this situation.' So not only was he not supportive, he was also very destructive."

Karen acknowledges that spouses can have a difficult time when such a tragedy happens to their mate. "In my own instance, he was not compassionate or sensitive to anybody's feelings—those of myself or my parents. But I think that although husbands and wives try to be supportive if they really love the spouse, noboby can truly understand who hasn't gone through it. They can't get inside your skin and feel it with you. And while they may want and try to be helpful and sympathetic, I can't imagine that they don't say sometimes, 'Oh, God, this is not the person that I married. Why do I have to suffer through this, too? This is not what I wanted for my life.' But it has a lot to do with the strengths of the individual people involved and the relationship they have with each other."

Karen explains what happened when her parents' household was diminished. "After I got married and left, that was one less person at home. Then my brother died. And after that, the dog died. So we went from having four people in the house and a dog, and being a very busy hustling and bustling home, to one with just my parents in it alone. My brother was dead and I was married. And the house was real quiet for my mother. My father works nights a lot because of erratic schedules. Sometimes weekends too. So my mother spent a lot of time alone. And my father was grieving so and kept saying, 'He didn't know how I felt about him. I wish I could do it all over.' All these emotional tears about how much he loved my brother, that's the part that got to me. I had seen my mother cry all the time, but I didn't feel as bad for my mother, in a way, because she and my brother had been very close. My brother knew that my mother loved him. I think he knew that my father did too, but my father doesn't know that."

As chairperson for a siblings group (of the Long Island chapter of Compassionate Friends) that ranged in ages from nine to thirty-two, Karen observed that many of the younger children wanted Mommy and Daddy to stop crying. "If Mommy and Daddy are so unhappy, who am I going to talk to?' This is the kind of thing they will say at meetings. Or, 'I don't want to upset them any more.' Many meetings have problems at which the siblings express dealing with the parents' emotions, saying 'They're not strong like they used to be.' I don't know how long a child wants to continue mothering the parents. Many reach a point where they are annoyed that no attention is being given to them, the children, and that role sometimes changes to anger. In my own situation, I still feel as though I want to mother my mother. Maybe someone a little younger than I would lose patience with her. But I don't think I want to stop, at least for now. I feel helpless and many siblings feel the same way. My parents feel helpless because they couldn't save my brother. They raised him and took care of him, but at the end, there was nothing they could do for him but hold his hand and watch him die."

Karen remembers wanting to protect her parents almost from the very beginning of the news of the tragedy. "At the hospital—and I've thought about this a lot since then—the very first thing that came out of my mouth to my mother were the words, 'I'm sorry.' When I think back on that, it seems like such a stupid thing for me to have said to her. I had lost my brother. It seems funny that I would have been saying I was sorry to her as though she had suffered a loss and I hadn't. It was as if I were saying something to her that a casual acquaintance would say, but it seemed strange that I would have said those words to her."

Karen had been asked if her divorce would have happened if her brother had not died and if she had not wanted to assume the protective role toward her parents. "It would have happened anyway," she explained. "But when my brother died, my eyes were really opened to the situation. It's easy to be in love and to have everything going along wonderfully without a crisis. But when something happens, you really find out a lot about a person's character. So, because we were thrown into this situation I was able to find out that there was nothing to this man. He couldn't give me any support or love, nothing. I didn't expect him to have answers for me. I just expected that perhaps I could cry on his shoulder once in a while. And I realized that this wasn't the type of person with whom I wanted to spend the rest of my life."

While the sibling in the preceding account tells us of the lack of support and sympathy from her former husband, the following account by a surviving sister tells of an experience that was quite different. Elaine Altman is very grateful for the warmth and compassion extended by her mate: "My husband, Martin, who also loved my brother very much, was extremely supportive. He understood the relationship between my brother and me, and that we were very close with many parallels in our lives." Elaine also recalls the help of Sue, a close friend. "Her father had died several years before, and she had also lost a dear friend. She called me every day and we talked a lot about it. She was wonderful."

As in the earlier story about Karen Eisen, another surviving sister who had never seen her father cry prior to her sister's death was Madeleine Toomey Pflaumbaum. "To see my father in such a bad way made me feel that I wanted to suffer *more* than he was suffering. Then I began to hurt even more inside." What saddened Madeleine greatly were the attitude and comments of her parents. "We've lived our lives. Why couldn't it have been us instead?"

Madeleine was angered when people asked her, "How are your parents doing?" She tells of events at a school meeting: "Last night I spoke at a PTA meeting. When I had finished, one of the ladies came up to me and said, 'How are your parents?' Now, I have never underestimated the grief that my parents have gone through or that of any other parent who has lost a child, but we siblings are constantly overlooked. The next time someone asks me how my parents are doing, I will tell them. 'They go to sleep, they get up, they eat, they go to work, and that's it.' Life for them is really considered as over. When Kathleen died they said they didn't want to live through burying another child. They both expressed that many times. But they did live to go through that again—when my brother died, too."

Cindy Tart, who, as we read in an earlier chapter, lost her eight-year-old brother Dennis, felt that his death broke into a camaraderie she had shared with her mother. "I had felt for a long time that I was very unusual because I got along great with my mom and dad. My mom was my 'gossip partner.' When I'd come home from school every day, I'd tell her everything, and we'd sit there and talk. But after Dennis died, I didn't feel comfortable telling her, because she would say things like, 'Save it for a rainy day,' or, 'Put it in your heart.' I never wanted to tell my mom that it was Dennis' fault, because it wasn't—it was his death that caused it, and that wasn't Dennis' fault.

"My mom gets upset at times over Dennis' death and she'll just blow up at everyone who gets in her path. After Dennis died, I was afraid to talk to my dad. I was scared, especially the night at the funeral home where all my dad did was to sit in this one chair. Then he'd get up and look at Dennis, and sit down again. (He said later on that he almost passed out.) Before we got ready to leave, he looked at Dennis once more."

When the family returned home from the funeral parlor, Cindy was concerned at the sound of her father's voice. "My father's got a fairly deep voice," she says, "but when he said to my sister, 'Please get me an ashtray,' his voice was high-pitched. That scared me. Then everybody started to say that they had never seen him cry, that Daddy never talked, and they were worried about him. But it's different now, because I feel I can go to my Dad with a whole lot more things than I could when Dennis was here. My dad and I are very close now."

In the above stories, we have read about the thoughts of some bereaved sisters. We will now hear from Billy Pfister, a bereaved brother who felt that his parents were being over-protective toward him after the death of his brother.

"My parents would go off the wall if they didn't know what I was doing at all times. At first, for about three weeks after it happened, they were very calm and relaxed—probably in shock. But as time went on, they began to get jittery. Finally, they said to me, 'You didn't learn from his death did you? You just don't learn. You're going to have the same thing happen to you.' It's not that I was going out on a motorcycle, which was how my brother was killed. But I think they made the association of the time it happened—at two or three in the morning—and when I was going to be out late, they were afraid that I might also fall into the same trap. They didn't know where I was and they had a fear of the unknown."

In an earlier account in this chapter, we read of a sibling who wanted to parent her parents. We now hear from Ellen Spector, who experienced the opposite—her parents wanted to protect her from the effects of grief. "When I get upset, they get upset to see me that way, but they try to hide it. I don't like to talk to my mother or father about my feelings, because I think that it makes them sad. So I try to keep busy. During the day when I'm occupied, I don't think about it. But at night, I think about it a lot and that's a bad time. I get really upset."

Susan Keats also felt that her father wanted to look after her. "After the unveiling, he asked if I was all right. He had cried during the ceremony and I thought that was good, because he hadn't shed a tear at the funeral. He felt he had to be the sturdy one. But at the unveiling, we just kept it to the immediate family. We didn't bring in other people because it would then be like another funeral. And I think knowing he didn't have to be in control made my father comfortable. The rabbi took charge and my father didn't have to do anything. He just cried and we hugged each other. My father and I don't talk much about emotional things, but there is a warmth between us. I think I've become used to that kind of wordless communication.

"But prior to the funeral, it made my mother unhappy, for she thought he ought to be more upset about what had happened. I think at the time he felt like he had to be the strong one and keep himself together while everyone else was falling apart. He had to make the funeral arrangements, and so I don't think he had much time to be upset. His apparent coolness was a source of conflict for a while because my mother thought my father should have been more emotional. She felt he was not allowing himself to cry, and she was angry because, in her view, he appeared to be almost entertaining people. That was something they resolved when she realized that everyone grieves in a different way, and she accepted his way.

"I also felt that my mother was suffering from guilt feelings, and my heart went out to her. My sister had been overweight, a matter of concern to my mother. She had also disappointed them by not going to college. Although she had a job, she wasn't earning much. All in all, she wasn't very ambitious and I think that frustrated my parents quite a lot. I knew my mother was feeling a lot of guilt, and I didn't want that. I longed to help her, to let her know she musn't feel guilty. At the same time, I knew there was nothing I could do to change her feelings."

The problem of people sympathizing with her parents' grief and not with hers disturbed Susan. "In a few instances, I was shoved aside. I'm not looking for more compassion than my parents, of course—I'm not competing for compassion. But I don't want to be treated as if losing a sister is any less than losing a daughter—it's just different. I understand full well that the situations are not the same and bring about different kinds of feelings. While I comprehend that, it sure has been hard for me. For example, we have friends in New Jersey whom I've known since I was six years old. When they called our house and I answered the telephone, they said, 'Oh, how are you? We understand you have a new job. And how is everything with you?' They didn't want to hear what I had to say about Carolyn or my reaction to her death. But when my parents got on the phone, they were speaking very quietly and sympathetically, and I didn't appreciate that. I simply wanted them to acknowledge that I was a sister who was grieving, rather than to address me in such a loud and cheerful way."

Jo Saulisberry tells of a time when her daughter reproached her for not understanding that she, Kathy, had lost a brother. "One day when I was really down and feeling sorry for myself, which I am very good at doing, Kathy said, 'Mom, I lost him too.' This made me think of how *into* myself I really was and that I didn't consider how my surviving children felt. I had just figured they were older, had their own lives, and would soon forget. I realize now how wrong I was and that they really hurt—not in the way my husband Chuck and I do, but as a brother and sister would. Although we cried together and talked a lot, I didn't want to burden them. I felt they didn't need help. I don't ever remember my son Dan really crying around us until one day many years later when he read a letter I had written to a friend about Tracy. When he put it down, he came over to me, held me tight, and just sobbed. Then he hugged his dad and said, 'I love you.'"

Allison Heitner admits to being selfish about thinking that her grief was the worst, after her sister died. "My mother is always very emotional about everything, so it didn't surprise me to see her in hysterics. She was just totally depleted. My father was the same because this very strong, big, tough guy was also crying. My parents did not deserve this, I felt. How could this happen to them? But I also felt that it was my loss more than anybody else's."

Allison's reasoning was that her parents had two other children to help them get through this horrible ordeal, and they had each other. "I tried to explain this to my parents, that they at least could comfort each other, and that they had me and my brother, but I had lost my closest and best friend, my sister just ten months younger than I. Even if I met other people whose brothers or sisters had died, I would always say, 'Well, what was the age difference?' Since ours was so close, or if it was a brother who had died instead of a sister, I felt they couldn't possibly have been as close as I was to my sister."

Her parents were disturbed by Allison's refusal to talk to her friends or to see other people. "I know this upset my parents greatly, but I wanted to be in our room, mine and Leslie's, with the two beds together so that I could be closer to my sister. I refused to leave that room because I felt she was going to contact me or come back. So I was determined to stay right there. For two months I remained in the house and had no contact with anybody. During that time, there was a big change in my personality."

The thing that did affect Allison deeply was seeing her father cry. "I had never seen my father cry until this happened. And that was a killer. As for my mother, she was like a basket case. Another thing that upset me when I finally went away to school was my parents' request to redecorate my room. They thought it would be a good idea. But, Leslie and I had decorated our room together, and had picked out the wallpaper and the paint color. To my parents, I said, 'No way!' To this date, six years later, it's still the same wallpaper, the same room."

Allison comments on the relationship between her parents. "My mother and father have an exceptional relationship and an exceptional marriage. It's much the same as the exceptional relationship that my sister and I had. People always commented about how close we were and how well we got along. I'm not saying we never fought, because we did. But she was always my confidante. I never confided as much in my mother until my sister passed away."

Barbara Capriotti, a bereaved mother, shares her observations of her eldest daughter after the death of her infant son to SIDS (Sudden Infant Death Syndrome): "My oldest, Cathy, made herself a sort of nurse-caretaker. She was always concerned about her father and me, and she did everything she could to make things easier for us, especially when we were upset. If she saw that we were having a rough time, she would do the laundry or the vacuuming. It was as though that was her way of showing that she cared about us and that she wanted to help us live our lives normally. It was a sad time for her, but I think she was all right. She had a friend who was a great help, whose mother had lost twins at birth. Her friend had never seen the twins, for she was born after they died. So when Cathy returned to school, Tricia was able to talk to her about her own mother who had lost children. I think it helped Cathy a lot to talk to a peer about something that had happened in her friend's family. I watched to see her grades in school and how she was relating to friends. I watched carefully but I didn't perceive her as having any special problems."

Marlene Levy not only lost her sister, but she literally lost her father as well. "My father left shortly after her death. He could not handle the emotional trauma and the guilt. He went to Las Vegas and two years later remarried and had two children. His son, he named after my sister, Sandy. To his daughter he gave the middle name of Madelein, named after the same person I was named after. As you can see, my father tried to start life all over to the point of trying to take my sister and me along with him to the West Coast. He's close to eighty now, has survived, and is very astute. Nevertheless, he's frightened and very depressed. As he said to me recently, 'Does one ever get over depression?' He's had a difficult life too.

"I was angry at my sister for hurting my parents. She had not only caused them to divorce, she had also left me alone. She left me without an older sister, someone to gain knowledge from. I felt that I'd lost everyone and that I was nobody."

Marlene takes a philosophical view now of the remarriage of both of her parents: "It's interesting how things work out, because my mother remarried about six years after my sister died. Her husband was ten years her junior and quite devoted. It was a new beginning. He handed life to her. He made her a beautiful woman, took her around the world, and cared a great deal. He had never had children and was very good to me. Had I been able to choose my father, I would have chosen him at that point. He gave me a tremendous amount of sympathy. He's always been there for me."

In the above account, a sibling talks about how the divorce of her mother and father affected her life after the death of her sister. Below we hear from a bereaved parent who addresses the issue of divorce.

Angela Purpura, social worker, former chapter leader of The Compassionate Friends and Metropolitan regional coordinator for the organization, was the first to establish a siblings group in Long Island. In working with the siblings, she gained tremendous insight into their many problems. She comments on the effects of divorce on bereaved families: "Many of us have heard of the alarming numbers of divorces which occur after the death of a child. The statistics are not as relevant as understanding that the death was not necessarily the cause but the 'last straw' in an already weak marriage. Consequently, regardless of the time factor, many surviving children have had an additional loss with which to contend.

"When faced with upheaval we are called upon to pool our resources," she adds, "in an effort to survive and endure, in order to continue. The more resources we have to tap, the more effective we can be in utilizing adversity to help strengthen us. A so-called 'broken home' can provide more closeness, love and understanding for the surviving sibling than one that had been plagued with anger and rage.

"It has been well over seven years since my eight-year-old daughter, Cassandra, died of a brain stem tumor, having been ill for three months. My only surviving child, Cara, is now thirteen years old and has developed into a vibrant, happy teenager with remarkable direction and purpose to her life. She has had many recent adjustments to make and has fared extraordinarily well.

"Last year, her father and I were divorced and I became a working mother for the first time. Cara will soon enter a new school, leaving the security of a private school she had once attended with her sister. It is apparent, however, that the most disturbing aspect of Cara's grief is that she became an only child and longed for brothers and sisters. A lot of her free time, when not in school or working two summer jobs, is spent at the home of our neighbors who have eight children. Although the youngest, who was Cassandra's best friend, is already in college, several children remain living at home. They have become Cara's extended family and no doubt have filled a great void. In her determination to further fill her needs, Cara is encouraging me to remarry.

"In order to understand Cara's growth, *I think it is important to know what I believe to be some key ingredients:* My grief was never hidden from Cara. From the very beginning, she was included and attended the wake and funeral. Although she was almost six years of age at the time, Cara was allowed to make certain choices. Would she remain for the closing of the casket? Did she want to wear any of Cassandra's clothes? How much did she wish to be a part of our involvement with The Compassionate Friends? In seeing her parents' openness about our sorrow, Cara needed no prompting and, in fact, asked to attend siblings meetings although she was only eight years old when the group was formed. She did have adjustment problems in school. However, we worked with with her teacher in that most difficult period.

"No matter how fragmented I was during those early years, Cara was always certain of my love for her. I had always been an overprotective mother and even more so as a bereaved parent. But I explained to Cara that I realized this behavior was often excessive at times and she would have to bear it for my own peace of mind. Although I have improved in giving Cara ample freedom to grow, "letting go" is still difficult. Cara, however, has come to accept this.

"We have both learned so much about life, ourselves, and closeness. Arguments are short lived. We are able to talk about our feelings. Cassandra's brief life and subsequent death has taught us to love more freely. Do I adore Cara? You bet! We have been through a war together. This bond will always carry us."

Marie Teague comments on the differences in the manner in which her parents grieved. "My parents dealt with Len's death in quite different ways. My dad, Carl Radtke, was fifty-three years old at Len's death. He internalized his pain, for I don't remember seeing him cry, but he probably did so when we weren't around. Fathers want so much for their sons, to live their youth again through them, and this Dad had only ONE son, who had not been anything like his Dad. Len was never destined to work thirty years for one company. He joined the Army instead.

"So when war took Len even farther away from him, I reckon my Dad experienced a longing for a relationship which would never be. As I said, he wasn't a weeper—that is, he wasn't until my son Brian died. These days, Dad does cry—for Len, for Brian, for his own parents, for injustices. He's a changed, 'liberated' sixty-nine-year-old.

"Mom cried easily. We visited the cemetery each Sunday after mass. For a while, prior to identifying the body, Mom had entertained thoughts that there had been a mistake, that it was another mother's son who had been killed. But she later told me, 'Marie, I looked at my baby and saw his cowlick, and I knew.' "

Marie also shares with us a very poignant note given to her by her surviving son, Mike, after a very difficult day that she and her husband were having soon after her child, Brian, was stillborn. Mike pasted it onto the refrigerator door—a loving gesture of a six-year-old child's caring and wanting to tell his parents so. It was written on the third day after Brian's death, printed very neatly, but in large letters:

I LOVE YOU MOM. AND I LOVE DAD.

LOVE MIKEY 1981 MAY TUES 12.

This loving gesture touched Marie and Don enormously and helped to make that day an easier one.

Sherry Sundland and her husband were getting ready for a trip to Florida with their surviving twin sons, age thirteen, but Sherry resented having to be a mother and wife. "The boys were asking if I had packed this and that, and my husband Tom wanted to know if I had remembered such and such. I guess it all came to a head and I blew my stack. I yelled that I was the one who had to do all the thinking for the wake and so forth and that I wanted to die and be with Chris and didn't they have any idea how much I was hurting? I was tired of being the strong one. For some reason, when a family member dies, I've always had the task of making the arrangements. After a series of deaths in our family, including my mother, my brother, my grandmother, and my great aunt, we learned that my father was dying of cancer and he passed away in September of 1980. The twins had helped take care of my dad when he was dying, as I didn't believe in hiding death from kids as it had been hidden from me. I didn't want them to be ignorant of death and not to know what measures to take when it comes. The twins said that knowing about wakes and so forth helped them when their brother Chris died, for they had an idea of what was done, how the dead person looked, and so on.

"We, as parents, allowed our surviving sons to express their emotions. If they wanted to kick the door or wall, we let them go ahead. Or if they wanted to cry, to heck with what people thought. They weren't shoved in a corner but were part of those terrible days. To them, their grief and guilt and loss were just as strong as Tom's and mine. *Maybe it was even stronger, for they didn't have the years we did behind us or the maturity.* We told them they could talk to us about anything they wanted and we told them how we felt. Being truthful to them and including them in everything helped. We showed that their opinion mattered to us just as their feelings did.

Russell Randazza tells how his parents dealt with the death of his sister Diane. "Since that time, my father has been apart from the family in many ways. Because of the severity of his loss, he no longer feels comfortable with us. He puts in a lot of overtime on his job. He's joined a health club. He goes out with friends who were not part of our circle. He spends most of the time with these new people and a minimal amount of time in the house. That's his outlet. I have sat down with him on three occasions, but it's like talking to the wall. He will answer me on any subject except the death of my sister.

"I try to tell him what my mother is going through, what help she needs, and what help he is not giving. I have also told him that my brother Charles and I are still here and we want to be his children. I wanted him to understand we were not just looking to my mother's needs. We were also concerned about what would help my father. My dad needs to accept what happened; he needs to realize that there is nothing he can do about Diane's death. We know *he needs* some space for himself, but he has a wife and two children who *need him.*"

Russell reflects back on the time of the tragedy. "When we walked into the funeral home that first time, my father fell to his knees. My brother and I had to lift him and carry him to a chair. My mother was in a very bad way, but my dad was completely out of control. From that point on, he has never been the same. My sister was Daddy's little girl. She was the oldest, and the only girl in the family. People who know my father say that no matter which of his children had died, he would have acted the same way. While he had never given us reason to believe that he loved her more than my brother or me, he and my sister were very close. As I said, she was Daddy's little girl, and in my opinion that relationship had a definite effect on his grief."

We have seen in the stories woven throughout this book the various ways in which bereaved parents may often be so overwhelmed by their own grief that they are not always able to provide surviving children with the parenting that had formerly been given. One mother, Judith Haimes, whose family we will read about in a later chapter, wishes she could apologize to all bereaved children in the name of all bereaved parents. She offers an **Open Letter of Apology** to surviving children in the hope that they will understand and forgive:

> I know over the last years since Michael's death that perhaps I have said or done things to make you feel less important than Michael, or made you feel that you were not able to take the pain away from me.

> I am now writing this letter to you openly, publicly, because I want you to know that the tears I have shed were not because you are inadequate in any way and not because I don't love you more than life itself. By inadequate, let me explain: I have often seen parents who grieved so much for the child who was dead that they forgot that the child who was living had feelings, too. Such a child would try to do something to make Mommy and Daddy feel better. Such a child would try everything from getting good grades in school to making a cake or a pot of popcorn, but the parent would still be so glum and down that the child would hang his head and walk into the next room, feeling "I can't do anything to make Mom or Dad feel better."

> In my own case, there was nothing anyone could have done to draw the acuteness out of the pain I was feeling—the same pain I would have felt if it had been *you* that was dead. I cry these tears because I am a mother who has lost a child. I would cry these tears if it were, God forbid, you and not Michael who had been killed.

> There have been times when I may have, without thinking, put my own feelings first. Perhaps I neglected to do something or go somewhere or share an experience with you because it would remind me of one I'd had with Michael. Maybe I didn't take you to Circus World for your birthday

because I had taken Michael once for his birthday, and to go there on another birthday would be too painful. That did not mean I was putting you aside. Nor did I mean to refuse to go to a restaurant whose hamburgers Michael liked so much. I realize now that hamburger place was also one of your favorite restaurants and I'm sorry that my pain outweighed my thoughtfulness for you.

When a parent is going through very bad pain, that is all she can think of. I don't want you to think that the experiences I share with you are less important than those I shared with Michael. If I have led you to think that, please forgive me.

When I sat at Michael's bar mitzvah, it was one of the happiest days of my life, because I was sitting there watching one of my children reach a high point in his life. When I sat at your bat mitzvah (a girl's bar mitzvah), Jakey, and tears rolled down my cheeks, it wasn't because I didn't feel as proud of you as I did of Michael, because I did. But, the music, the prayers, everything there brought back to me that sudden pain, the realization that a piece of my heart was missing. That is not to say that your bar mitzvah was not one of the most beautiful experiences I have ever had with you. And you, too, are a piece of my heart. I know that you suffered because he was not there, but you did not make it more painful for me. Sometimes children teach the parents how not to act.

If I tend to glorify Michael as one who was perfect, while you have so many faults, understand right now that that is not true. I have raised my voice to Michael as many times as I have to you. I have put him on restrictions for not studying for a test. I have hollered at him for getting grass stains or grease on the seat of his new pants and I have punished him for coming in ten minutes after dark when he knew he was supposed to be home before that. While we all love Michael, he was not perfect.

Michael was a wonderful boy and I love him as much as I love you, but I don't love any one of my children more than the other. I love each of you in a different way. My love for Michael is different now because I can't reach out and kiss him as I can you. I miss the things that I will never have with him—his graduation, his wedding, his children—joys that you will be able to give me that he cannot. Thank God I can kiss you and hug you and hold you and talk to you and share with you any time I want. I cannot do that with Michael and that is the cause of my pain.

While there are regrets that I have for not sharing in Michael's future, don't feel that your future is not important to me just because I won't have a future with him. If I have ever said, 'If only Michael were here, it would be perfect,' I did not mean to spoil any special occasion for you. If you ever thought that, I ask your forgiveness because no one taught me about being a bereaved parent.

I try to show you how much I love you, but I am only human. I am beginning to realize that you too are only human and my actions may have hurt you. Sometimes in my own pain, I did not see that you, too, were suffering for your lost brother. You were missing the future that you will not have with that brother, for the things you cannot share, for the little secrets, the jokes. It took me a long time to comprehend that you, too, suffered as much as I, only in a different way. You may have though, 'Yes, I missed him at the bar mitzvah. Sure, I don't have a future with my brother. And sure, you're wallowing in your pain, but who was there for my pain?'

Maybe you didn't want to hear a funny story or an anecdote about Michael because at that particular time you wanted to do something else or perhaps it was too painful for you. Maybe there were times when you did want him immortalized a bit because he was such a big, strong brother to look up to. Forgive me if I have hurt you by not understanding, and please open up to me the way I am opening up to you. I never wanted you to feel, 'Wait a minute, Mom. I lost a brother, too. I lost a sibling. You're not the only one.' I want you to be able to come to us and say, 'Mom, that hurts.'

For all the times you sat quietly in the corner, suffering, when people were comforting Dad and me, I am saddened. And, for all the times you were sent to a movie because Mom and

Dad were grieving alone and you wanted to grieve also, it's not that we are sorry—*we are sorry that we didn't know any better.*

No one knows how something like this is going to affect us. And for all the times when I didn't want to talk about Michael but you needed to, and for all the times I did want to talk about him and you didn't want to hear it, I'm sorry. But that was a thoughtlessness. I guess it's because none of us knew—you didn't know and we didn't know. It kind of works both ways.

The point I really want to make is, your mother might be stupid and your mother might be doing the dumbest things you could imagine, but this is why she's doing them—because she's in so much pain she has no idea what's happening. And I wonder how many times have you hurt your parents by doing the same thing that I am apologizing for?

It's all a part of our not being experienced in handling a tragedy like this—and that is natural, too. Nobody set out to make any of this happen and God knows if we could change it we would. If there was anything I could do to make a difference, I would. But I can't and you know that. So the best that I can do is to say, 'Talk to me. Whatever you are thinking about, or that may be troubling you, open up to me. Let me open up to you. Let's be honest about our feelings. *If we can talk, we will never need to apologize to each other for the pain again."*

We cannot undo what has happened. We can't undo Michael's death and we can't undo the pain that's there, but we can try to prevent anybody from causing more pain to each other or ourselves.

Chapter Eleven

At School

"Often a child will come to school and pour out his soul to a teacher, and she doesn't know how to handle it," says Eloise Shields, a mother who is a psychologist in the Torrance school district in California. Mrs. Shields bemoans the fact that young children need help in their grief, as do the teachers: "Many teachers have come to me, asking about emotional support and information for children who are experiencing grief and loss in their classrooms. Generally teachers are so busy they don't try to take on too much therapy with a child, but just listening is often all that is needed if the emotion in the child isn't too strong. If the child experiences deeper grief, the parents are contacted and asked to come in. At that time the teacher can obtain more facts and see if the parents are aware of what the child is going through."

One explicit direction given to the parent, Mrs. Shields stresses, is to *make* the child come to school whether he wants to or not. "It is not uncommon for a child to want to stay home if he has lost a sister, a brother, or parent. The loss can be so overwhelming he is frightened of leaving home, just in case someone else leaves him forever. So he dreams up the reasoning that if he never leaves home, he'll always be around to prevent anyone else from leaving him unexpectedly. Parents have to be shored up to remain firm, that life is to go on at school as usual. This alone is a great help to both parent and child—for the school to tell them this rule. We have found this prevents the child from developing a school phobia, which is much harder to treat than the death adjustment, as it compounds the child's emotional problems."

Athena Drewes, a psychologist in Orange County, New York, offers some guidelines for helping children at various age levels. The advice, while geared to bereaved parents, can also be very useful to assisting teachers in understanding children's grief. After all, everything that happens to a child in life affects him or her in school.

- Prior to five years of age, children's points of reference are intensely personal and they are still very egocentric and self-centered. Their thinking is magical and omnipotent. Whatever they wish for, both good and bad, is believed to come true. Everything that is perceived or felt seems to be common to the whole world. It is difficult for them to grasp the concept of personal danger, death and its finality. Death is disturbing to children under five because of the separation involved. Also, young children don't see death as final.

- At the age of five, children begin questioning more actively about their world. Emotions are strong at this age. Fears and anxieties are usually temporary and concrete, and are manifested in thunder, sirens, darkness, nightmares and the strong fear that mother will leave and not return, which carries over into concerns over death in general. They are likely to believe that the inanimate objects are "alive" in the same way as humans. They are beginning to empathize and can begin to grasp that death means finality. For five-year-olds play is important. In dramatic play children take on roles such as mother, father, baby, sister, and brother. From five years of age and on up children's imaginations have developed to the point where they can try to put themselves in other people's situations and imagine dangers they've not yet experienced. They are interested in details and desires for realism.

  This stage can be very disconcerting for parents during their bereavement. Surviving children, especially around five years of age, will press for explicit details. Can the dead sibling breathe, see, feel, etc. in the grave, and will they, the surviving sibling, die too? Where does the person go after death? Will they come out of the grave after they wake up?

- Between the ages of five and nine children give death a form that is recognizable such as a scary figure or angel. They can envision death as something final but believe with luck you can avoid it if you do special things, run fast, etc.

- By around the age of nine, children may be able to grasp death as final and inevitable. Older children are able to understand the concept of time better but their feelings of vulnerability (Will I die too?) as well as anger, sadness and questioning about death will still surface.

- If the parent feels emotionally unable to handle the child's questions about death, they should be direct about this. Tell the child, regardless of age, you're not able to answer all of them now, but will at a later time. By choosing the time to discuss the child's questions, you are making sure that some discussion will take place. By having your spouse present as well, this will help in avoiding placing the burden of explaining on one parent. Waiting for the child to bring up questions can leave a parent at a disadvantage, catching you off guard or not being able to give the best response to the question.

- *Talks should be brief since children can't handle a lot of information at once.* Between planned talks there will be questions as situations arise and these should be answered so the child is not confused by what she or he sees or hears. But children also need parents who are realistic—it's just not possible to have all the answers.

- Answer questions simply and honestly. Parents sometimes avoid talks as a way of avoiding tears. It's healthy for children to see their parents cry, but don't force feelings in a child. Some may show no sorrow. They may not be at the age of comprehending finality or may simply deny the event and pretend it didn't happen. Some may react with anger, laughter, guilt or misbehavior. If a parent is too upset to discuss things or too overwhelmed with grief, counseling for the child should be sought.

- It may be helpful if another adult who is not as emotionally involved spends time with the child to help in discussing feelings and answering questions. By sharing in the family's grief, it allows the child to share his own grief and work through feelings.

- Parents frequently make the mistake of keeping a child away from the funeral and grief process. Excluding a child only adds to feelings of guilt and may be viewed as a punishment for something the child did or didn't do. Children between four and eight years should attend the funeral, if only for five minutes. Children over eight should attend all services and children under four should be encouraged to express their feelings of grief but won't understand what is happening at the funeral. However, a parent should use discretion if hysterics or anything frightening to the child is expected. Each parent must carefully take into account their child's age and ability to handle the situation. A child should never be told a dead person has "gone to sleep" as they may fear going to sleep as a result.

- Birth order can affect how a child responds to a sibling's death. A younger child may feel jealous and lonely because they are too young to go to the hospital or participate. They may be jealous of all the attention the other sibling is getting, even in death.

- An older child may feel the burden of having to take care of the younger children or help the parents. Consequently they may have to put off dealing with their own grief. Children of all ages and birth order feel a lot of guilt over having wished the sibling's death or that they are the survivor and not the one to die.

- The one thing I would want to stress the most is for the parent to share information about the death to the surviving child, no matter what the child's age, for children pick up from those around them that something tragic has happened. Never assume the child is too young to understand. They can sense something is wrong when they hear whispering or abruptly-stopped conversation with their presence or see looks of concern. When not made part of the grief process, the child's fantasies become greater than the reality of the situation. Once the truth is explained in a simple manner, children can come to grips with it and cope in their own way. Opening up communication allows them to share their feelings and thoughts and lets them know they are still part of the family.

In the preceding guidelines, Athena Drewes has offered insight to teachers who can utilize the knowledge to better understand the child's actions in school and what the child may be experiencing overall at home. Later in this chapter, we will hear from Dr. Roberta Temes who tells us how these emotions carry over into the schoolroom.

Surviving children not only have to deal with their emotions at home, they must also cope with insensitive comments of classmates and friends. The brother of a young boy who had died of cancer suffered bitterly at the hands of his school chums who taunted him—both prior to as well as after his brother's death. The boy who died was eight years old. His brother, ten, originally harbored feelings of anger at his brother for being sick and receiving so much attention. Later, when his brother came home during a period of remission, the ten-year-old became the younger boy's protector. Having lost his hair to radiation, the young boy had to wear a hat. Friends would tease him unmercifully in attempts to push his hat off. The boy's brother defended him and later suffered consequences after his brother died. "The kids didn't know how to act. They thought what my brother had was catching, and they wouldn't come near me."

Other children tell of being taunted by classmates on the school bus or while in the schoolyard. "Hey, where's your brother?" "Yoo-hoo, what's your sister doing now?" When children don't know how to cope with a problem, they often revert to taunting or making jokes. Witness what one teacher experienced after the 1986 explosion of the *Challenger* spacecraft: "After the death of the seven astronauts, we spoke to several children at different grade levels to determine the impact. To our great surprise, many of the children reverted to jokes about death. In the case of the *Challenger*, the question they asked was, 'Do you know what NASA means?' They all chimed in to give the answer: 'Need Another Seven Astronauts!'"

In other instances, siblings say that teachers who have taught more than one child from the same family, often revert to calling the surviving sibling by the name of the deceased child. Each of us wishes to be properly identified in life—and that identification can be crucial to the surviving sibling. One sister makes the point: "I wish teachers would pay as much attention to getting our names right as they do to our giving them right answers to their questions."

Another surviving sister, Cindy Tart, fifteen, tells of an incident that happened to her in school, which served to enlighten her fellow classmates: "I had a strange experience at school. The guidance counselor came in and gave us little cards that we had to fill out, which covered all the abuse problems in our county, like drugs and alcohol. I remember it was seven months to the day my brother was buried. So when the counselor came in and passed out these cards, and with Dennis on my mind, I raised my hand. I said, 'I can tell you one thing that's needed on that card, which is missing from it.' She was surprised and said, "What?" And I said, 'Something to help with the loss of a sibling.' All the kids in the class were going, 'What?' 'What's that?' 'What does that mean?' And the lady simply said, "A child that has lost a brother or sister to death.' Then everybody in the class knew that I had lost a little brother to death.

"I started mentioning the group that my parents went to, called The Compassionate Friends, and how we had gone to a siblings group there for surviving brothers and sisters. The kids around me started asking questions. It made things a lot better than when I had first gone back to school, which was the Monday after Dennis was buried on Friday. On that day, I got funny looks from a lot of people. But there was one girl who came over to me and said, " 'I'm so sorry about Dennis. If I can do anything, let me know.' And I thanked her. Later on, as the day went by, I couldn't concentrate on my work. I couldn't do anything, so I went to the Guidance Department to check out, which they let me do. On Tuesday I went back and I stayed all day. Some of my close friends made it better for me. They even made me laugh a litte."

In the following account, Billy Pfister tells how he found himself in a slump when he began college following the death of his brother, John: "There was a big transition to begin with because my brother died when I was just between high school and college. So, I had a few months to deal with his death— July, August, and September—before I started college. But it was a strange kind of feeling, as if nothing was the way it was supposed to be. Here I was trying to take the step from high school to college and my brother dies. When I started college, I was in a slump. I had slowed down, and couldn't function as well as I would have if my brother was still alive. If the tragedy hadn't happened, I think I would have had a little more on the ball when I went into college. I think I would have been a little more aggressive in my approach to the whole thing. It just didn't seem fair to me that my brother had died."

No matter what their age, surviving siblings quickily learn that life is not fair, says Dr. Roberta Temes, clinical assistant professor, Department of Psychiatry, Downstate Medical School, Brooklyn, New York, and author of Living with an Empty Chair. Dr. Temes counsels that children under five feel frightened, whereas children five to ten have other problems: "The younger children are bewildered and often regress to previously outgrown 'babyish' behavior. Children who are five to ten at the time of the death usually have sleeping or eating difficulties, and have trouble separating from their parents. Ability to concentrate diminishes. Schoolwork may suffer. School behavior may change radically—the quiet student 'acts out' and becomes the class bully, while the hitherto popular child becomes withdrawn."

Dr. Temes states, "First feelings of identity come from familial roles. A daughter, a kid brother, a middle child—our family defines our place. A surviving sibling wonders just who he is when he's no longer the big brother or his sister's tag-along kid brother.

"At school," Dr. Temes observes, "children who have lost a sibling are different from their classmates. Their family has become horribly reshaped and they feel at once guilty, angry, abandoned, and frightened. Children need to talk about the death with other family members. They may not be ready for professional intervention—bereavement counselor, psychotherapist—for years; and that's perfectly normal. Eventually, usually at the time of another loss or severe stress, the death may need to be spoken about to a professional."

Although Dr. Temes indicates that children need to communicate with other family members about the death, she clarifies a seemingly paradoxical point. "Pre-teenagers and teenagers on the one hand hate being at home and constantly run to friends' houses. On the other hand," Dr. Temes asserts, "Teenagers resent the attention from well-meaning neighbors and extended family, and may persist in trying to deny the tragedy." More details concerning the grief of adolescents appear in chapter 18.

Whether at school, at home, or at work, surviving siblings often have trouble responding to the question, "How many sisters and brothers do you have?" The reason, Dr. Temes believes is that a sibling's death makes an indelible mark that will remain throughout the survivor's life.

Jeanette Colburn, herself a surviving sister, teaches at Grant Middle School in Springfield, Illinois. During her first year of teaching, the father of one of her students died, followed by the sudden death of the school principal three weeks later. "I had been ill-equipped for dealing with death when I was growing up," says Jeanette, "and I didn't know how to help the students. I then went into counseling and became aware of how the death of a sibling or other significant person can affect kids. I also learned ways adults can be of support to them. A number of my Special Education students have verbalized about the deaths of people close to them, some of whom were siblings. One of the most dramatic examples was one of my students whose eight-month-old sister died due to Sudden Infant Death Syndrome. Within one month this twelve year old gained ninety pounds, and by the end of the year had gained 125 pounds to a weight of 350 pounds! Prior to her sister's death, she had functioned at grade level. Within two years she was functioning four grade levels behind, was tested, and made eligible for Learning Disabilities services. School systems are often not aware of the impact of grief on children." Tragic consequences can occur when children's attendant problems go unheeded.

Jeanette also joined SHARE (an organization for bereaved parents, which we will read more about in the "Helping Hands" chapter). As editor of the SHARE newsletter, she received a great deal of input from parents who have suffered neonatal losses. "One of our SHARE parents told what happened after her baby daughter died. Her three-year-old son started acting very much unlike himself. Finally his mom said, 'Mommy can't help you unless you tell Mommy what's wrong.' The child replied, 'I never got to see her.' Luckily, the parents had pictures that were taken at St. John's (the hospital in Springfield, Illinois, where SHARE was formed) and were thereby enabled to help this young sibling cope with the death of his baby sister. His comment 'I never got to see her' was a telling one—one we hear a great deal about from SHARE parents."

The preceding story about the young sibling is one that Jeanette relates to personally: "My own brother was delivered stillborn at five and a half months. I had been anticipating his birth, but never got to see him. It was something I came face to face with when I was a student in a Pastoral Care Program at St. John's. A little boy was brought into the emergency room. He had been hit by a car while roller skating. His name was Christopher, and that was my brother's name. Coincidentally, his sister had the same name as mine. I was with the youngster and his family when he was admitted into the hospital, and was with them the next morning when he died. It didn't occur to me that I was saying good-bye to my own brother until I went to this child's wake. Then I felt a sense of sadness for the boy who had died, but at the same time a real sense of relief—and that's when it dawned on me."

Jeanette counsels that teachers and parents alike need to understand the many questions that children have after the death of a sibling. She believes the surviving sibling's emotions spill over into the classroom with many parents unaware that their children are experiencing confusion and a "mixed bag" of emotions. Jeanette, agrees that the preschool-age child as described earlier by Dr. Roberta Temes, believes death is temporary and reversible. "They equate it with going on a trip," Jeanette asserts. "This is validated if the child is told that the loved one went on a journey. It is difficult to find the right words to use. Simple explanations can be very confusing to a preschooler. When told that the body is in a casket, or special box, they are quite apt to ask, 'How will he eat or go to the bathroom?' or, 'What will he do when it rains?' It is helpful for the parents to explain that dying is when breath, warmth, and movement stop. It is best to use terms that the children can understand and at the same time assure them that most people live to be an old age. Children ages six to eleven know that death is 'real,' but prior to age nine or ten view it in a personified way—as a ghost, angel or space creature. They perceive that only the weak and the old die because they can't run fast enough when death comes for them. They ask matter-of-fact questions such as wanting to know why the body is cold."

Jeanette urges teachers to be especially observant of the needs of adolescents: "Many in the field of thanatology believe that adolescents have a most difficult time dealing with death as it shatters their sense of invincibility. They are in a double bind, being torn between independence and dependence. They vacillate from wanting comfort, yet being expected to comfort. Yet because of their desire to show maturity, they may not allow themselves to acknowledge that need. They may even appear to draw away from their parents and not talk about their own feelings, or they may do things to anger their parents in an effort to bring them out of their depression. They may also become 'model children' who appear to be doing so well. Teenage siblings are ofen told, 'Take care of your parents.' The resulting sense of responsibility can be very burdensome. In striving for independence, they may turn more to their friends for understanding, but even then they may want to 'look good' to their friends by maintaining a strong image. Teenagers may be embarrassed to cry. This is generally an outgrowth of comments to them such as, 'Don't cry. You're not a little kid.' Instead, one might make the suggestion to them that some people do their crying when they go to bed, or when they are in the shower. Students have approached me and commented on how helpful that was, for it gave them permission to cry.

"Teachers and parents should be alerted to three emotions that are commonly experienced by younger children and adolescents. They are fear, anger, and guilt, but most children are unpracticed in talking about these feelings. When asked, they may say, 'I don't know,' which may also be a means of covering up or of suppressing their feelings so they won't be 'different.' It has been well documented that children who experience a loss are very vulnerable and at risk for future emotional problems if not given adequate support. They may have difficulties if they come from families in which death is a taboo, when someone must be to blame, when emotional relations are ambivalent, when things must go on as before, and when loss means chaos."

Jeanette points out that many children may internalize their anger and express it in passive-aggressive behavior both at school and at home. "For example, they may lose things or impede the movement of others. They may not clean their rooms. Some who experience guilt may feel responsible as if 'wishing made it so.' Unconscious guilt may surface in acts of self-hurt, neglect of health, or even self-defeating life choices. A denying of real feelings may result in the individual responding to life in an uncaring manner."

Jeanette notes that schoolwork may be affected by grief after delays of up to five years. "It is common for bereaved students' grades to drop. Girl's grades tend to drop farther and take longer to recover than those of boys. Subjects such as Social Studies and English may be especially difficult for the siblings. Adolescents often show the effects of grief in Science or Math. It is not uncommon for them to be able to solve equations involving addition and multiplication but to have difficulty with those involving subtraction or division. Younger children usually show declines in language skills. Surviving siblings may also have difficulty following directions—being told to do three things but only doing one."

Jeanette believes teachers are in a difficult position: "A vast majority of teachers have had very little education about grief," she asserts. "It does little good to tell bereaved students to 'try harder' or to label them 'lazy' and so on. It is more helpful to give them concrete advice. An example would be to indicate they should use an assigment book and subject notebook (Trapper) so they won't be as apt to lose things, or to provide time for them to talk about how they are doing." Jeanette believes it is more important for the students to see school as an understanding environment rather than a hostile one. "But," she admonishes, "because teachers, social workers, school psychologists, and administrators are generally unfamiliar with grief, school systems may treat the bereaved students' 'symptoms' rather than the 'cause' of their difficulties with school."

A growing number in the field of education are recognizing the need for workshops and in-services designed to assist them in being a source of support to bereaved siblings. Jeanette states: "Some social workers have indicated that making such students eligible for Special Education classes, was the only alternative they had, as no other supportive services are available other than psychotherapy. We can't take pain away from children and adolescents. However, we can provide support as they go through their 'ring of fire.' As Dr. Glen Davidson, Ph.D., says, 'We don't have the choice of if we will grieve, but we do have the choice of when and how.'"

In school, the decline in attendance by the sibling, coupled with behavior problems or poor school performance (which can last from one year to eighteen months), may necessitate that the child repeat a grade or be referred for psychological testing. Jeanette urges, "It is essential that school officials be notified when a death occurs so they can hopefully provide necessary assistance and support for the child. A teacher who is unaware of the situation may label the child as being lazy, a sneak, stubborn, or defiant and thereby compound the problem. Psychological testing may identify areas in which the child is having difficulty and reveal *symptoms* of the child's grief but be misunderstood. Consequently, the child may be labeled 'learning disabled' or 'behavior disordered' and placed in alternative educational programs when in reality, the child is grieving. The school is then treating the symptoms rather than the cause."

Jeanette offers an uplifting overall view: "After experiencing the death of a child, the family will never be the same, but there won't always be the intense pain. If things were the 'same,' the family would have to deny the child existed. The family will view life differently, but with communication and patience throughout the mourning process develop compassion, empathy, and a deeper appreciation of each other. With love and support, most children resolve their grief and live normal lives."

EMMAUS PUBLIC LIBRARY
EMMAUS, PA. 18049

Chapter Twelve

At the Workplace

Some of the problems encountered by adult siblings when they return to the workplace are exacerbated by the fact that most co-workers do not accept the grief that follows the death of a brother or sister as they do the mourning after the death of a spouse. An example is Elaine Altman. She and her brother were very close, went to the theater together, liked the same books. Elaine and her husband, along with her brother and his girlfriend, went on vacations together, and the four of them were planning to rent a house.

Elaine's brother was on the verge of becoming a psycho-therapist—something for which he had worked hard. He had not done too much with his life, but now, he was on the brink of achieving his dream. Then he died. This was a heavy blow to Elaine who grieved not only at his death, but at the trick of fate that closed the door to the fulfillment of his dream. She had a hard time accepting his death.

At work, although most of her co-workers were very supportive, Elaine encountered criticisms such as "I can't understand why you are mourning a brother so much when you have a husband." Elaine describes the hurt she experienced. "My grief was made worse by the realization that many people can't understand how deeply I feel my brother's death. The relationship between a brother and a sister is not always as close as ours was. We were very much in tune with one another, and talked frequently on the phone as well as person-to-person. We shared so much. How could I not be grief-stricken at his death? Why didn't they understand that? Yes, I had my husband, but this was a brother who was very dear to me and I miss him terribly."

Elaine was afraid that if she didn't return to work immediately after Michael's death, she might never go back. "I felt that if I didn't return right away, I wouldn't ever be able to return. Although I was very shaky and weak, I went back. Everything was unreal to me. I couldn't believe that everyone was going about things in their normal way, because my whole world had changed and nothing seemed normal. Somehow, I just went through the motions of my job. One person with whom I once shared an office was not usually that warm, but she hugged me and cried with me. She had heard conversations I'd had with Michael and understood how important he was to me. Another woman came and told me that her first husband had died when she was very young. She wanted me to know I could talk to her, and occasionally I did. It helped to have a person there who had also suffered a loss."

Billy Pfister had just started a job as a day-camp counselor and returned to work the very day his brother was killed. "I kept breaking down and my employers told me they thought I should go home. But I told them that I could do the job and that I wanted to get it under my belt. I went through a full day of work. The people who knew he was dead, the counselors, kept an eye on me. I didn't say anything to the kids, of course. Afterwards, I was glad that I had been able to work that first day, because I don't know how I would have handled the pain of John's death otherwise. Being at work enabled me to have a chance to pull myself together."

Russell Randazza described how he handled returning to work after his sister, Diane, died. "When I went back to my job, I tried not to show my feelings. I wanted to be professional and keep my work and my private life separate. I tried very hard not to mix the two, but it was difficult. Most of the people from work came to the funeral, and my co-workers were sympathetic, but not overly so. They gave me space, which is what I wanted."

At first, Susan Keats found it hard to accept mundane things such as work when something so devastating had happened. "I work on an account at an advertising agency. People are all excited about things like toilet tissue products. And I thought it was not possible for me to become involved with things so insignificant compared to Carolyn's death. But after she died, there were so many nice people around. They made me feel that life was short and that I should accomplish things and be proud of those achievements. I should make my mark and make myself feel I'd actually done something worthwhile with my life."

While riding to work, Karen Schlesier Eisen would buttonhole fellow passengers to talk about her brother's death. "In the beginning," she says, "when I was riding the Long Island Railroad to work, I'd tell anyone sitting next to me on the train that my brother had just died. I'd go into all the details about the accident. I would tell anyone who would listen. Somehow, I wanted everyone to know that he had been here but that he's not here now and you should have known him. I wanted his presence to be felt."

Karen believes that a lot of people are afraid to talk about the one who died for fear the bereaved person will burst into tears and they would not know how to handle that person's emotions. At work, Karen was annoyed at the treatment she received. "After two weeks of everyone's being so nice to me, it was sickening. Everyone treated me completely different than before. No one allowed me to function properly." Karen felt as if she had leprosy. She marched into her boss's office and said, "If I've done something wrong in my work, I want to be treated accordingly, like anyone else in the office." Having said that, it seemed to clear the air, and things returned to normal.

One day soon after, however, a co-worker had a fight on the phone with someone who was obviously a family member. When she hung up, the woman passed the comment, "Does anyone here want a brother?" Yes, Karen most certainly did— and shook her head in disbelief that this person would offer to give away something so precious.

Many bereaved adult siblings experience apprehension of what co-workers will say to them when they return to work. In greeting a person who has had a loss, there are many things business associates can do to make the bereaved feel better. One of them is to go to that person, appropriately touch his or her shoulder or arm, and simply pause. That silence lets the person know everything. It is also quite proper to say, "I'm very sorry to hear about your loss." If you are fairly close to the person, it would be helpful to make it known that you are available to listen.

Dr. David Meagher, Professor of Health Sciences at Brooklyn College and bereavement counselor and consultant in death and dying, explains why it is so difficult for co-workers and friends to make contact with bereaved siblings. "As we grow up, we practice going to a dance, or a party, or we ask how we should act when visiting—but no one tells us how to talk to one who has lost a family member. As a society, we require verbal communication." Dr. Meagher continues, "Because we are not comfortable with nonverbal communication, we feel that when encountering another, we must say something. After we say, 'I'm sorry to hear about the loss, and if there is anything I can do for you, let me know,' we are stuck and search for something else to say."

Because of the standoffish approach to mourning in our society, grief experts say, the co-worker who wants to say something but is afraid of the bereaved person's reaction may think the proper thing to do is to ignore the fact of the death or to try to distract the mourner from his or her grief. It has been noted that even professionals such as doctors, nurses, the clergy, and others may be unable to help the bereaved through grief. They may feel helpless in the face of such suffering and be unable to provide the support needed by the bereaved. They may remain silent rather than say something that could increase the grieving person's pain or evoke his or her anger. Nonetheless, bereaved siblings at work have to cope with the loss, and co-workers and management can help them to do this without making them feel ostracized or alone.

One of the worst things a co-worker can say is, "Shouldn't you be over this already?" Or, "Shouldn't you be getting better by now?" "Shoulds" are not words the bereaved feel comfortable with, because everyone's clock ticks at a different speed when it comes to recovering from the loss of a loved one. There is no time limit, but an adjustment and a moving toward "recovering." Some problems that have been observed at the workplace include tardiness, crying spells, or a lack of concentration. Or, there may be physical symptoms of headaches, loss of appetite, or perhaps symptoms that the deceased sibling suffered before they died. The grief, or inability to express that grief, can affect the bereaved brother's or sister's morale and can carry over to co-workers and management. An example is when an employee is unable to function well on the job. Co-workers may "cover" for the bereaved person, thinking it will be just a matter of time until the worker will return to normalcy. But co-workers who take on the extra work initially will eventually want to relinquish it. At that point, the bereaved person can become a problem to both co-workers and mangement.

One of the difficulties that grieving adult siblings may have upon returning to the workplace is an overreaction to any additional type of loss. It doesn't have to be a death, grief experts advise. It can be the loss of an office, the transfer of a friend, or the death of someone in the organization whom the bereaved barely knows. Although the sibling may react inappropriately to the "second" loss, such reactions are normal.

Some grief therapists caution about getting well *too soon* and putting on the air of "professionalism" at work. The paradox, they warn, is that the scab on the wound may start to heal, but the wound itself is still festering. A bereaved brother or sister who may appear to be getting over a loss very quickly may suffer setbacks at a later date. This seems to be especially true, the experts say, of professional men and women who believe they have to maintain an image of "being in control."

The grief process may last longer than most people think. Time—and help with going through the grief process—are the healers. One step that personnel and management can take in assisting with that healing is to familiarize themselves with the growing number of support groups for the bereaved in their community, and to offer employee-assistance programs to include help for the bereaved similar to those for rehabilitating employees with other problems.

The bottom line, grief counselors stress, is that it will be up to the bereaved to show co-workers how to help, particularly if it is an anniversary date of the death. There will be good days and bad days. Employers and co-workers may want to help ease the pain, but may not know how to extend the helping hand. Anne Rosberger, psychotherapist and Executive Director of the Bereavement and Loss Center of New York, advises that acute depression may set in around the first anniversary of a death, because many bereaved carry about with them an unconscious timetable that allows only one year for mourning.

One bereaved brother had returned to work and for an entire year had masked his grief, believing that he had his feelings under control. His fiancé called him at his place of business, not realizing it was the anniversary of his sister's death, and discovered he had not gone to work on that day. She later learned that he was at home. "Now, this was a man who never missed work, was never late a day in his life. So, I was very worried as to why he was home. When I called him, he said to me, 'I never thought I was going to feel this bad a year later.' "

Dr. Rosberger stresses the importance of seeking help when needed, but with someone experienced in grief. "The grief counselor does not help one to forget the pain, but rather helps the person to realize it." She also maintains that all people have their own individual calendars when it comes to grief. Grieving may take months or years. It is not an unnatural function. It is not a disease. It is a natural and necessary process in bereavement."

Chapter Thirteen

The Haimes Family

"I luv-v-v-v you, Jakey," said Michael Haimes, age sixteen, as he teased his younger sister. Jakey, who was nine years old, retorted, "Well, I hate you!" To which Michael continued his caressing tone, "But, I luv-v-v-v you, Jakey." Michael and Jakey had gotten into a fight, and Jakey was in no mood for making up. In fact, when Michael left in his car to go to the library, Jakey refused to accompany him.

Jakey recalls the incident. "Mike said, 'Do you want to come?' And I said, 'No, get away from me.'" Her final statements to her brother played heavily in the guilt Jakey felt after Michael was killed in a car accident en route to the library. "I almost went in the car with him," Jakey reflects. "So it could have been both of us." The last words she spoke to her brother, "I hate you," tormented Jakey for a very long time.

After Michael died, Jakey tried to put her own grief aside to help her mother and father. "I pretty much helped everybody else. Mom was really upset and Dad was always depressed. Josh and Ian were still quite small, so I helped take care of them, and Mom and Dad were in so much pain, I tried talking to them to help them." Jakey suggested to her parents that they think about Michael's death the way she was trying to view it. "I would pretend that he went away to college; that he was gone during the day and then while I was asleep he would come back home, take a shower, and go back out. When I woke up he'd be gone. I told that to Mom and Dad because I figured if they could think he was away at college, it would help them. They said that might be okay for me, but they know he's gone so they couldn't look at it that way."

Jakey also found herself in the position of comforting her teachers at school when she returned. "When I went to school, a few of the teachers came up and gave me hugs and started to cry and I said, 'Don't worry about it.' It's as if I were the strong one. But the teachers were all extra nice to me. An article had appeared in the newspaper about Michael, and they wanted me to read it to everyone in the class. And so I did. I felt good about it. The only thing that bothered me was whenever somebody said, 'I know how you feel.' Because they didn't know."

Jakey fondly recalls an earlier time in school. "We were making snowflakes for Christmas. I made one that Michael said he liked a lot and I gave it to him. Every night when I came in to kiss him good night, he'd say, 'I have your snowflake right here.' It was sitting next to him on his night table. So when he died, I wanted him to have that with him and I put it into the coffin. I wanted that little piece of me to be with him."

On the anniversary of Michael's death, Jakey doesn't go to school. "Most of the time it's during vacation. But when I have school, I don't go. That day is a very hard one for me. I take it pretty good all year, but that day can be rough. We usually go to the cemetery. I want to go, but when I get there it's really upsetting. All the memories come back, good and bad. Sometimes I feel like, 'Oh my God, that's him in the ground.' And other times I feel that he's here with me. It depends how I feel on that day. Sometimes I just wished that it would happen to me so that I wouldn't have to go through the pain of missing him."

One of the other issues that Jakey has faced is hearing her two younger brothers argue. "Sometimes they'll fight and say, 'I wish you were like Mike'—meaning dead. And that hits me right between the eyes. I tell them, 'Don't ever say that, because I remember when I wished that and it sort of came true.' Josh and I are real close when it comes to that. When it hits Ian, he cries and I have to talk to them and explain it to them." You have ups and downs and better days and not such good days. When I get upset, I usually write down my thoughts and let it out that way, or I tell my best friend. Now, my mom got me a diary to write in. I think it's important to do that or to talk about it.

"For example, a friend of mine had a sister who died last year of a brain tumor," Jakey explains. "Her sister had been in the hosptial for about a year. My friend left on a trip on her sister's birthday, and the day she got back was the day after her sister had died. She was really upset and felt very bad that she wasn't able to spend those last three or four days with her sister. She felt she wasn't there for her sister on her birthday. So it's important to talk about your feelings with someone who can really understand what you are going through. It makes you feel better."

Jakey's own sister, Lorrie, was a source of concern to her after Michael's death. Lorrie had gotten married and had been having problems with her pregnancy. Jakey explains her worry. "Lorrie planned to name the baby after Michael, and I thought that was kind of neat. Some people say that when you name a baby after someone who died young, it will be bad luck. So, when Lorrie had problems from the beginning, I started to believe that. But now I don't, because Lorrie and her husband, Lenny, have a healthy baby girl and everything's fine. They named her Michaela—that's Michael with an 'A' at the end."

Another issue troubling Jakey is the way many people view teenagers. Now a teenager herself, Jakey wanted to address that issue because of an experience she had. Her mother, Judith Haimes, describes the incident: "Jakey's friend, Karim, with whom she had attended school for six years, was spending the night with his friend. After everyone in the house was asleep, the two kids got up and on a lark decided to take the mother's car for a ride around the block. They had never before done anything wrong, and were nice kids who got good grades. But, while they were driving the car, they saw a police car, panicked, and crashed. Karim was killed and his friend was seriously injured. A few days later, Jakey received an upsetting phone call from a friend who had unpleasant things to say about the accident. She became concerned that when you are a teenager, people think the worst.

"Jakey thought this might have been what people thought about her brother Michael, too. Jakey felt someone had to defend Michael just as she had defended Karim to the friend who called. Michael—whose car was hit broadside by another driver—was also a teenager, she thought, and people—even his peers—might judge him simply as a teenager rather than learning the facts. Jakey recalled all the times she heard adults reminiscing. 'Remember the time we all went swimming in the lake that was off-limits,' or, 'Remember the time we all climbed on the roof.' Because she felt all teenagers were entitled to be accorded that same chance at memory, she wrote the following to those adults and peers who may have forgotten."

Did You Hear About Those Two Dumb Kids?
By Jakey Allayne Haimes

A close friend of mine died. He was just 14 years old. When I was sitting in my room crying, I realized that I was also crying for my brother Michael who died in a car accident when he was only 16 years old.

The telephone rang and it was a friend of mine who said, "Did you hear about the two dumb kids who stole their parents' car and wound up in an accident? Serves them right!" After setting him straight, it dawned on me that there may be other people who feel this way, particularly those who did not know him.

So many times people choose to see only the negative things that teenagers do. So I wanted to speak out and say that my friend, Karim Said Petrou, did not die because of alcohol or drugs, or because he was a wild teenager, but simply because of one foolish mistake that he and his friend Jonathan Grigsby made.

If Karim and Jonathan had not been involved in that car accident, then maybe ten or fifteen years from now they might be telling their children about the mischievous deed that they once did when they were only 14 years old.

Judith Haimes sheds some light on the effects of Michael's death on her other surviving children. "Joshua was three years old when his brother died. Michael had been very close to Joshua, had given a great deal of time to being with his younger brother, had gotten up in the middle of the night to give him his bottle." Joshua had been told by his parents and knows that Michael is no longer here. From the beginning, Joshua would walk along and he would suddenly ask, "Where's Michael?" "Isn't Michael coming home?" "When is Michael coming home?" And then after a time Joshua started saying things such as, "Michael's up in the sky with Superman." Although his parents, Judith and Allen, tried to convey to Josh that Michael was dead and that he was with God, and although Josh is a very bright little boy, it's very difficult to tell a three-year-old child that his brother is dead.

Judith tells a story of the time when Joshua asked her, "Why did God kill Michael?" Judith sat the boy down and told him that God was not responsible for Michael's death, that God had not killed Michael, that God was taking care of Michael, and that Michael had been killed by a car. A short time afterward, Joshua said, "Oh, then God's going to fix him up good, make him all better, and Mike's going to come back, because God can do everything." His mother comments, "So, you see, even the most intelligent little three-year-old had difficulty understanding that death in this form is forever. Sometimes, out of the blue, Joshua has been in an up-mood and he'll just start talking about Michael for no reason, saying, 'I miss Michael.' 'I wish Michael were coming come.' And then, having a very down moment, Joshua will say, 'Michael's not coming home anymore.'"

Several years after Michael's death, Judith encountered another situation with Joshua, one that she cautions other parents about: "There is a very important point I would like to make about how one child may very much want to be like the dead child. For example, Joshua has been told how much he looks like Michael, which he does. And in action, he's a great deal like Michael. Now he's starting to ask questions like, 'Did Michael like spinach? Because if he did, I love spinach.' Or, 'Spelling is my best subject. Was spelling Michael's best subject?' This can become a whole different problem unless nipped in the bud, by showing Joshua that he is his own person.

"We say to him that yes, Michael liked some of these things or Michael didn't like some of those. Or, 'You look a whole lot like Michael because you are brothers, but you are not Michael and you don't have to be Michael to be loved. We love you just the way you are.'

"Parents need to be made aware that sometimes a child feels so inadequate in their own way, they may feel overshadowed by the dead sibling. And, he figures if he's like that sibling, then perhaps his parents will love him more. It's something to look out for with surviving children."

Judith's youngest child, Ian, was about a year old just three months prior to the time that Michael was killed. "It was weeks until he wouldn't run around yelling, 'Mike, Mike,'" Judith remembers. "On the day that Michael was killed, just as Michael was leaving the house he turned to me and said, 'Mom, I want you to hear this. I want you to listen to this.'" Michael wanted his mother to hear the first word he had taught his little brother to say, which was "Mike." Michael was adept at playing the piano and he used to put Ian on his lap and play with him. Shortly after Michael died, the song, "The Music Box," was playing on the radio. This was a song that Michael played very often on the piano. As soon as Ian heard the song on the radio, he ran into the other room toward the piano and yelled, "Mike, Mike." Judith continues, "This was the reaction of a child who was only one year old. Michael was very fond of his little brother. He hugged him a lot and used to call him his 'Little Bruvver.'"

Michael's older brother, Bobby, who was nineteen, was attending school out of state in Pennsylvania. Because it was impossible for him to get home so quickly, his dad had to tell him the news by telephone. "Bobby took it very hard," Judith comments. "When he heard his father's voice telling him that Michael had died in the accident, Bobby began to sob and scream. Michael and Bobby were competitive, yet very much like so many siblings with all the rivalry that brothers and sisters have. Whatever Bobby could do, Michael could do better or would always try to. Bobby, of course, tried to outdo anything Michael did. They were always teasing each other with the very things that siblings will say to each other.

"Bobby was home on his school break in December, which was several weeks before Michael died. Since he wasn't going to be home for the Chanukah holiday, the family devoted an evening to Bobby so he could receive all of his gifts. Each person in the family presented their gifts. Michael gave his last and it was a very special gift. It was a T-shirt imprinted with the saying, 'That's right, pal.' It was an expression that Bobby used all the time. Bobby was very touched by this and for the first time since they had been very young kids, about three or four years old, Michael reached over and kissed Bobby. Ordinarily, Bobby's reaction would be to pull back or scream. But, instead, Bobby kissed Michael back. Just at that moment their dad took a photograph of the two boys—a priceless photograph. The whole family had many memories of Michael to talk about when Bobby came home between semesters.

"My son Bobby is a big, strong young man, my six-foot three-inch football player, over 200 pounds. And big boys don't cry is what our society teaches. Bobby said that although he felt the pain, he found it very hard to cry. Bobby came home many months later and saw a picture of Michael in our bedroom. He also saw a poignant poem his dad had given to me on my birthday. It was about Michael. When Bobby saw the picture and read the poem, the tears finally flowed. He came out of the room a short while later, saw me, and shared his feelings. It was the first time he had really cried since Michael died. 'Don't think that because the tears don't come out of my eyes that the pain isn't in my heart.' Bobby said that he thinks about his brother almost every day and although time does make it better, there are still difficult days."

Lorrie Haimes was not quite twenty-one when her brother Michael died. "They shared secrets and were so similar in personality. They liked to play tennis together and used to go to the movies. They were very close," their mother says. Judith describes the transformation in Lorrie when she saw her parents in pain. "Lorrie sometimes had a great tendency to be wrapped up in herself, but when Michael died she just took over, as the firstborn often does, and became very strong when she saw her foundation—her parents—were falling apart. She went to the car in which Michael had been killed and took out his personal things. She had even gone to pick up the police report. She did everything that had to be done, handling details she knew her parents couldn't—and never complained. She put us first and kept her own grief to herself or shared that grief with Lenny Churilla, the boy she ultimately married."

Before proceeding with the dramatic events leading to the birth of Lorrie and Lenny's first child, we will first read about the issue of naming a surviving siblings's child—a complex one for many brothers and sisters as well as bereaved parents. In the following article, reprinted from THANATOS, Judith and Allen Haimes address some of the many questions.

Naming A Surviving Sibling's Child

by Allen and Judith Haimes

Recently we were asked by a friend how we would feel about our surviving children naming a child after our dead son—and how the surviving siblings would feel about it.

Our immediate reaction was that everyone would want to name after the child that died. But, after talking to others, we soon realized not everyone feels this way. Here we were thinking "how right it is." We find many people do not, cannot, will not wish to name after a dead child. The question turned out to have many complexities:

While naming of a sibling's child may help some parents, for others it may create trauma. The question often arises: does a surviving child name their newborn after a dead sibling because they really want to, or because they feel it will please their parents? It follows that often there is concern as to whether grandparents will treat the newborn named after their dead child in the same way they would treat other grandchildren without that name. Apart from the grandparents' reactions, would a surviving sibling who named a child after a dead brother or sister be able to react to this child the same as all other children they had—and how does this affect the spouse of the surviving sibling?

No two families are alike in the way they grieve.

What complexities in human nature—and what complexity evolves in inter-family relationships in the aftermath of the death of a child! Many of these questions cannot be answered. We are faced with the reality that no two families are alike in their emotional responses—no two families are alike in the way they grieve.

Some parents welcome the idea of perpetuating their child's name and would feel hurt if at least one, if not more, of their surviving children did not do so. Some parents may have underlying fears connected with other superstitions that existed prior to their child's death and not necessarily caused by the death. Therapy may help in this instance. And counseling may help if parents move too much in the other direction and become terribly upset because everybody they know does not choose to take their child's name for their new baby. Many bereaved parents cannot bear the thought of handing down their dead child's clothing to another child, much less the name.

One parent was very apprehensive about a grandchild bearing the dead child's name lest he meet the same fate at an early age. Other parents scoff at the idea of a name being "jinxed." Each family has so much turmoil going on. Losing a child is a horrible thing—and each of us breaks in a different way.

In our own case, in our hearts and minds, we honestly believe that naming after a dead child will enable everyone to remember the person who died. Fifty years from now, our grandchildren will be telling their grandchildren, "I was named after an uncle who was killed when he was very young." Thinking of our heritage and who we were named after gives us a sense of continuity, a sense of belonging. But it is not useful for anyone to sit back and say, "you should" or "should not" name after the dead.

Superstition may play a part, and we can only explain how we feel. For us, Fridays have *not* become the worst day of our lives because Michael died on a Friday. Nor is the 19th a jinxed day for us because he died on the 19th—any more than the 17th is a blessed day because that is the day Michael was born. We talked with out daughter Lorrie, 21, recently married, who hopes to have a baby soon. "But of course I will name the baby after Michael," she exclaimed. Then we asked, "Well, would you ever have any feelings that the baby would be jinxed with that name?" Lorrie looked at us, annoyed, and answered: "Mom, Dad? Are you kidding? That's like saying I would be jinxed if I rode in a brown car because Michael was killed in a brown car." Lorrie thought of it as being perfectly ridiculous. She feels she would want her children to remember a man so important to her, whom they never knew. "I want them to remember they had an Uncle Mike, and I want to tell them everything about him." She misses Michael and wants to perpetuate his name.

We must each follow our own hearts.

We are dealing with human emotions—those of familes who don't want to hurt anymore. We sat down to put together a logical way of dealing with this issue; we discovered this was totally illogical because no two families feel the same way. There are those who feel comfortable in naming after the dead; and there are those who do not. The only applicable "Golden Rule" after the death of a child is: "There are no rights and no wrongs for bereaved parents and siblings." There are right ways and wrong ways, but what may be right for one person may not be right for the other. We must each follow our own hearts.

As we have seen in the preceding article, Lorrie Haimes was determined to name her baby after Michael. "There was never any question in my mind about that," Lorrie states. "I know if the situation had been reversed and I had been the one who died, Michael would have named a child after me. It is just a love you feel for each other, and wanting to perpetuate the name. I will remember Michael, but maybe the next generation won't. So, in naming my child—either Michael Steven if it's a boy, or Michaela Stephanie if it's a girl—after my brother, that child will grow up to know who its uncle was and to be proud of the name they have inherited. In my case, my husband was not really keen on the name Michael, only because it was his own middle name and he never cared for it. But, he knew how much it meant to me to have a child named after Michael and because he understood that need, he consented."

After Lorrie and Lenny were married, they tried and tried to have a baby, but Lorrie could not get pregnant. Following two years of trying, Judith explains how she learned of Lorrie's news: "On my birthday, Lorrie and Lenny sent me a card that said, 'Happy Birthday, Grandma!' Lorrie was then six weeks pregnant and that's what she gave me for my birthday. When Lorrie was two-and-a-half months pregnant, she began to have dreams about Michael. Soon thereafter, she started having some problems. It began by her feeling a little uncomfortable. Having never been pregnant before, she didn't know how to react to this. One night, she felt particularly bad and went in to take a shower, she felt nauseous so she got a glass of water. She drank the water and put the glass on the side of the tub. At this point Lorrie remembered having a sharp pain in her stomach. She fell into the tub, the glass falling with her. She got up out of the tub with her head bleeding profusely. When she grabbed onto the towel rack to pull herself up, she started to faint. The towel rack was pulled out of the wall and Lorrie fell on the broken glass. She sat on the glass and the broken end went into her bottom about two inches. She lay there in a stupor, continuing to bleed. When her husband came in to help her, she thought it was Michael coming through the door. She was rushed to the hospital in an ambulance, but had already lost a great deal of blood. She had also lost the baby. Her doctor performed major surgery and had to remove a part of her uterus. She was given five pints of blood.

"Lorrie recuperated and tried, but couldn't get pregnant again. She even took fertility drugs but to no avail. Finally, as a last resort, she cried aloud, 'Michael, you're up there with God. I want you to do me a favor. I want a baby. I need a baby. I'm going to name the baby after you. I can't live like this. It's so hard and so long. The doctors tell me that it doesn't look too good for me. You've got to help me, Michael.' A month later, Lorrie woke up on the morning of April thirteenth and said, 'I know I got pregnant last night. I know it.' Sure enough, she went to the doctor and he confirmed she was pregnant."

Judith describes how Lorrie was convinced her baby would be born on the day that Michael had died. "The doctor told Lorrie the baby was due in the middle of January. Lorrie exclaimed to him, 'No, it's not!' I asked Michael to help me and I know that he did. My baby is going to be born on December nineteenth, on the fifth anniversary of Michael's death. I know it.' " The doctor said that was impossible. Lorrie was insistent, 'I know it. The baby is going to be born then.' She would hear nothing else. She went through her pregnancy talking to Michael every day about this baby; decorated the room with Michael's picture hanging over the baby's bed. 'This is going to be Michael's namesake. The baby's going to be born on December nineteenth.' "

This time, Lorrie went through a normal pregnancy. She and her husband had the baby's name picked out and it didn't matter to them if it was a boy or a girl. "On December eighteenth, she started into mild labor," Judith relates. "She went to the doctor to be checked. At four in the afternoon, the doctor admitted Lorrie into the hospital. I was in Lorrie's room with her husband, and the doctor came in to tell us that they were giving Lorrie something to speed up her labor. I asked him why, was she having a problem? He replied, 'No, she's not having any problems. But let's just get it over with fast.'

"The baby was born at 8:30 on the night of December eighteenth, a beautiful little girl, Michaela. When it was all over, the doctor told me, 'Look, it's bad enough that this baby will have to live in Michael's shadow.' My reply was: 'This is going to take the worst day of my life and turn it into the best day of my life.' He answered, 'No, the nineteenth of December will always be the worst day of your life. The baby shouldn't have to share that day. As it is, the baby's birthday will be a reminder that that was the day her Uncle Michael died.' So that's why the doctor speeded up the delivery. We all knew that Michael had a hand in this, and that if things had been left alone, the baby would have been born on Michael's anniversary. Instead, we gave little Michaela her own identity.

"Lorrie says she is not immortalizing Michael. We spoke about this and Lorrie simply believes that although Michael is dead, he's still as close to her as he was when he was alive. None of us feel that Michaela is going to be burdened by carrying Michael's name. Rather, she is going to be reminded that she had an Uncle Michael who was very much loved and who would have loved her very much in life."

Chapter Fourteen

Chuck Akerland

When Chuck Akerland was ten years old, he and his family were living in Bangkok, Thailand. It was there that his sixteen-year-old brother, Trey, jumped off the roof of their apartment building and killed himself.

Now age twenty-six, Chuck reflects on the events of that day: "I was the first one in my family to know that Trey had jumped. But let me explain what led up to the day he committed suicide. My brother had been involved in drugs for some time. We were living overseas during the sixties and the Vietnam War, and my dad was an Air Force colonel and a consultant. One afternoon, my mother saw Trey out on the streets in Bangkok at a time when he should have been in school. After he got home around 5 P.M., my parents asked Trey where he had been. My father, demanding an honest answer, pointed out that we had always been open in our family, and that we didn't keep things from each other. My brother became angry and refused to tell where he had been.

"I was standing in the living room as my brother ran by and up to the top of the apartment building. My father followed him and they had a confrontation on the roof. As Trey began to move closer to the ledge, my father left him to ask the police to bring a net in case Trey should decide to jump. All this excitement and movement made me wonder what was going on, and I went out to our balcony. There I saw Trey on the ledge. For some reason I turned my head away and, as I did, he jumped. When I turned back again, Trey was on the ground below. I knew that my mother, with my father gone off to get help, was alone inside the apartment. As soon as she saw my face, she knew what had happened. I have always felt fortunate that I didn't actually see him leap."

After his brother's death, Chuck's deepest pain was that there was no one he could talk to. "All I've ever wanted was for people to realize how much I hurt, but nobody would listen to me. I said this to my mother recently, and she replied, 'I was always there to listen to you.' That may be true, but it would have been difficult for me as a ten-year-old to say to my mother, 'This is how I feel about Trey's death.' I knew how upset she got whenever that subject was brought up, and I decided not to mention it.

"It was to my dad I really wanted to talk about Trey, but he wouldn't talk about it. He felt too hurt, I suppose. He seemed to draw away from me as if he didn't want to take the risk of getting hurt again by being close to me, and I never spoke to my mother, for fear of upsetting her. So nobody ever knew how much I was hurting."

Chuck yearned for a one-on-one relationship with his father, especially after his brother's death. "I was envious of my brother's relationship with my dad, even though I knew their talks were centered on the drugs my brother had been involved with for about a year. Furthermore, they always talked behind closed doors. Yet I envied my brother for those talks, father to son, man to man.

"After Trey died, I remember the biggest question I wanted to ask my dad was, 'Is Trey dead?' Just to confirm the fact. Just to have it said out loud. Yes, I knew he had jumped off the roof. You know—I saw him on the ground. But I wanted to have it said. I wanted to have that one-on-one conversation with my dad, but I never did. Not until many years later, when my father called me two weeks before he took his own life."

Two days after his brother died, Chuck returned to school. He tells of his behavior. "I walked into class and glibly said, 'All right, ask me anything you want to know about my brother's death.' I really wanted to talk about it. I wanted people to ask me, 'Well, how do you feel?' But the sight of this flippant ten-year-old back in class only two days after his brother had committed suicide shocked my classmates, particularly when I opened up with the statement, 'Okay, ask me whatever you want.' People were completely put off by that and probably thought, 'Oh, this kid has flipped his lid.'

"At that time, I remember hoping that one of my parents would also die a year later so that I would get more attention. Perhaps then, a year later, my other parent would die. I was getting a lot of attention from my brother's suicide, the kind I'd never received before, but I'd probably get even more if a parent would die, I thought."

When Chuck was twelve, he and his family returned to the States. "I had only close friend back home, but when we got back to Maryland, he had moved to another part of the state, so I couldn't talk to him about Trey. As a result, I never really got to talk to anybody about it, and as time went on, there seemed to be no reason to do so. I thought, 'Well, Trey's gone now. He's dead and my parents will take care of me.' All I needed to do in life was to go to school and do my homework, so what's the need to talk about my brother's death."

During the years that followed, Chuck continued to think it was unnecessary to talk about his brother's death. In being denied an outlet for his grief, his pent-up questions, and the desire to be recognized as his father's son, Chuck suffered a startling revelation as he entered his senior year in high school. "I had been living for years as if I were in a fog. I had thought there was nothing to do in life but go to school and do my homework, and so it was quite a shock for me to realize that next year I would no longer be in school. I had not prepared myself to go out and work. I was terrified because I had grown up thinking, 'Well, you don't need to do anything, but go to school. Your parents will take care of you and you'll always have a house, a bed, and food.' I was petrified of going out into the world and working. Since Trey's death, I had spent all my life just being taken care of."

To Chuck the only solution was more schooling. "The only route I could see was to go to college. Then I would be taken care of. My parents would pay for my meals and my room and board, and I would have to do nothing but go to school. There would be no need to talk about Trey as long as I was taken care of by my parents. But then I began to act out my need for attention by getting poor grades and by refusing to mature. For example, when I was fourteen, I was still carrying my teddy bear around. I remember one time my father remarked, 'My God, he's fourteen years old and still carries his teddy bear with him. What's going on?' The truth is that all I wanted was for somebody to come up to me and say, 'Charlie, what's going on? Anyone looking at me would have thought I was trying to get attention, which of course I was. But I was really saying, 'Will you pay attention, open your eyes, and see there's something wrong with me? Will you please let me tell you that my goddamned brother died? I'm upset and will you start addressing the issue?'"

Chuck reveals that he had also felt a sense of euphoria at his brother's death. "One touchy issue that is seldom mentioned by young siblings is one I experienced: *I was really glad that Trey had died*, for then I had my parents all to myself. I had the bedroom all to myself, no one to snitch on me. There would be more gifts for me. All those thoughts went through my head. It wasn't until I was fourteen or fifteen that I began to miss him.

"I had the idea that with Trey's death all the bad things that were going to happen in my life had gone with him. By the age of ten, I had already had enough experience to know the good from the bad, and I felt that his death would spare me from any further evils. I thought, 'From now on, Mommy and Daddy will take care of me and everything will be fine. I'm sorry that Trey is gone, but at least he took everything bad with him.'"

Chuck now says, "I think there are many other ten-year-olds who think as I did but don't dare tell this to their parents. While it may be true that ten-year-old children do go through the pain of loss, some may also feel glad because the loss has brought them personal gain and the attention of their peers. However, if young kids are left to harbor such feelings, guilt can develop that will make them depressed and sad for the rest of their lives. We must also watch out for kids who will take advantage of their parents' pain. One nine-year-old sibling, when she didn't feel like doing her homework one evening, said to her grieving mother, 'I've been thinking of my sister and I couldn't concentrate.' The mother, of course, excused her. In another instance, the sibling told her mother one morning that she didn't feel like going to school. When the mother inquired why, the girl said she had been dreaming of her sister and was upset. Tears filled the mother's eyes and she said to her surviving daughter, 'I understand. It's okay.' Many siblings will utilize the death to their own benefit when they cannot express their true feelings to parents. This is another pitfall that remains as a hanger-on to siblings later, when guilt rears its ugly head."

Chuck also sheds some light on questions that other siblings may have: "Are parents able to understand the true feelings of young siblings who cannot express their real feelings? I was scared and I'm sure other siblings of that age are too, but I thought that since my parents had been children once, they would know what was going on with me. However, the truth is that when a child dies, the parents *haven't* been there before. *They're going through it as adults at the same time you are going through it as a child.* So, it's nothing they understand because, unless they were a bereaved sibling, they are adults who have never experienced what you are experiencing as a child.

"If I had to give advice to a ten-year-old sibling now, I would say, 'Your parents don't know any better than you do, but you need to talk to someone. Perhaps there is a counselor at school who can help, or a siblings group of some kind, either at a local church or at a Compassionate Friends group in your city. It's painful for parents to hear that they don't know any better than their ten-year-old child. It knocks down their parental authority and sounds like you are trying to undermine them. But it's true. Just recently, my mom said to me, 'I think we were three people all trying to find a way to exist.' In our family, we never communicated with each other as a unit, for in order to do that, each person has to be willing to give."

Until Chuck was twenty-six, he was deluded by one great misconception. "Up to this past year, my biggest misconception was my belief that everyone else was happy. This idea took form four years after Trey's death. Even in my early college years, a lonely cloud of sadness hung over me because my brother killed himself. I used to think, 'Oh my God, how awful. There isn't much worse than having your only brother kill himself.' As long as I continued to think that other people were happy, but that I was unhappy because Trey had died, there was no hope for me. My conclusion was that other kids were *happy* because their sibling *hadn't* died—and I was unhappy because my sibling *had* died. Since there was nothing I could change about my brother's death, I assumed that I would remain unhappy the rest of my life."

Chuck describes the shock he experienced when he realized that people who had not lost a sibling were unhappy for other reasons: "When I discovered that people were not the happy individuals I believed them to be, I thought, 'They're unhappy and they didn't even lose a brother. If they're unhappy because their car got stolen, or because they're not the vice president of a company, their unhappiness stems from insignificant things, while I'm unhappy because I had a brother who died. "With this realization, Chuck felt himself becoming truly content. "I realize that others are sometimes unhappy for trivial reasons, and I understand I was unhappy for very good reasons. I'll always miss Trey and wish that I had my brother, but I'm starting to be satisfied with my life. Remember, there was a time when I thought high school should be the happiest years in a person's life. But if I was sad in those years, what did that mean for the rest of my life? I was convinced that happiness was not for me. I found out differently in this past year and now feel I have come very far."

Chuck also believes he has come far in understanding his mother. "When I went home to visit my mother for her birthday, we had a great time together. The following Sunday afternoon, however, we got into an argument. She made the point, 'You have a tendency to pick arguments.' That was the first time I had ever been told of that trait in myself. I replied to her, 'You know, Mother, you're right; I do pick arguments. It's because I have all this rage inside.' She told me she didn't have any rage;

she just had a lot of sadness. We then discussed our different lifestyles, and she told me she had been raised to 'do it on your own.'

"What I'm starting to discover in this whole issue of suicide, and the so-called epidemic of it, is that it's not so much suicide per se as it is our changing culture. We're not just fighting against the death of children by suicide, we're fighting a whole culture that says you should do it on your own instead of sharing with others. My mother said she didn't believe in baring her soul at support groups. If you have the attitude that you must 'do it on your own,' nothing outside you is going to help.

"As that scared ten-year-old, I would have loved to have asked, 'I'm in pain. Why don't you reach out to me?' But that would have been opposed to my mother's true belief that you had to do it on your own. In her mind, she felt she was doing the right thing by giving me privacy. In trying to cope with such ideas, it's as though I'm fighting an entire cultural tradition, not only my mom's belief. It's as if it has nothing to do with my mom and not her fault at all. But experience has taught me that there's a flaw in that tradition."

A friend once asked Chuck, "What does it take to get through the kind of pain you experienced?" Chuck remembers the discussion: "He wasn't particularly talking about a surviving sibling; he was talking about surviving depression and pain, and whatever causes that pain. I replied, 'What it takes is for somebody to hear you.'"

Chuck has now taken many steps to make certain someone is indeed hearing him. After his father's death, he spent two years in therapy. "I finally realized what I had been going through during the twelve years after my brother died, and I didn't want to go through another twelve years after my father shot himself." Later, Chuck contacted The Compassionate Friends and subsequently became co-facilitator of their siblings group. He also attended meetings at various suicide groups.

Chuck tells how a visit to a nutritionist unearthed the reason for a problem of his of long-standing: "I went to a nutritionist and body therapist, and told her I had no appetite. I happened to mention to her that Trey had died at about 5:45 and that dinner was usually scheduled for 5:30. She immediately pinpointed that as the base for the eating problem I'd had for all these years. 'You don't eat,' she said, 'because your brother died at supper time. Since then you haven't given yourself permission to eat dinner.' " Chuck then began to realize the tremendous long-range impact that the death of a sibling can have on a surviving sibling. He now believes he has begun to accept the deaths of his brother and father.

Chapter Fifteen
A Father's Thoughts on a Surviving Son

Abe Malawski recalls that upon returning from the cemetery after burying his older son Harvey he was concerned about the impact on his younger son Steven. "I wanted to be certain that Steven understood he was loved no less than his brother. I realized there had been a tremendous number of people at the funeral services for Harvey. Anyone would have been impressed by this turnout to pay respect to my son. But I wanted to make sure that my surviving son Steven knew, after seeing the huge crowd there for his brother, that this had no bearing on our love for him.

"When we returned home after the funeral and were sitting in the kitchen, I put my arms around Steven and we both began to cry. I said to him, 'Just remember one thing, Steven. I loved your brother because he was Harvey and I love you because you are Steven. One has nothing to do with the other.' I remember Steven's answer to me was, 'I know, Dad.' I was glad he said that because I never wanted Steven to have to say, 'Hey world, I'm here, too.' Steven is as much a part of my world as is Harvey."

Steven, a senior in high school when his brother died, graduated three months later in June. In September, he went away to an out-of-state school. The only thing his parents asked of him was to call home twice a week. Abe comments on those early days. "Whenever Steven called, his conversation was guarded. But I think he knew that his mother and I needed to hear his voice more than anything else and it was not what was being said that was important." Abe also noted that Steven is now doing graduate work and still manages to call them twice a week—and it's six years later.

Abe recalls that on other occasions it was difficult to discuss with Steven personal things about Harvey. "He would squirm if I asked questions about how he took his brother's death, would try to tell me as swiftly as possible and then change the subject. On one particular occasion, though, about two years after Harvey died, we had a conversation in which he surprised me by opening up and sharing his thoughts.

"I had become chapter leader of The Compassionate Friends in Babylon, New York," says Abe, "and I had been asked to give a lecture at a local high school where a course in death and dying is an elective available to the senior English class. The course invited guest speakers to discuss the subject. I had just picked up Steven at the airport, and in the course of the conversation I told him about the lecture. Then I said, 'I don't know what to say to these kids. Do you have any suggestions? How was it for you when you first went back to school after your brother died?' Steven replied, 'I didn't want to talk about it, but I accepted my classmates' sympathy. If they wanted to talk any more or say anything else, I just said, 'Please, I don't want to discuss it. I wanted to be left alone in those days. It was too painful to talk about my brother.'

"And then Steven added something very poignant. He said that he not only had lost his brother, but he had also lost his best friend. I choked on that. I was very glad I had a cigar in my mouth because I did not want him to see me crying. He opened up and started talking, and I didn't want to stop him. He went on to say that until about two years before Harvey died, they used to tease each other unmercifully, but that in the last two years, they had become closer. I wished we'd had another two hours of driving time, because Steven was remembering all the good things and all the bad things that he and his brother had done in those days.

"Something else that Steven said touched me deeply. He said that although he was left with his memories, he would never be able to discuss with his brother all the things he would have taken up with him. 'I'll never have the relationship that you and Uncle Lou have as brothers growing older together,' he commented. For me, it was very difficult to sit and listen to Steven's thoughts. It was taking me back to the very beginning when this whole nightmare started. But later when I got home, I was very glad and grateful that my son had felt comfortable enough to share his thoughts with me.

"I wondered how often Steven had been able to discuss his feelings and whether he had ever shared his thoughts with his classmates. I do know that when the first anniversary of Harvey's death came around, we sent Steven a memorial candle. And when he called us a few days later, we learned he had lighted it. His mother asked, 'How did you manage that?' 'Well,' Steven replied, 'the fellows in my room wanted to know what it was, and I told them and then I talked about Harvey.' He said there were about six of his classmates in the room. In parting, they said to Steven, 'Anytime you want to talk about it, we'll be glad to sit and talk with you.' It made my wife and me feel good that they were so caring and could surmise what he was going through."

As chapter leader of The Compassionate Friends, Abe has been able to observe that one of the things bereaved parents complain about most is, "My children don't want to speak of their dead brother or sister because they're afraid it will make us cry." Abe tells how this issue arose in his own household. "In our case, our surviving son did not mention his brother's name for over a year. Whenever Steven was home on a school break, he would walk on eggs rather than mention Harvey's name. We had not told him how upset we were about his refusal to speak Harvey's name because we thought perhaps Steven was having a problem saying his brother's name."

One of the most difficult situations Judy and Abe endured in connection with Steven not speaking his brother's name had to do with television. "We have two television sets in our home, one in the den, the other in Harvey's room," Abe tells us. "Whenever my wife and I were watching a program and Steven wanted to watch something else, he would announce, 'I'm going to the *other room*'—not to *Harvey's room*, but specifically to the *other room*. It used to put a knife into his mother every time he said that."

Abe explains what happened when Steven learned that

they wanted to hear his brother's name and that it was okay for him say it. "I had been asked to return to lecture at the high school class I mentioned earlier. This time I spoke about how a father grieves for his son. One of the points I brought to those children was how important it was for surviving siblings to mention their brother's or sister's name after he or she has died. I explained that most parents are hurt or very uncomfortable when their dead children are ignored. I asked how they would feel if no one were ever to speak their names again. Soon after the lecture Steven came home for the weekend, and his mother said to him, 'Your father gave a talk at the high school and it was taped. I haven't heard it yet and I'm going to play it now. I'd like you to listen to it, too. So we all sat and listened.

"Steven heard me say how important it was for bereaved parents to hear about their dead child, that not hearing it was almost a sign that he had never existed. After the tape was finished, Steven was very gracious about telling me he had enjoyed the tape as much as my audience had. He also said he learned about a few issues that he was not aware of that had existed in our family. Then, ten or fifteen minutes later when we switched channels in the den where we were watching TV, he got up and said, 'I'm going to *Harvey's room* to watch something else.'

"And that was the very first time since his brother's death that he had said, 'I'm going to Harvey's room to watch.' The tape gave him permission and he realized it was okay for him to say his brother's name. Although we have never discussed it, I suspect he was afraid of hurting us by mentioning Harvey's name. I believe many surviving children in the beginning want to protect their parents from pain, many of them to the detriment of their own feelings, which surface later. Others feel they want to become everything the dead child was to their parents, a feeling of wanting to make it up to their parents for having lost so much."

Abe explains that bereaved parents carry burdens of guilt about their surviving children as well as about the child who has died. "Months and even years after the death, parents— in recalling the early weeks—wish they had been able to help their surviving chidlren more than they were capable of doing at the time. The most important thing for parents to do when they lose a child is to let their surviving chidren know they are really loved very much. The reason this is so important is that most surviving children have seen their parents disintegrate, deteriorate both mentally and physically until all of a sudden their parent becomes their child and must depend on them. The parents become nonfunctional. The food is not taken care of. The cleanliness of the house is not attended to. The nurturing is not there because the parent is completely out of focus. These parents become like a boat without a rudder—it's going around in circles in hurricane weather. The whole family unit seems to flounder.

"What we are talking about here is that what the surviving sibling formerly called 'home' is no longer a true home, and the sibling has no comfortable place to be. The surviving children see their parents broken up and they wonder, 'Would our mother and father act this way if we were to die?' These siblings have been through all the trauma of their own pain and added to that is the grief of their parents. A surviving sibling may think, 'Well, maybe I'll show them that I also count,' and this attitude may bring about a suicide. A child may take his own life to prove to the parents that he existed apart from the unit that's completely out of control. But, thank God, there are not many such instances. It is vital to our remaining children's continued survival that they know it was nothing they did or said that caused the death.

"What surviving siblings must be told over and over by our actions and by our words is that, yes, they most certainly *are* important—more than they could ever imagine. In fact, they are the only reason for our existence. They don't realize that we are so mentally shattered and despondent that they are the only reason we do not take our own lives. Mourning a dead child doesn't in any way decrease your love for your surviving chidlren. You love each of your children, and love each one in a different way. I wish I could apologize to every surviving child for every bereaved parent who loves them, but who is so devastated by that horrible punch in the stomach that they are feeling, and simply unable to convey for a time any feelings other than the pain they feel from that knockout blow."

Abe realizes that holidays can be very difficult for bereaved siblings. "Most families have a hard time with the holidays. Some surviving children want things to proceed as usual; they want their parents to be as they were before. Other siblings find it difficult to cope with the holidays, especially if the parents are displaying unhappiness at the prospect of celebrating festive occasions.

"Anniversaries and holidays are not easy, but we want Steven to understand that we love him and that it is important for us to make that effort, just as he wanted to make the effort to speak his brother's name because of his caring for us and our needs. More importantly, because Steven—as does every surviving child—deserves to have his place in the sun, to enjoy holidays and all the other good things in life.

"Steven's girlfriend is a student nurse and she also happens to be the sister of a bereaved parent, for her sister's youngest baby died of SIDS. So, if anyone understands Steven, she does. In addition, she's a very sweet kid. I think that will make things easier for him. Because Steven is now an only child, I feel good that his girlfriend has brothers and sisters to whom Steven is very close, and that's important. Meanwhile, we have tried not to be overprotective. I am thankful that Judy and I have always been of one thought—we are here as poles attached to a young tree, so when the strong winds buffet it, we keep him from breaking. But the young tree grows strong and is later able to withstand that wind on its own. That is what parents do—help their children to reach maturity and to be on their own."

Chapter Sixteen

A Mother Talks of Her Surviving Son

On a cold wintry day in February 1974, Ann Witty Niemela was hurrying her three sons to get ready for school, while she was readying herself for work. "Being the mother of my clan, I was barking orders to hurry and eat while making sure shirts matched pants, hair was combed, and so on. Rusty, who was nine, and Brian, age six, were running out the door to catch their school bus. My youngest son Darren, four, and I were rushing to our waiting ride into Hyannis to the baby-sitter and work. Brian called out, 'Bye, Mom.' I tried to see him, but he was down the road out of sight. I yelled back anyway, 'Bye, hon, be good.' That proved to be our final farewell, and was the last time I saw my two older boys alive. I have always wished I'd taken a longer look at them, given them more than a quick hug, and I truly wish I could have seen Brian yelling his final good-bye."

Ann's day at work was an ordinary one—nothing untoward happened to warn her of the crushing events about to take place. After school, Rusty and Brian were in the care of a sixteen-year-old baby-sitter who lived across the street and who stayed with the boys until Ann came home from work. On this particular afternoon, Ann returned a half-hour late because her car ride was delayed. "I remember feeling frustrated because I had planned on going bowling that evening. It was to be my first night back after having major surgery the previous month. When I got home, I asked the sitter where the boys were, and she said they were out sledding in the snow.

Ann asked the sitter to find the boys while she heated up a pot of soup made the day before. "She came back after a few minutes and said she couldn't find them," Ann remembers. "I felt a minor annoyance that they were disobeying my orders to never play out of the sound of my voice. With that, I sent the baby-sitter home and said I would call her when it was time for me to go bowling. I bundled myself and Darren and got in the car to drive around to find Brian and Rusty. The road we live on was like a cul-de-sac. It was being developed, but there were no houses down at the end of the pond. The pond was not visible from the houses that were occupied."

When Ann reached the pond, she got out of her car and found the boys' sled by the boat landing. "I could see their footprints going down to the pond. I remember looking out over the snow-covered pond and seeing a black opening out about fifty feet. I didn't think about it consciously, but the pit of my stomach sank. I think my whole body knew, but wouldn't tell my brain what I saw. I rushed back into my car, drove home, and called the police. The rest of that evening is a blur of police, friends, rescue workers, questions of what they were wearing, if they were prone to wandering off or going to friends' houses to play, and making millions of phone calls to see if they were here or there or had been seen by anyone.

"Their father and I had been divorced about eight months. He was a police officer in a nearby town, and he and every available policeman from his force came over to join in the search for the boys. I remember sitting at the kitchen table and hearing the big generator truck with iceboats on it going by the house. It was the most gruesome sound I have ever heard. I remember feeling very confused by what was happening, like floating in and out of a horrible dream.

"There was a two-way radio on the table. We could hear what the men in the team by the pond were saying, but to someone who is not used to hearing rescue lingo on a radio, it was hard to understand just what their words meant. After a few moments of silence on the radio, I remember hearing some jargon and what sounded like the word, 'Affirmative.' My ex-husband jumped up and went into another room with his buddies following. I kept asking, 'What did they say?' But no one said a word to me. Finally, a woman from the rescue team just nodded and said, 'Yes, they found them.' I screamed and said what no one dared to say to me, 'My babies are dead, my babies are died.' "

The rest of that evening was nothing short of a nightmare for Ann. The one thing she was grateful for was that her surviving son was asleep. "Darren had been put to bed long before any of this happened and, surprisingly, he slept all night. I thank God for that. Two of my closest friends stayed with me all night. A doctor, the one who pronounced the boys dead, gave me a strong sedative. I must have slept a few hours, because all of a sudden it was daylight and there were several people there and Darren was awake. I went into the kitchen to have some coffee, and Darren came up to me. He asked if I was still worried about Rusty and Brian. I glanced at my girlfriend, and she shook her head to indicate he didn't know anything yet."

Ann tells of the poignant scene when she took her son in her lap to explain that she was no longer worried about his brothers. "I held my son in my arms and asked him if he knew what an angel was. He said, yes, he knew. His Grandpa Witty was an angel and so was his Grandpa McCombs, and his little sister (Tamara Lynn, who had been stillborn) was an angel because they all died and went to Heaven. I told him that was right and explained that last night Rusty and Brian died and they were Angels in Heaven now, too. He and I both cried and hugged each other. We were all we had left."

Two funerals were held for Rusty and Brian—one in Massachusetts where they lived and one in Indiana. "We were all from Indiana, and that's where I wanted my boys buried. I remember in the couple of days before the first funeral, I asked Darren whether he would like to stay home or go over to his cousin's house and play. Either one would be all right with me. He chose to go to play with his cousin. He stayed there throughout the wake and the funeral. I called to make sure he was having a good time and told him I would be over to get him soon.

"Their funerals were on Valentine's Day in Massachusetts. We flew to Indiana right after the service. Two days later, we had their final funeral in Indiana. I took Darren to that one to say good-bye to his brothers. He cried throughout the funeral, going from my lap to his father's," Ann reflects. "After the funeral, Darren had two very distinctive questions. He wanted to know why I kissed Rusty and Brian if they were dead. He also wanted to know if I would put him in the ground when he died as I had done with Rusty and Brian. I explained to Darren that I kissed his brothers because I still loved them even though they were dead. To his second question, I said their souls were in Heaven and only their bodies were being buried. I tried to explain that the soul is the part of us that feels happy and good when we get a surprise or a hug. That part went to Heaven and they are with Jesus, playing, I said. The body didn't know anything, and Rusty and Brian didn't know about being in the ground. I found this to be a very thin line to deal with at his age. I wanted him to understand that it was good to die naturally, but not good to want to be dead. I just tried to talk to him on his own level about the things I hoped he understood and still be as honest as I could. Instinctively, I spoke of his brothers as being dead, not merely sleeping or passing away. At the age of four years and nine months, Darren was given a very grown-up problem to deal with and, unfortunately, I could not do other than meet it head on. I could not try to paint a nice picture for him."

Ann tells of the many pitfalls ahead. "There were a great many everyday obstacles to deal with and no knowledge or guidance as to how to cope with our tragedy. So many steps backward to the few we'd taken forward. I began to see signs in Darren that all was not well with him. In time, he took to hitting smaller children and deliberately doing things that could harm himself, like riding his bike carelessly and on purpose into the street. My first thought was that I had to get help for him. This started a long line of child psychiatrists and child psychologists, but to no avail. I was told I was overreacting to this situation, that Darren was so young and his capacity for understanding death is limited and not to worry; children of his age forget things they don't understand.

"I couldn't believe them because I knew Darren did

understand what had happened. He just didn't know what to do with it and neither did I. I became overwhelmed, watching my child go downhill. I soon turned to thoughts of suicide. My problem was not the wish to die, but how to die. I couldn't leave Darren by himself and inflict the pain of losing his mother too. Furthermore, I certainly couldn't harm a hair on his head, kill him, and then myself. I started to have fantasies of Darren and me walking down the road and a big truck going out of control and running over us and killing us. We would die together—but I didn't do it, and no one could blame me. I didn't cause it."

It was at this time that Ann realized she needed help for herself. "It scared me to think of how thrilled I was about a truck killing us. I called a psychiatrist recommended by a friend. This was the beginning of salvation for Darren and me, for by receiving help for myself, I was able to help my child. I know now that what a mother is, her children will be. We are their reasoning power, their teacher of emotions whether it's fear, sadness, happiness. If I'm overwhelmed and anxious, so will my child be, I reasoned. Also, I assumed that it was harder and more harrowing to Darren to lose his brothers when he was so young and all he knew was his brothers. He had lost his brothers who were also his playmates. I had lost my hopes and dreams and my future, but it was important for me to take care of my emotional needs so I would be better equipped to help Darren adjust to becoming an only child in need of the lost companionship."

Ann expresses a great concern for surviving children who enter or re-enter school. "Darren had a very rough beginning in the public school system. Also, if anyone could, would, or should benefit from a book about surviving siblings, it is my largest goal in life to educate the educators. They were our biggest and most threatening force during Darren's and my struggle in life. I find it hard to say that it was ignorance on their part, because so many professed to be trained and educated in dealing with children and their needs. I at first relied on them and their educational knowledge to help me and my child. After all, I thought, what did I know? I hadn't gone to college. I didn't have the discipline of a higher education. I was only a wounded mother with a wounded child.

"Darren was in an open concept kindergarten. It was one large room with three different classes in different parts of the room. I was unaware of many of the problems at school, because no one had told me. At parent-teacher conferences, I was just advised that Darren was a bit disruptive and his attention span was short. His next year at this particular school started with a brand new young principal. I got a phone call from him to come down for a meeting with him about some problems with Darren. At this time, Darren was seeing a child psychologist in Dennis, Massachusetts, by the name of Dr. Waxstein. He was truly a catalyst to the road of recovery for both Darren and me."

Ann tells of her meeting with the new principal: "I walked into his office and introduced myself. Immediately this man ranted and raved about Darren, about what a disturbing factor he was throughout the entire school and that he wouldn't stand for one child disrupting everything and everyone. He spoke of how he would see to it that Darren be committed to the school for mentally deranged children. I could only stare at him and let him rant on. I finally cut in on him and in a louder voice than he was using, calmly told him that if he cared to calm down, I might be interested in discussing Darren with him, but that if he continued in this manner, I would leave."

Ann continues with events. "After the principal calmed down, he asked me to have a seat in his office. He told me that 'they' had had it with Darren and all had decided that Darren should be examined by a neuro-psychiatrist. They felt there was something neurologically wrong with the child, and based on whatever the findings of this examination, they would decide if Darren would be allowed to continue school there. I was shocked that things were so serious at school. I said to the principal that if Darren were mentally deranged, wouldn't there be signs of derangement at home, too? I told him I saw no sign of this with Darren at home. He didn't even bother to comment. He told me that as soon as I took Darren to the doctor he had named, I would have to attend a meeting to discuss Darren's future."

When Ann arrived home, she called Dr. Waxstein. "I was in a state of hysteria. Dr. Waxstein gave me the name and number of a renowned neuro-psychiatrist in Chatham, Dr. Olssen, as he felt it would be wiser to choose our own doctor than to have one selected by them. Darren was checked out from head to toe by Dr. Olssen who also asked me numerous questions about delivery, early childhood, and such. His final assessment of Darren was acute anxiety with nothing neuro-logically wrong. He said he would send the appropriate findings to the school and to Dr. Waxstein."

Ann asked Dr. Waxstein to attend the meeting at school, after Darren's results had been sent there. "I was so afraid that I was trembling," she recalls. "After I arrived I trembled even more when I saw how many people were there—Darren's teacher from kindergarten, his first grade teacher, his prospec-tive teacher for next year, the school psychologist, the school nurse, the principal, and the superintendent of schools! Also present were myself, Dr. Waxstein, and Darren's father. The principal opened by stating we were all there to decide a program to help Darren in his special need. They all took turns telling of their personal encounters and projections with Darren. His kindergarten teacher spoke of how Darren dis-rupted the entire class with his antics. Not only did he disrupt his own class, she said, but the other classes as well. His present teacher added that he was no better this year; if anything, he was worse. She told of all the bad and wrong things he had done. The nurse and psychologist spoke of the numerous occasions on which they had been called in and were at their wits' end as to how to treat Darren. (I found out later they had been trying different things with Darren even in kindergarten, *without my knowledge*—things like putting him in a box on top of a table to isolate him from the rest of the students and to give him time to reflect on his inappropriate behavior, as well as numerous tests to make their own assess-ments on what to do with him!)

"The special needs teacher gave her expert advice on

'these types of children' and their negative effects on their classmates. Then Dr. Waxstein told of his own tests and findings. Darren had a very high IQ, an unbelievable memory, and the vocabulary and ability to put into words how he felt and thought. Dr. Waxstein also injected Dr. Olssen's findings, which were positive. Then I was asked if I had anything to say. I told the group I thought this meeting was called in order to find something to help Darren. I asked of each and everyone there how they expected to help my child when I had heard nothing positive out of their mouths about Darren. I asked since when has a negative force provided anything positive. I felt they only wanted to rid themselves of a problem they had helped to create rather than trying to solve it, and felt that they weren't qualified to help my child. I felt Dr. Waxstein's and my hard work and efforts were being undone.

"As it turned out, Darren was placed into a special needs program geared to a highly anxious person, almost on a one-to-one basis. Darren proved to them that he could learn as fast as they could teach, and he excelled in everything.

"Darren is a senior in high school now in New Hampshire. He is a very well-mannered, sensitive young man. Soon he will be going into the U.S. Army to become a military policeman and hopes to have a career in law enforcement of some degree. Obviously some of the things Darren and I did were right. Today, we are well adjusted, happy, and we still miss and love Rusty and Brian. We still indulge in our feelings and tears for them."

Ann stresses that the most important factor in dealing with a surviving child is touch and communication. "They go hand in hand. I always tell Darren what I think and feel and he does the same, telling me what he thinks and feels. It's been hard work for both of us, but we have maintained our close communications. I am proud of the fact that he has learned the concept of weighing pros and cons and looking at every angle to help before he makes a decision. This life experience has proven him to be a very loving, considerate, compassionate human being. For someone who was labeled a mentally deranged bully, that's quite a feat!"

Chapter Seventeen

Lynn Gardner and Children

Lynn's son, David Dohrenwend, died when he was eight and a half years old. He had been born with one upper heart chamber and only one pump. "The other pump had never developed and the upper chamber had a hole in it," Lynn states. "Open-heart surgery was performed on him when he was seven months old. The operation was so serious that the doctors considered it a miracle that there was no further damage to his heart. They also said he was no longer in the hands of the medical profession. Those words stuck with me," Lynn remembers, "and I decided that David, the youngest of my eight children, was going to live at home with us. He was not going to live under rigid and protective circumstances. We were not going to try to prolong his life in isolation from the rest of the world."

Lynn explained to her other children that their brother had "a very special heart." She describes the time when David's siblings learned of his illness. "I told my children that it was thought David would not be with us long, but that during whatever time was left to him, he was going to have a normal life. When David came home, I don't think the other children totally understood the problem. Their youngest sister had been born with some brain damage, so they had been used to that. However, I don't know how the news about David hit them. We tended to live a normal life, and as David grew up he got into trouble and he earned spankings just like the other children. His older brothers and sisters had to scold him many times, but he scolded them too. During the remaining years of his short life, there were examinations and hospitals, with many doctors looking at him, constantly checking him. They used him almost as a teaching model because his external physical body never indicated what was on the inside. Through it all, he was a picture of perfect health."

About two months before David died, Lynn's instinct told her his time had come. "A couple of months before David made the actual transition, I was sitting at the kitchen table thinking about my job," Lynn reflects. "I was then working for the governor in the field of energy and on that day I had gone through some kind of yuck situation in the office. I broke into tears. I was crying when David came in, put his arms around me, and said, 'Are you crying because you know I'm going to die?' 'No, honey,' I replied, 'I'm crying because of people's inhumanity to one another.' But it was typical of David to want to comfort and he understood that I knew he was dying. My oldest daughter, Carolyn, is also extremely intuitive and always has been. She was away at college when she began to feel that David was going to die. She became panicky and hysterical. So she came home from college for a while and visited. She was close by enough to do that."

All of Lynn's children took their mother's view: "Hey, this is the way it is. Each day is a gift of life. Each day is precious and if he's with us, he's with us and if he isn't, he isn't. That's the way it is when you've been told, 'Take this child home. He can't live.' When David kept thriving and thriving, we learned to live with it in a different way. You appreciate the fact that the child is never ill, even though the doctors said he would be ill; he never got ill. He enjoyed phenomenal health. They said his energy would be low and that he would sleep a lot. Well, that was exactly the opposite of what happened! He had so much energy, I would have to stop him and say, 'Your mother needs to sit down; sit down and relax!' That was David."

Lynn tells of a standing family joke about shoes. "Our home sits on two acres of woods and someday when the ground cover's all gone, a storehouse of shoes will be discovered on the place. David always had a thing about shoes. He had a habit of coming home with only one shoe and saying, 'It walked away.' We'd ask, 'Where's the other one?' And he'd answer, 'I don't know. It left.' And we would say, 'Go back and find it.' He would retort, 'But it walked away.' 'You just go back and walk until you find it.' Although we knew we had a serious situation with David's health, we tried to find humor in everything he did, and to let him lead a normal life for as long as he could." David went to school and, like the rest of the children, he had no restrictions. He went swimming. He would do things like jumping off trees. He got in the car once and backed it into a tree. "In other words," says Lynn, "he had no taboos."

In November, David reentered the Mayo hospital in Rochester, Minnesota. "We did all the Christmas shopping together while he was up there for tests and shipped everybody's gifts back to Indianapolis where we lived. Prior to having surgery, David wanted to buy Christmas gifts for his brothers and sisters. And he did. In the process, he wanted to buy himself a new shirt and trousers. It seemed like a logical thing that he did. Those things he had picked out for himself were the ones in which he was buried. The kids were prepared and knew that this was serious and that he might not pull through. There were many masses and prayers going on simultaneously."

Lynn relates what happened after David's surgery. "The operation was performed on the twenty-third of November and he died on the twenty-fourth. The significance of its being Thanksgiving Day is I think, pretty remarkable. After the surgery, the doctors insisted, 'We're still hoping for a miracle.' I told them, 'We've had a miracle'—meaning that we'd had David for a much longer period than they'd expected. I was feeling at peace with the idea that if he didn't continue, at least the time we'd had with him was a gift. I was surprised at the medical profession for not recognizing that and not being comfortable that I could accept it. They said, 'We're going to try some very experimental things,' but they added, 'You need to get some sleep. Go back to your hotel for a while.' So I did, but about 5 A.M. I woke up and called the hospital immediately. I was told, 'Yes, he's beginning to slip. You had better get back here.' His body had started to deteriorate and the doctors said they didn't expect him to live. I don't know how to explain it, but there was a calmness about me, for I didn't believe that David was meant to continue."

Lynn asked that a priest be summoned to perform the last rites. "I also asked that someone call his father who was staying in another hotel. Then I got up and went to the hospital. David was comatose. He had never opened his eyes after surgery. He was lying on his back with his hands open just like a big airplane, a big bird with this whole wingspan. I put my finger in his right hand and he grabbed it. I said to the nurse, 'Get some doctors. He's moving, he's functioning!' But she said, 'Oh, no. That's just an involuntary movement.' But it was a different kind of squeeze and it was a continuing one. Tears started to come out of his eyes and down his cheek. We started to say good-bye with each other in a telepathic way. It was as if we were talking to each other. I had my eyes open and although his eyes were closed, I was hearing his voice on an inner level. We were saying good-bye and there was no need to hold him back. And while my hand was in his, it was as if he was pulling me down a tunnel. He was racing, he wasn't even walking. He was running down this dark tunnel, all the while pulling me. I left my eyes open while I was experiencing this. All of a sudden there was an incredible light. There was not a feeling of fear, but one, really, of ecstasy. It was a good feeling, not a bad feeling. And as he went toward the Light, he was happy and joyous. And then there appeared a sort of abstract bridge with, on one side, a greeting party of abstract faces without bodies, as such. But they were so bathed in light as to be like transparencies, as if you were seeing them through veils, and David went to them through the light. At that moment I was back out of the tunnel, and my 'experience' had lasted only seconds. But I knew it had been given to me for some reason. Within the next ten years I learned that I'd had a cross-over experience which later led to 'channeling,' a term used for this type of spiritual experience. I feel it all ties in with human potential and that it has a lot to do with self-esteem. I call it spiritual wisdom and that's how I see it, as very normal and natural."

"When I was told it was doubtful that David would survive the day, I called the kids. The children made a decision—to wait for Thanksgiving dinner. My mother had flown out from New York to be with them, but they wanted me home for Thanksgiving. I decided after David's passing that I would honor my children's wishes, and I flew back to Indianapolis that night to be with them. When I arrived home, I learned that several priests who were good friends had been with the kids for the day. There were not a lot of tears, just a sense of appreciation, a giving of thanks for the time he was with us. One of the priests, who had been part of the celebration for David's first communion at our home, asked each of us to write a letter to David or to God about what David meant to us, and sent us off by ourselves to write."

The following are excerpts from some of the letters written by David's sisters and brothers—Carolyn, Cathy, Linda, Jim, Mark, Michael, and Lisa:

"David, you're a very special person. You touched so many people with your enthusiasm. . . . Remember our trips to the library, going swimming, the airport, bike riding—I really did have an advantage, my legs are longer (giggle, giggle, tee-hee). You really shared so much with so many. I'm sure God sees how proud and thankful we are."

"Do you remember the silly Pink Panther cartoon, the one where he bounces the man's head and the eye follows him? I think it's one of the funniest things we shared. Making faces at people in other cars—the old Raspberry trick. Spending the night outside in a tent in the backyard. Playing games of silence, games with closed eyes and drawing. Games we played ever since you were little—dropping the diaper pins, stealing the blue blanket, and oh so many things. I really love you. Because of that I can accept your dying. I'm one to believe strongly that there is a reason for everything . . ."

"I remember sitting in the car with the CB, following the creek in back of Dad's apartment, going to the top of Monument Circle, teaching you to do back-flips off the furniture, walking a secret path along White River, and watching firecrackers. I really cared for you and I am extremely thankful for the time you shared with us. I will always miss you so please visit me occasionally. Maybe we will still make it to the Cincy Zoo or square-dancing, or the thousands of things we have yet to do."

"All those places we used to go together, I'll have to now go alone. I'm going to miss holding your hand in the park, feeling you tug at my purse when the elephant swung his trunk too close, holding on tight to you when the carousel song you picked turns out to be a jumper. Even more, I'll miss afternoon talks with you sitting on my lap in the rocking chair and laughing so hard at times that we both would fall out. I'll miss having you run up and hug me when I come home. But most of all, I'll miss feeling your warm hand on my shoulder and hearing you say, 'Don't worry. It's all right.' "

"Dave knew what was going on when others didn't have the foggiest idea. Although eight, he lived a full life by talking his way out of almost anything, and by talking people into things he wanted to do. Even if he didn't get his way, he had fun trying. Above all, he brought happiness to all he knew.

"God, thank you for sharing David with us. We are richer in this life for having experienced your love through your child and our brother, David. David was one of your greatest expressions of love. David was joy. David brought laughter— and we eagerly await the day of rejoicing when we will join him in laughter, sharing with you the beauty of his soul and his presence."

"God, I guess I really don't have to write a letter to you. You know I loved him and that was all that mattered. You know I still love him . . . What did I love best about him? Well, nothing was distinctive about him because everything about him was special, so very special! What did I love best about him? His soul. I love David's soul, whether it was the part of his soul that made him laugh or made him cry or whether it was the part that made him play or made him fight. Oh, and by the way, I loved the way he could touch people's lives."

The entire family returned to Carmel for the funeral. "We had left David's body at Mayo's. I had given them permission to do some further medical examinations. When we arrived at the funeral home, I asked that the shoes be left off of David's feet. If you remember earlier we told you how David didn't like his shoes on. When we looked at that body in the casket, there was no semblance of the child we had lost. The hair was neat and he never had a neat head of hair even when he came out of a barber shop. We knew it was the physical body, but it just didn't bear any resemblance and it was a horrible shock. The kids began to say, 'That's not David.' I prayed for words to help them understand. And I said, 'Yes, it is. What you're looking at is the shell. Without the soul there is no life. The life you knew and the joy and the beauty you knew were the soul of David. When the soul is not there—it's just an empty shell.'

"We all agreed that David's hair looked impossible. He looked like a slicked-down dude and he *never* would look like that. So, we all leaned over the casket and messed up his hair. And we rumpled his clothes a little bit. We made him look like David as best we could. Our final touch was to concede that David would not have wished to wear shoes—and so we made sure he wasn't. It was not that they were participating in making David appear as we wished him to appear, but as they remembered him. I think that was really a major point for all of us."

At Christmastime, one of David's sisters made a marker for his grave. Lynn explains: "I remember Christmas was a very quiet one that year and we visited the graveside for a while. Because of financial limitations (funds were tied up and money was unavailable to us), it was an unmarked grave. One of my daughters, Linda, took a log, to make a marker for his grave. She put on the marker what I thought was the most beautiful thing that could have been said. She wrote: "When you were born on June 6, 1969, you cried and we smiled. And when you died on November 24, 1977, you smiled and we cried.' "

Chapter Eighteen

Holly Shaw

Holly Shaw is the equivalent of a tooth fairy to many bereaved siblings who find routes to survival through the help she offers them.

Holly, a bereaved parent, is also Nursing coordinator of the Division of Adolescent Medicine at the Schneider Children's Hospital of the Long Island Jewish Medical Center. There, a variety of health care services are provided to young people, ages twelve to twenty-one. As part of the program, the Center also participates in an outreach and community educational and prevention service. Holly explains how and why the program for loss and bereavement began:

"The project started in an effort to assist high schools that were experiencing sudden deaths among teenage students, the kind of tragedy, for example, that occurs when four kids are killed in a car accident. What we do here at the Center in response to such situations is to go to the schools and work with the teachers and administrators with a view to guiding them, and through them their students, in methods of coping with life- and health-threatening situations. We help to identify students who are at risk.

"However," Holly clarifies, "when we say 'students at risk,' we are talking about young people in several categories. For example, an adolescent who experiences a loss by death faces a crisis that must be added to the crisis he or she is already burdened with, for all teenagers go through the very real crisis of leaving childhood behind and learning to become men and women. To have another crisis imposed on top of that may present teenagers with burdens too heavy to handle."

Holly tells how the program helps to identify those teenagers who are heading for trouble. "Adolescence itself is a high-risk time and when teenagers come up against too heavy a burden, they may easily fall prey to such other problems as substance abuse, suicide, depression, vandalism, truancy, sexual promiscuity, and other forms of high-risk behavior. Experience has taught us that teenagers often become victims of such problems after the loss of a sibling. Sometimes we'll see a good kid with a serious problem, but no one will know what has caused it. However, the difficulty may be traced back to a real loss, one that is frequently the death of a sibling. The death of a brother or sister is a catastrophic event for any child, but it can be especially disastrous for a teenager.

The kinds of difficulties experienced by teenagers are described by Holly: "When a death has caused the crisis, we often find two contributing problems. Many times parents and other family members seem to forget about the teenager, doing one of two things. They often treat the adolescent like a young child and do not include him or her in any adult conversations or decisions, treating him as though he's a baby who can't handle anything. That's devastating for a teenager. It makes him feel left out of the experience, injures his self-esteem, and deprives him of the opportunity to participate in the family crisis in a way that will promote his personal growth.

"The other thing that families do, which remains with these kids as a regret for the rest of their lives, is to force the child to behave and respond as an adult. That can leave long-term scars." Holly describes the type of comments that put teens in such a position: "People will say to a teenager, 'You have to be strong for your parents.' 'You're the man of the family now.' 'You have to take care of your mother.' They put the teenager in the position of having to parent the parents. Teenagers are adolescents, not adults, and such statements place great stress on them, sometimes more than they can handle. Holly states that teens mourn differently than do adults, yet they proceed through a series of stages similar to those that grieving adults experience. "There are four distinct processes most teens will pass through. The first can be described as a feeling of numbness at the time of the loss, followed by a period when the child is actively yearning for the reappearance of the lost person or feeling. The third phase is one of despair and disorganization. The fourth and final stage is one that is a road back, beginning to pull life together, reorganized behavior, and an ability to function in the real world. Young people should be made aware of the feelings they'll be dealing with and the stages they'll pass through on that road to accepting the loss."

One of the important things people must realize, Holly believes, is that teens need to be helped to understand what is a normal grief reaction. "The youngster will need time to attempt to rest and relax, along with a bit of pampering and permission to act a little "babyish." But teens need to understand that normal reactions to grief can include feelings of great sadness, guilt, self-reproach, loneliness, and helplessness. Often physical symptoms will appear—a sense of tightness in the chest or throat, a feeling of great fatigue, and sometimes just a generalized feeling of disorientation and of being preoccupied. Youngsters should be helped to understand that, although these symptoms are frightening, they are almost always temporary." Holly stresses that kids who aren't made aware that these are normal reactions often compound their grief by assuming they are losing their minds. "They conclude, by themselves, 'I must be crazy to feel like this.' Children should be made aware that these feelings don't mean they are going crazy. They need to know that it's the body's way of becoming used to the fact that their sibling is gone, and to understand that feelings will pass. It's tough for teens, but those who mourn properly can reap the benefits for the rest of their lives."

Holly urges that parents, when conveying details about a death to a teenager, be honest and specific. "Teenagers are in a transitional period between childhood and adulthood. They have to behave and be responded to in that manner. That means they should have full knowledge of what's going on. Someone should present them with as much information as they can about what has happened, if it were an accident, if it was an illness, even if it was something awful. Remember, they're going to be exposed to those facts in a distorted way through the newspapers or possible police investigations. Parents aren't doing kids a favor by protecting them from the truth. The more they know and the more lovingly it is presented to them, the better they're going to be able to deal with it."

The issue of a teenager's participation in the funeral is one of concern to Holly. "Some families feel that anybody below the age of eighteen should not be permitted to go to a funeral. However, for many children as well as teenagers, it's meaningful for them to attend such a service. Something positive may happen to a youngster who is with people who share his feeling of grief, and who sees that adults can have these feelings and can handle them in a healthy, constructive way. So teenagers who are left out of that experience are the ones who might be much more likely to get involved in drugs, because they haven't seen how mature people handle these feelings.

"If you lock teenagers away," Holly continues, "or send them off to relatives, they aren't going to be able to master their feelings. They're not going to be exposed to adult behavior to help them cope with a crisis. A teenager usually wants to be at a funeral and feels that it's important to go. However, such a child should be there as a member of the family to share the family's experience and *should not* be there to take care of a despondent mother or father or grandparent. Very often, family, neighbors, and relatives forget this." On the other hand, Holly cautions, "Some teenagers might not want to go to the funeral and should not be forced to participate. Parents should talk to them and say, 'We're going through this family problem together. Let us know how you want to be included and what is best for you.' I realize full well how much parents are hurting after the death of a child, but the surviving child's needs must not be shoved aside. We can't always do what the teenager wants us to do. But we can at least give them the message that we are considering what the teenager would like and allowing them to express their opinions."

As stated earlier, Holly stresses that teenagers don't

grieve as adults do. She describes some of the differences: "Often teenagers are not going to feel comfortable about their own feelings. A lot is happening to them anyway. After a funeral and during the bereavement period, the grief might not be with them at all times. They might put it out of their minds for some time. They might cry alone in the bedroom, but they might be laughing and fooling around with their friends. We need to make sure we don't make judgments about that kind of behavior. It doesn't mean they don't care. Sometimes family members, teachers, even classmates say, 'Oh, what a cold, hard kid. Look at him having such a good time.' But, that doesn't mean the kid doesn't care; it just means that is the way he or she is handling grief."

Holly bemoans the fact that in many cases nobody talks about the death to the teenager. "What happens most frequently is that no one wants to talk to the teenager about what's happened to the brother or sister who has died. Other kids are afraid to bring it up because they don't know what to say, and the teenagers themselves don't know how to talk about it. Recently, I spoke with a fifteen-year-old brother of a ten-year-old who had died. The fifteen-year-old had made a suicide attempt because of his depressing feelings, and because he had no one to talk to. He longed to discuss the death of his sibling with his friends, but no one ever mentioned it to him. He felt that meant they either weren't interested or couldn't handle it and he didn't know how to bring it up to them. But it was painful for him because his sad, depressed feelings were constantly with him. He just couldn't ignore them. He actually made an attempt on his life and wrote a note talking about the kind of pressure that he felt, about not being able to talk about this with other kids. It's something we see all the time; other kids avoid the adolescent griever. They may not avoid the kid entirely, but will avoid discussing what happened. This can put an extraordinary amount of pressure on the teenager."

A word of caution is given to those in the educational field. "Very often in school," Holly asserts, "the teachers and the guidance people think they're doing the best thing when they say to the kid, 'If ever you need to talk, just come into my office and let me know.' That's a generous offer; however, most teenagers will not respond to it. So the teacher or the guidance person thinks the kid is doing fine, but the kid *isn't* doing fine. All it means is that the kid doesn't know how to take the first step—how to go into an office and talk about it because he or she can't think of what to say. You know, teenagers think that they have to know what to say before they go to talk to someone."

As a psychiatric nurse, Holly offers suggestions to teachers and guidance counselors about what to say and how to reach out to the teenager: "Just say, 'I know what happened. I understand that this must be a very difficult time for you and I'd like to help you. I'd like to offer you my support. I'd like you to know that I care about what happens and I'd like to help you in any way that I can.' This should be put in words and an effort should be made to do more than just wait for the kids to show up at the office. It's not inappropriate to schedule an appointment with the kid, say with a guidance person, for instance. The kid may say, 'Well, there's nothing wrong with me. I'm not crazy, I'm fine.' The response to that could be, 'Glad to hear it, but I want to make sure. Something very painful has happened in your life and I want to be certain you feel that we're around and supporting you. I want to make sure that you're going to be all right, so I want to see you every week (or every month, or whatever time is possible) to give us a chance to talk about it or maybe to talk about something else. But we know this can have a profound effect on your life and your well-being, and we want to make sure you're going to be all right.'" Holly stresses that the guidance person "should be informed and have the kind of educational resources to know something about what's likely to happen to this teenager, or what the grief process or post-traumatic stress syndrome is like so it can be recognized in case the child does demonstrate such types of behavior in school."

Teenagers are at a point in their lives at which they question a great deal, Holly states. "They're beginning to develop philosophical kinds of questions and inner, intrapsychic discussions. Many of them have terrible feelings of survivor guilt—why did I survive and my sibling did not? That may happen in the case of an illness, accident, or anything else. The teenager might think, 'Why didn't it happen to me?' While some of this is survivor guilt, some of it is simply trying to make sense of that experience and trying to integrate it somehow into their life scheme. In asking 'Why wasn't it me?' It's not always an answer they are seeking—often it's just an effort to find some rhyme or reason to an event that makes no sense. But that may take some time, for the teenager has to come to terms with the fact that sometimes things happen that make no sense, that are totally unjust and unfair, and we don't always know why.

"This is an area that can lead to anxieties on the part of teenagers, however, wondering if it can happen to them. Sometimes we see that they'll almost tempt fate to see if it is going to be them. They will take exceptional risks. Part of their developmental process is risk taking and learning by experience. And one of the reasons why this is so devastating to a teenager is that it comes at a time when they really believe they're invulnerable—that nothing bad can happen to me or my family. Then to learn that something bad *can* happen is a shocking awakening to reality. So the teenager may cope with that shock by almost tempting fate, taking more chances and living more dangerously, or by saying, 'Nothing matters anymore. If this could happen, then going by the rules doesn't count. I can do anything I want.' But very often kids who are angry and guilty believe they don't have a right to go on living because their sibling has died. Part of the counseling that's very important in helping teenagers restore themselves to health is the emphasis on the fact that they are entitled to have a life, to experience joy and pleasure, and that they can go on."

To help convey that sense of worth, Holly has made a video tape about what the healing process was like for sixteen-year-old Wanda Carrion. Wanda's seventeen-year-old brother, Tony, was killed in the fire at New Jersey's Great Adventure amusement park, which took place in the Haunted House. Wanda, her brother, and other teenagers were on a class trip;

her brother and four other children were killed. Holly says, "All the survivors developed a feeling of 'what happens to me now? How can I go on and enjoy myself when my brother is dead?' They put their life on hold."

Holly describes Wanda's grief: "The video is based on Wanda's struggle to come to terms with the pain of her brother's death. It is a dramatic portrayal of her feelings, what things were like for her before her brother's death and how things changed afterward. Following her brother's death, Wanda wasn't able to return to school. She was withdrawn, sullen, and lonely, and when she finally did return to school, she would burst into tears in the hall. Her dancing teacher said she stopped dancing. Dressed in black from head to foot, she went to the cemetery almost every day to sit by the grave of her brother." Holly explains more of the content of the video: "In the film, there is a meeting with the principal, assistant principal of guidance, and the teacher to explain the impact of the tragedy at the school, how the school (Franklin K. Lane High School in Brooklyn) reacted to the deaths and the change they saw in Wanda after her brother's death. Later, Wanda explains that she didn't know how to talk about her pain."

Holly continues, "In the time we spent together, our many conversations both at school and during home visits, we formed a bond of trust and friendship. She wanted others to understand her pain. She said, 'My parents lost their only son, but I lost my only brother.' Wanda was able to develop the ability to talk about her feelings and her loss. In the film, she tells how important it was for her to have someone who listened when she was down, depressed, feeling hopeless, that it meant a lot to have 'someone who was there for me.'"

A second surviving sibling Holly has worked with is Nelson Ruiz, nineteen, who was a Marine when his sixteen-year-old brother, Lenny, died in the Great Adventure fire. Nelson and Wanda were friends. When he came home on leave and saw the progress Wanda had made, he went to Holly and said, "Can you help me the way you helped Wanda." Holly tells of Nelson's pain: "Although the fire happened over two years ago, Nelson is just now beginning to deal with it. He had a very close relationship with his brother. To me, Lenny was something very important in my life. He was the only one next to my mother who I could go to and tell him how I feel and what I was going through. And even though he was three years younger, he'd always try to help me as much as he could."

Nelson had learned about his brother's death shortly after he entered boot camp. "The chaplain came to me and said he needed to talk to me alone. In the beginning, I was in shock because he told me my younger brother had been in an accident. Then he started giving me the details of the accident. He asked, 'Do you have a brother named Lenny?' I said, 'Yes.' Next he told me, 'Well he went on a Great Adventure trip in New Jersey.' And I said, 'Yes. I gave him the money for that.' Finally he said, 'Well, your brother died in a fire in the Haunted House there along with several other people.' At the time he told me about Lenny, I had just returned from the training grounds. I was tired and couldn't comprehend what was happening. I just didn't realize what was happening to me."

The chaplain was with me a long time, about an hour or so. Afterwards, he took me downstairs to his private office and made me call home. I talked to my sister. She told me it was true, that my brother had passed away. I was feeling such pain—something I had never experienced in my life. I thought, 'Why did he die?' From that moment, nothing was the same for me. Before I took the plane home, the staff sergeant talked with me. He told me I had to be strong and tough. I didn't feel that way at all. I couldn't seem to pull myself together. However, on the plane, I thought, 'At some point I have to be strong, not just for myself but for my mother and father.' But I felt confused and didn't know how to act."

"Nelson recalled, "I had to take care of my parents and my younger sisters for such a long time and I had no one to talk to. I had to protect my parents from hearing more about the fire." When he went back to the Marines, nobody wanted to hear about his own personal sorrow. There was no way for him to talk about it. He commented, "You know, I thought that being in the Marines and going to another country would help me forget. But I now realize that I carry those feelings inside me wherever I go. And the pain is sometimes more than I can bear."

Holly Shaw recognized that Nelson Ruiz (and hundreds of other surviving siblings) had no one to talk to about his grief, his personal sorrow after the death of his brother. As a result, she has helped many teenagers who feel alienated and isolated from others, and who, when something so painful as this happens to them, don't know how to share that pain with others. Holly also recognizes that when siblings do try to express their pain to someone, the response can be just as devastating as the pain. "Such statements as, 'Well, it's just your brother. Think how your parents felt in losing a child. That's much worse,' or 'You should be over that by now. After all, your brother died three months ago,' have negative and destructive effects on a sibling. These thoughtless comments ignore the feelings of the sibling. Many kids who end up completing a suicide might not have necessarily wanted to die, but they wanted to stop the pain. They may have died accidentally or without realizing that dead is dead and that they're going to be dead for a long time. They just think of a way to stop the pain that seems for them, at the moment, endless."

Talking to the right person is the key to recovering. The most basic need of a surviving sibling is to have someone nearby to listen, to share in the pain, and to care, whether it be a close friend, a relative, a co-worker, a member of the clergy, the family doctor, a counselor, or a therapist. For Wanda and Nelson, it was the caring nurse, Holly Shaw.

Chapter Nineteen

Messages of Hope

Surviving siblings are helped when they take steps to give their lives purpose and meaning. In Harold Arlen's and Johnny Mercer's classic song, "Accentuate the Positive and Eliminate the Negative," we are given the key to recovering. Negative thoughts don't help—they only destroy. By pushing them aside and allowing positive thoughts to take over, we can make life worthwhile.

Because each individual is different from all others, so are their reactions to anger, fear, and guilt. Each of us deals with these emotions in our own way. In this chapter we will hear from many of the surviving brothers and sisters who enlighten us by sharing their experiences. They now offer their words of encouragement and hope to others who must travel the path of bereavement.

Madeline Toomey Pflaumbaum explains that although time doesn't cure, it eases the pain. "Although this may sound trite, time really does help. It takes that stabbing pain away, even if only for a short while. When you do have good days, don't feel guilty. Go with those feelings because, in the beginning, good days may be few and far between. When you are feeling bad, let yourself mourn, because that's all right. We have to do that just to get through our grief. Take one day, one step at a time.

"At first," Madeleine advises, "all you have to do is get yourself out of bed and propel yourself forward. Just live for that moment. The most important thing to remember is that it's okay to express your grief. Pay no attention to anybody who says (which has happened to me) 'All right, it's been six months. You should be over this now.' There is a proper place for your memory of that loved one. If you want to think about that person for a whole day, go ahead and think about that person for a whole day. And in so doing, remember that tomorrow you're going to have a better day." Madeleine has become president of the Long Island chapter of M.A.D.D. (Mothers Against Drunk Drivers) and apart from her efforts with that group, spends a good deal of her time sharing with bereaved siblings newly come to grief.

Another surviving sister who believes strongly that people underestimate time's healing power is Susan Keats. Eight months after her sister's death, she had this to say: "I definitely think I'm getting better and attribute my growing recovery to time. Yes, of course I still think about it, and I still haven't accepted everything. It's just that I have never stopped my life. I never sat down and said, 'This is horrible, how can I go on?' I've always been busy and I've kept that way. I've always been able to talk with my family, but it's time that is the main healing factor."

Susan believes healing depends on which stage of recovering you have reached at the moment. "We have discovered that it comes over you in waves, and you can feel fine one moment and a few moments later you can be crying again. But strangely enough, you're never constantly crying, and this, I think, may be your body's way of getting you through your loss. If you were continuously crying, you would never be able to pick yourself up off the floor.

"In time we realized that we must allow people to deal with things in a natural way instead of inflicting on the sorrowing the way we feel about things at that moment, in the belief that they should react the same way we do. Each of us grieved in our own separate way, and we learned a great deal about ourselves, we really did. What we all tried to do was to take an adverse situation and learn something positive from it.

I think we were able to discover a few good things about ourselves, and about other people, and about what we wanted to do with the rest of our lives."

Jay Goldstein has advice for other siblings who suffer from grief and guilt: "It's better to talk about your feelings and get them out into the open. If there are others who have suffered a similar loss, with whom you can talk, it's helpful to do so, because you learn from them that you're not alone and that others feel just as you do." Jay was able to convey some of his feelings in a talk that he gave at Smithtown High School West. There, Mrs. Barbara Okst teaches a course entitled, "Death: A Fact of Life." The course is so popular with teenagers that there is a waiting list of students to get into the class. Mrs. Okst has brought in dynamic speakers who present views on death from all standpoints. She also allows ample time for questions from the students.

Representing the siblings group for the Long Island chapter of The Compassionate Friends, Jay spoke to the class. He was able to tell his peers how he felt when his brother died. He spoke about his guilt feelings and his learning to cope with them. "I wasn't able to talk too much to my parents or anyone else, but at the siblings group, I could open up and talk because I knew the others there would understand."

Several years after giving these lectures, Jay found the need to lecture no longer existed. "Things are different now and I haven't had to give lectures for a long time. It's been five and a half years and the emotions are there, but they're not as predominant as they were. In addition, I think that being away at school really helped me a lot. Just hang in there, I'd say, for the rough days will pass. You may not think so, but they will. Each day gives you more time, and time is what heals. I think there will always be a bad day now and then, but that's normal."

Karen Schlesier Eisen gives us a warm message of hope in a touching story about two beautiful people who met after a time when Karen thought she would never get to know anyone who would understand how much her brother meant to her. After her divorce, Karen tells of happier days that followed:

"Jonathan and I met through a friend and then began to see more of each other. We were introduced in November and decided to get married the next summer. His grandmother had just died and we were with relatives on Long Island. So we drove another hour and went to the cemetery where my brother, Billy, was buried. Jonathan was very willing to go and was very calm about the whole thing, but I didn't really know what was going to happen when we got there. He had never met my brother and I was apprehensive and thought perhaps I would feel strange about him being there. After all, my former visits with Billy had always been the two of us alone."

Karen describes the poignant scene that took place. "When we got to Billy's grave, I just stood there. Jonathan introduced himself. 'Hi, Billy. My name is Jonathan and I'm going to marry your sister. I just wanted you to know that I will take care of her, and that I love her.' It was very natural and comfortable and as if he were really speaking to a person. It was really touching that he was trying to communicate with my brother in some way. I cried because I felt it was very thoughtful of him to recognize Billy in that way."

Karen also shares with us the soul-searching she did after her brother's death. "I've spent a lot of time looking within myself—searching for the strength to somehow deal with Billy's death. I'm the oldest. Billy always wanted to be my older brother. It's been quite a bumpy road my mind has wandered down, one filled with extreme anger, panic, guilt, and so very much love—all of them coming at me at once. My mind has been crowded with details. It amazes me that I've been able to make rational, important decisions along the way. I don't cry very much anymore. Not on the outside anyway. But I do cry on the inside when I hear a sad song—or a happy song. Or if I see a boy my brother's age or do something we did together.

"People ask me if I'm over 'this'—if I'm all right now. They simply don't understand that 'this' never goes away. Sometimes I will find myself having a really rough day and I may not even know the reason why. Jonathan is very understanding, though. He will just say, 'Are you having a Billy day?' And then he will leave me alone for a while. I just wish Jonathan had come along a little sooner, but I'm very happy he's here now. I have learned so much from Billy since his death and in reflecting on how he shared his life with us and loved us so unconditionally. And in addition to Jonathan, I've taken two other very special people deep within my heart—my mom and dad. I think I've really grown up, Billy. Thank you."

Allison Heitner shares with us the day when she knew she was on the road to recovering: "I realized I had started to recover from my sister's death when one day I said to myself, 'Eventually I am going to die. One day I will see my sister again. Why rush it? I have been put on earth to live and have children. After I do die, there will be all eternity to be with Leslie.' After she died, I was going downhill at a rapid pace. I didn't realize it, but I was in a constant depression. I could never imagine at that time in my life that things could change and get better."

It was at that point in her life that Allison left New York and went to California with a girlfriend. "I needed a change of scenery. As soon as we arrived, I got a lot of job offers. However, I wanted to start my own business. I began making sequined sweatshirts and hired a rep to help sell them to stores. Although I was doing a lot of business, I still remained both lonely and depressed. All I was doing was sitting in my apartment, making those shirts. My girlfriend suggested that I go out and get a job that would take me out into the world. She had seen a job in the paper for a receptionist in a color animation studio, and she knew that I had two degrees in art.

"Although the thought of working as a receptionist again didn't thrill me, I knew myself and said, 'Once I get into that job, and get my foot in the door, I'm going to go for the top.'" After three months, Allison was promoted into the art department. "Within a short time, I became the head of the department and I love what I'm doing. We produce animated cartoons and movies and I swell with pride whenever I see my credits. They say, 'Color Design by Allison Heitner.' My position in the TV business is called a color key artist. I have already told my company that I'm interested in becoming the first female animation director. They're behind me and even pay for my courses in animation design."

Today, some ten years after her sister's death, Allison has these thoughts to convey to other siblings: "I began the road to recovery about four years after Leslie's death. Now I am a healthy, functioning, normal individual. I know I will never forget or forgive her death. At times, I still get angry at the hospital. I would still like the real story to be told. But I don't even think about dying anymore. Believe me, I want to live and I'm making every effort to make a good life for myself." Allison urges other surviving siblings to give themselves time to deal with their grief and to understand that other sisters and brothers have walked in their shoes and have made it. "If I can make it, you can, too. You deserve a good life, just as I do."

In the following messages of hope, three surviving sisters found they were helped by thinking back to happy times before their personal tragedy.

Leslie Boden says that the strength she and her brother and her parents have had through "all of this" is being able to cry together and laugh together. "We've been able to talk about him and to remember him walking around, bouncing through the door with his backpack on, or whatever. It is important to have these little moments and not feel that any mention of his name is charged."

Betty Tucker agrees with the above philosophy. "To someone who has suffered the loss of a brother or sister, it's essential to just try to remember all the good things and the happy times. That's what I tried to do, to recall the pleasant memories. Put pictures around, *because the important thing is not that our brothers or sisters died, but that they lived.* That's it exactly."

During the years after her brother died, Froma Lippmann often remembered the laughter they had shared. Those memories were generated by small happenings. "I looked forward to the season for eating tangerines because they had been Charles' favorite fruit. I reveled in the fact that our son, his uncle's namesake, was a sports fan par excellence, just as my brother had been." Froma remembers pet phrases of her brother and the fact that the surgeon who performed her appendectomy would not permit Charles to visit her in the hospital for fear his jokes would cause her to laugh so much that the stitches would rupture.

Upon reflecting, Froma recalls that Charles thought of his kid sister as a friend and looked out for her safety and interest whether she was being teased by the kids playing street hockey or invited out on dates by one of his fraternity brothers. Today, Froma values the continuing closeness of Charles' widow, who married his best friend sixteen months after his death and "whose family became family to ours."

Many surviving siblings have found that the insight of a grief counselor or going to siblings' meetings have helped them after their loss. Billy Pfister found another source of understanding and compassion in a clergyman. "Although you can go to your family to help ease the pain, everyone is grieving and so that's not always easy. The first person who really helped me was a priest who was somewhat like a chaplain at my high school. It was funny because all through high school I had never really had any relationship with him. I'd say hello to him when I saw him and that was it. Suddenly, I just became friendly with him. When I had my bad days, I'd go to see him. I'd be in school and when I was down, I'd go visit him and sit and talk. He would talk to me like a friend. I wasn't as if he were a priest. He totally dropped the priest-presence. It wasn't there when I spoke to him. I felt the warm friendship he was extending to me, and he helped me a lot."

Dan Saulisberry offers a brief, but inspiring, message of hope: "Although I can do little to ease someone else's grief, I can relate to it. And I can tell them that life does go on, something positive always comes out of negative, and that time is a good, good friend. In the words of the psalmist, 'Weeping may endure for a night, but joy cometh in the morning.'"

Chuck Akerland was able to find a source of inspiration in his high school teacher. "There were a couple of things that kept me going, and I hope maybe I can do that for other people. I was hurting very much. I had lost my only sibling and was trying to find some way to get my life back on an even keel. In high school, I had a teacher who, to me, just seemed to be completely content with life. I thought, 'That's the way I want to be. I don't want to live the rest of my life like this. I want to be like him—honestly, truly content.

"I kept striving for that. I was afraid to grow up with my parents who were so unhappy because I thought I'd wind up unhappy, too. But here I saw a person who could be content, so I figured it might be possible for me to be that way. I kept holding onto that concept—that if he could be content, if there was *one person* out there who could be content like that, then goddamn it, I could be content too, and I kept going for that. By degrees, I am becoming content—and I mean truly. Yes, I miss Trey. I will always miss him, just as you will never forget your brother or sister. And sadness or confusion will be there at times, but you don't have to feel guilty if you have good times, happy times that a normal kid should have and enjoy."

Chuck also explains how seeking help at a siblings group was of benefit to him. "I remember when I first went in. I said to myself, 'You know, I think it's too late. Here I am, twenty-six years old. College has passed me by and high school years have passed me by, and they weren't pleasant for me. But it's *never* too late, even sixteen years after my brother committed suicide.' At the meetings of The Compassionate Friends and later at Survivors of Suicide meetings, they had said that it's never too late—and really, it isn't. Yes, it's too late to go back to college and be able to say, 'Those were the best times of my life.' In that sense, yes, it is too late. But as long as you're alive, life is worth living. *Life is for living and death is for dying—it's really as simple as that.* If you want to be dead, die. If you want to be alive, live. So, in a sense attending the siblings' group and the parents' meetings provided a moving-through process. It was very important for me and my future."

Ellen Spector says the thing that aided her was communication—talking about her loss to her friends. "I had many people around, and that was good for me. At the beginning, nothing helps. The reality may not hit you for a while. It didn't really hit me until I went back to school and was away from home. I was close to my roommate, and the only thing that gave me any relief was talking. I like to remember how, when we were little, my brother used to watch me when our parents went out. He took care of me and played games with me. He had a very good personality, and we did a lot of things together, such as traveling. When he came home from college, we saw a show together. Then I found that he had really gotten interested in music—the words, the lyrics, everything. It's helpful to remember all those good things and our nice times together."

The author has shared with the reader in an earlier chapter the telephone call received from Linda Bellucci, who confided her fear that she might have caused her infant sister's death. Linda was burdened with guilt, as is often the case in a SIDS family, and felt she didn't deserve another sister. This feeling was reinforced when two brothers were later born. During our phone conversations, Linda and I discussed some of the things she liked to do. She yearned to play tennis. I urged her to 'go for it.' From the content of a postcard I later received from The Nick Bollettieri Tennis Academy in Bradenton, Florida, she did! It read as follows:

Hi Mrs. Donnelly,

I just wanted to share my happiness with you, for you add joy to my life. I've been here at one of the most important tennis academies in the world for almost 3 weeks. I work real hard, 7 hrs. a day in the Fla. heat, but it's worth it! I've had the opportunity to meet some young tennis pros who are students here. It's been a wonderful experience. I hope all is well with you!

Your friend,

Linda Bellucci

One of the greatest rewards of any author is to reach the audience to whom her work is directed. To receive such a card, in which this young surviving sibling, fifteen years old, has obviously decided to 'go for it,' and who is striving so eagerly to reach her goals today, evokes a feeling something akin to what Linda wrote: "It adds joy to my life."

Similarly, it is hoped that the messages from all the brothers and sisters throughout this book will offer to every surviving sibling and their families the encouragement and support that will enable them to go on with their lives, remembering the good things. Recovering does not mean you have to forget.

Chapter Twenty

Helping Hands

Helping hands come in many forms—through other siblings who have experienced a similar tragedy, support groups, individual or group therapy, religion, and "bibliotherapy" with listings of books to read. Because each person is different, no one helping hand is the right one for everybody—*but there are many helping hands.* If you try one and it isn't good for you, make a change. Try another way. For example, some people may like to ride a bicycle, whereas others may prefer to drive a car. Still others may take a train or a boat to their destination. Although all of these may get to the same place, some people are more comfortable with one means of transportation than another.

So it is with bereaved siblings; some may be more at ease in meeting with other surviving siblings, either by telephone or in person. Some may be more at ease in a group setting; others may not. Some may find organizations extremely helpful, but others may discover it is simply not for them. Some may prefer the intimate setting of a family doctor's office, their clergyman, or a school teacher or guidance counselor. Others may have to look further.

In that search, a question often asked is, "Do I need help?" Another question that follows is, "How and where can I find it?" Bereaved parents and siblings alike have written to me from all over the country, bemoaning the fact that time frames were imposed on them by their psychotherapists. One sibling called to say, "I went to a therapist because I wanted to talk to someone who could help me understand what I was feeling. At the end of the twelve months, he said to me, 'It's been over a year now.' As soon as I heard that judgment, with the implication that I should be better because a year had gone by, I handed this guy his walking papers."

Many bereaved parents and surviving siblings express the view that unless professionals have suffered the loss of a loved one, or have had some training in grief, they may simply be uninformed about how surviving siblings and bereaved parents get better. One parent commented, "The symptoms of severe grief can be so similar to mental illness that they are sometimes misinterpreted and perceived as pathological by the professional when in fact they are normal signs of grief. More so than in other situations, bereaved siblings and bereaved parents are really at the mercy of professionals."

Siblings and parents are urged to understand that if they went to a doctor for a physical illness and did not like the diagnosis or disagreed with it, they should go for a second opinion. Don't hesitate to do the same if you feel the person you are seeing is inflicting more harm than help.

Judith Haimes offers some advice: "You have heard many war stories in this book where psychologists and therapists are concerned. But, those are horror stories of survivors who are sharing their experiences with you and are in effect saying, 'Don't let this happen to you! Use your common sense.' For example, if you were pregnant, you wouldn't go to an orthopedic doctor but to an obstetrician or, in smaller communities, to a doctor experienced in delivering babies. Use that same philosophy when you are looking for help in your grief. There are psychologists who specialize in phobias, in injuries, and in divorce; they may be the very best in their fields, but not the best for you if they have had no experience in grief. However, once you find doctors, psychologists, therapists or counselors who either specialize in grief or who have a keen empathy for or understanding of grief, you can then select the person best suited for your own personality and needs, and chances are that you will find a good one."

In many instances, siblings, as with bereaved parents,

just want to verify that they are not crazy and simply want the comfort of knowing that what they are experiencing is "normal." Perhaps surviving siblings can best be guided as to when help is needed by the counsel given by other siblings: "You need help when the pain becomes an overwhelming thing in your life, when it starts interfering with your everyday activities, whether that occurs immediately after the death or months or years later."

Psychotherapist Athena Drewes clarifies the issue: "Most people who seek out professional help are urged to do so by friends or relatives, when they become 'stuck' in the mourning process. But for most people, grief *counseling* is supportive help that should be available and sought after early on in the grief process. Usually there is intensive family and community supports for the first few months. Then people assume you've gotten on with your life, and that the grief is past. They withdraw their support. It is at this time that the pain and sense of loss may have its greatest impact and counseling can help continue the support that is still needed to grieve.

"You cannot handle the emotional impact of loss until you first deal with the fact that the loss happened. In grief counseling," Drewes maintains. "The goal is to help the person so they don't carry the pain with them for life. I view mourning as a process, not a state. Consequently it is more that a person is doing 'grief work' since going through the tasks of mourning requires work."

Again, it is important for bereaved siblings and parents to understand that recovering doesn't mean they have to forget. One parent, Vivian Kessler, summed it up best: "As we recover from a serious accident or surgery, so we recover from the emotional traumas of life; the sharp pain fades to a dull ache; the wound heals but the scars remain forever. We learn to live with the memories, the lost hopes and shattered dreams. We never 'get over' the death, but we can 'recover,' adjust and learn to live with our pain."

And so we see that there are many helpful routes available for surviving siblings; talking to friends and family members; sharing with other siblings; the counsel of a clergyperson or family doctor, funeral director, teacher, counselor, psychologist, social worker, therapist or co-worker. What is important to realize is that there *are* alternatives. There are many helping hands, including support groups to help siblings in their grief. Younger children in bereaved families are often helped by teachers in school who are finding ways of talking about death, and courses on death and dying are appearing more and more in the high schools and colleges. Also available are many useful books for those who prefer to read. A suggested reading, prepared by Froma Lippmann, educator and bereaved sibling, appears at the end of this book.

As we mentioned in the beginning of "Helping Hands," if you tried one way and it wasn't right for you, then check out the other routes and find one that you feel comfortable with. Don't despair that there is no other way. *You will find one that is right for you.*

Following is an alphabetical listing of organizations in the United States and Canada that help bereaved families, with descriptions of their activities, together with addresses and telephone numbers where available.

Bereaved Families of Ontario, Canada

A self-help organization for bereaved families, this group has chapters across Ontario that provide support and counseling to the newly bereaved. Programs vary according to city, some including French, and Portuguese speaking groups. Trained volunteers, themselves bereaved, offer help to bereaved parents, bereaved siblings, bereaved spouses, and families of suicide victims. These volunteers have been specially selected by a committee of health care professionals in their community. Upon completion of their bereavement sessions, they are chosen for their ability to listen, to care, and to honor confidences of those who come for help. Each volunteer not only leads a small group with a co-leader or acts as a support person on a one-to-one basis, but also must meet with a member of the health care committee who is their professional support. Funding from municipal governments, foundations, corporations, individuals, churches, funeral directors, coin box campaigns, and others make it possible for this group to reach out to newly bereaved people.

To contact a chapter in your area, the following listing is provided:

Pembroke . . . . (613) 732-7894
Ottawa-Carleton . . . . (613) 731-5511
Cornwall . . . .(613) 939-2824
Durham Region . . . .(416) 434-8111
Metro Toronto . . . .(416) 440-0290
Owen Sound . . . .(519) 376-7110
Oakville . . . .(416) 842-3012
Peel Region . . . .(416) 842-3012
Kitchener-Waterloo . . . . . .(519) 742-3611 ext. 2165
Brant County . . . .(519) 752-4101
London . . . .(519) 686-1573

For additional information write to:
Bereaved Families of Ontario
Les Families endeullees de l'Ontario
33 Bloor Street East, Suite 210
Toronto, Ontario M4W 3H1

Candlelighters and the Candlelighters Foundation

Candlelighters is an international organization of parent groups that have or have had children with cancer. Some groups have youth auxiliaries for teenage cancer patients and for teenage siblings of cancer victims. The group provides guidance in coping with cancer's effects on the family and seeks to ease frustrations and fears through the sharing of common experiences. Candlelighters includes more than 165 chapters, affiliated groups and contacts in the United States, Australia, Belgium, Brazil, Canada, Chile, Denmark, England, France, Guatemala, Germany, Indonesia, Mexico, New Zealand, South Africa, and the West Indies. It is a nonprofit organization with emphasis on promoting an emotional support system of "second families" to each other. Candlelighters also hold social functions where families can meet and relax in a supportive nonthreatening setting.

The Candlelighters Foundation is the coordinator and educational arm of the parents' groups. It helps new groups to form, acts as liaison to existing groups, and offers communication services. The free services and publications are supported through tax-exempt donations and a grant from the American Cancer Society. Should you wish further information please write to:

The Candlelighters Foundation
Suite 1001
1901 Pennsylvania Ave. NW
Washington, D.C. 20006
Telephone: (202) 659-5136

Centers for Attitudinal Research

The Center for Attitudinal Research in Tiburon, California, is a nonprofit, nonsectarian group, originated largely through the efforts of child psychiatrist Gerald Jampolsky, M.D. Programs were intially established for children with life-threatening or catastrophic illnesses. Traditional health care is supplemented by providing an environment in which the children can actively participate. For a child experiencing a catastrophic illness, there is a temptation to feel anger toward the world, a sense of being different and alone. Dr. Jampolsky and the staff at the center strive to ease these stressful tensions.

The Young Children's Group directs its attention to children aged six to sixteen, and offers a sharing, loving, supportive program with the use of art and music.

Similarly, siblings of children with life-threatening illnesses need to share their fears and anxieties, their feelings of loneliness and unhappiness. Often they feel less loved than the brother or sister being given so much attention by their parents. In the siblings' group, common fears, anger, and guilt feelings about sick or dying brothers and sisters are discussed in a supportive atmosphere. A phone pal/pen pal program has been established whereby children, their siblings, and their parents can relate via phone or letter with people who have had similar life experiences.

Offshoots of the Center for Attitudinal Research are being established throughout the country. All the programs at the center are provided free of charge. The center participates in workshops locally and nationally and offers assistance to those wishing to start other centers. For further information, contact:

The Center for Attitudinal Healing
19 Main Street
Tiburon, California 94920
Telephone: (415) 435-5022

The Compassionate Friends, Inc.

This voluntary self-help organization offers understanding and friendship to bereaved parents and surviving siblings. Its main purpose is to assist families in the positive resolution of the grief they experience after the death of a child, and to promote their physical and emotional health. The organization charges no dues and has no religious affiliation. Beginning in Coventry, England, the organization has now expanded to almost 525 chapters throughout the United States. There are also chapters in Canada, England, Australia, South Africa, the Netherlands, Israel, and Switzerland. The Compassionate Friends has also prepared informative pamphlets as guides in understanding grief—for bereaved siblings, for teachers, for doctors, nurses, for friends and family members. They may be obtained by contacting national headquarters listed below. For other information regarding nearby chapters in the United States that may have siblings groups, all inquiries may be directed to:

The Compassionate Friends, Inc.
National Office
P.O. Box 3696
Oak Brook, Illinois 60522-3696
Telephone: (312) 990-0010

U.S.A. Chapter Locations

ALABAMA
Anniston
Birmingham
Decatur
Dothan
Jasper
Mobile
Montgomery
Silverhell
Talladega
Tuscaloosa

ALASKA
Anchorage

ARIZONA
Mesa
Greater Phoenix
Phoenix (W.S.)
Tucson

ARKANSAS
Conway
El Dorado
Fayetteville
Fort Smith
Hope
Rogers

CALIFORNIA
Anaheim
Barstow
Fairfield
Fresno
Grass Valley
Hesperia
Los Angeles
Palo Alto/San Jose
Pomona
Redding
Riverside
Sacramento
San Diego
San Francisco
San Lorenzo
Santa Maria
San Rafael
Tulare

Van Nuys
Ventura
Walnut Creek

COLORADO
Colorado Springs
Denver
Evergreen
Fort Collins
Grand Junction
Greeley
Nunn
Pueblo
Salida

CONNECTICUT
Bridgeport
Groton
Hartford
Meriden
New Haven
Rockville
Stamford

DELAWARE
Wilmington

DISTRICT OF
  COLUMBIA
Washington, D.C.
  (Bethesda, Md.)

FLORIDA
Boca Raton
Bradenton
Brooksville
Clearwater
Daytona Beach
Ft. Lauderdale
Ft. Myers
Fort Walton Beach
Gainesville
Hernando
Jacksonville
Lakeland
Miami
Naples
Ocala

Pensacola
Plantation
Sarasota
Tallahassee
Tampa
Titusville
West Palm Beach

GEORGIA
Albany
Atlanta
Atlanta (No. Atlanta)
Athens
Augusta
Columbus
Cornelia
Monroe
Moultrie
Savannah
Warner Robins

HAWAII
Honolulu
Kahului
Kailua-Kona

IDAHO
Boise
Burley
Coeur d'Alene
Idaho Falls
Pocatello

ILLINOIS
Arlington Heights
Aurora
Blue Island
Champaign
Chicago
Chicago (Spanish
  Speaking)
Elgin
Galesburg
Gurnee/Milburn
Hinsdale
Hoopeston
Jacksonville
Joliet

Kankakee
Mattoon
McHenry
Ottawa
Pana
Peoria
Rockford
Springfield
Sterling
Waukegan (Prairie
   View)
Wood River

INDIANA
Anderson
Bloomington
Bluffton
Columbia City
Elkhart
Evansville
Fort Wayne
Greenwood
Huntingburg
Indianapolis
Kendallville
Kokomo
Lafayette
Logansport
Muncie
Shelbyville
South Bend
Terre Haute
Valparaiso
Wabash
Warsaw

IOWA
Algona
Caroll
Cascade
Clinton
Davenport (Moline, Il.)
Des Moines
Dubuque
Independence
Indianola
Marshalltown
Mason City
Ottumwa

Sioux City
Spencer
Storm Lake
Waterloo

KANSAS
Attica
Council Grove
Emporia
Garden City
Kansas City
Lawrence
Manhattan
Newton
Phillipsburg
Tescott
Topeka
Wichita

KENTUCKY
Ashland
Cynthiana
Elizabethtown
Hopkinsville
Lexington
Louisville
Owensboro
Paducah
Princeton

LOUISIANA
Alexandria
Baton Rouge
De Ridder
Lafayette
New Orleans
Shreveport
Sulphur

MAINE
Bangor
Camden

MARYLAND
Annapolis
Baltimore
Cumberland
St. Leonard
Salisbury
Walkersville

MASSACHUSETTS
Amherst
Boston
Chatham
Concord
Fall River
Falmouth
Gardner
Hingham
Holliston
Pembroke
Springfield
Worcester

MICHIGAN
Alpena
Ann Arbor
Flint
Grand Blanc
Grand Rapids
Hancock
Kalamazoo
Lansing
Muskegon
Ortonville
Pigeon
Port Nuron
Saginaw

MINNESOTA
Annandale
Battle Creek
Brainerd
Breckenridge
Crookston
Detroit Lakes
Fairmont
Fosston
Mankato
Minneapolis
New Ulm
St. Cloud
St. Paul
Warroad
Willmar

MISSISSIPPI
Columbus
Greenwood

Gulfport
Jackson
Laurel/Hattiesburg
Meridian

MISSOURI
Blue Springs
Columbia
Independence
Joplin
Kansas City (Greater)
Kansas City
  (Northland)
Lamar
Maryville
St. Louis
Sedalia
Springfield
West Plains

MONTANA
Billings
Bozeman
Glasgow
Missoula
Miles City

NEBRASKA
Kimball/Sidney
McCook
Norfolk
North Platte
Ogallala
Omaha
Scottsbluff
Valentine

NEVADA
Carson City
Las Vegas

NEW HAMPSHIRE
Concord
Dover
Jaffrey
Nashua
Plymouth

NEW JERSEY
Audubon

Brookside
Clarksboro
Flemington
Holmdel
Manville
Medford
Northfield
Nutley
Old Bridge
Princeton
Roselle
Teaneck
Toms River
West Milford

NEW MEXICO
Albuquerque
Sante Fe

NEW YORK
Albany
Bardonia
Binghamton
Brooklyn
Buffalo
Cobbleskill
Dunkirk
Fairport
Flushing
Geneseo/Naples
Horseheads
Jamestown
Kingston
Lockport
Long Island Chapter
Madrid
Malone
Middletown
New York City
Orchard Park
Purdys Station
Rochester
Schenectady
Staten Island
Star Lake
Watertown
Wellsville
Warsaw

NORTH CAROLINA
Asheville
Concord
Glen Alpine
Greensboro
Mocksville
Raleigh
Statesville
Sylva
Wilkesboro
Wilmington

NORTH DAKOTA
Bismarck
Devils Lake
Fargo
Grand Forks
Valley City

OHIO
Akron
Ashtabula
Athens
Belpre
Carrollton/Massilon
Cincinnati
Cleveland Heights
Cleveland-Southwest
Cleveland-West
Columbus
Medina
Middletown
Mount Vernon
Niles
St. Henry
Van Wert

OKLAHOMA
Bartlesville
Clinton
Enid
Lawton
Midwest City
Norman
Oklahoma City (N)
Oklahoma City (SW)
Ponca City
Stillwater

Tahlequah
Tulsa

OREGON
Bandon
Bend
Eugene
Niles
Portland
Roseburg
Salem
The Dalles

PENNSYLVANIA
Altoona
Ambler
Beaver
Butler
Ebensburg
Erie
Greensburg
Hanover
Honesdale
Indiana
Johnstown
Kittanning
Lancaster
New Castle
New Hope
New Kensington
Oil City
Philadelphia
Philadelphia, N.E.
Pittsburgh
Pottstown
Pottsville
Reading
St. Mary's
Scranton
Valley Forge
Warrington
Williamsport
York

RHODE ISLAND
Pawtucket

SOUTH CAROLINA
Anderson
Charleston

Florence/Hartsville
Greenville
Hilton Head
West Columbia

SOUTH DAKOTA
Sioux Falls

TENNESSEE
Athens
Bristol
Chattanooga
Clarksville
Knoxville
Memphis

TEXAS
Abilene
Amarillo
Austin
Beaumont
Bonham
Borger
Bryan
Corpus Christi
Dallas
El Paso
Fort Worth
Graham
Greenville
Houston (SE)
Houston (W)
Houston (Northwest)
Lake Jackson
Lubbock
McAllen
Nacogdoches
New Braunfels
Odessa/Midland
Palestine
Rockport
San Angelo
San Antonio
Temple
Uvalde
Victoria
Waco

UTAH
Ogden

Salt Lake

VERMONT
Lyndon Center
Montpelier
Rutland
Windsor

VIRGINIA
Burke/Springfield
Charlottesville
Dublin
Falls Church
Grafton
Leesburg
Lynchburg
Richmond
Staunton
Warrenton

WASHINGTON
Bellingham
Bremerton
Clarkston
Kennewick
Longview
Marysville
Mt. Vernon
Seattle/Bothell
Spokane
Tacoma
Walla Walla
Yakima

WEST VIRGINIA
Beckley
Bluefield
Chapmanville
Huntington
Martinsburg

WISCONSIN
Appleton
Ashland
Beaver Dam
Elkhorn
Fond Du Lac
Green Bay/
   Brown County
LaCrosse

Madison
Manitowoc
Milwaukee/
   Whitefish Bay

Oshkosh
Platteville
Rhinelander
Tomahawk

Waukesha

WYOMING
Cody

The Compassionate Friends of Canada
Les Amis Compatissants du Canada

An international organization offering friendship and understanding to bereaved parents.

Un organisme international offrant amitie et comprehension aux parents affliges.

CANADIAN CHAPTER LEADERS & CONTACTS
(National Board members underlined)

BC ABBOTSFORD—Lea Foreman, 2679 St. Moritz Way, Abbotsford, BC V2S 5W4 Ph. (604) 859-1359

COLUMBIA VALLEY—Paula Petras, Box 115, Fairmont Hot Springs, BC V0B 1L0 Ph. (604) 345-9579

COQUITLAM—Barb & Ron Patterson, 1850 Harbour Dr., Coquitlam, BC V3J 5W7 Ph. (604) 936-9708

FORT ST. JOHN—Harold & Charleen Spooner, 9324-107 Ave., Fort St. John, BC V1J 2P3 Ph. (604) 785-8931

KAMLOOPS—Linda & Mike Foster, 1338 Kenora Rd., Kamloops, BC V2B 3X7 Ph. (604) 376-1346

Carol Dreger, Knutsford, BC V0E 2A0 Ph. (604) 374-4647

KELOWNA—Judy Taylor, #93-1929 Hwy. 97 S. Kelowna, BC V1Z 2Z1 Ph. (604) 769-6352 (Contact)

KITIMAT—Bev Gustafson, 44 Omenica St., Kitimat, BC V8C 1Z4 Ph. (604) 639-9759 (Contact)

NANAIMO—George & Myrna Skaling, 3768 Uplands Dr., Nanaimo, BC V9T 2T8 Ph. (604) 758-3816

PRINCE GEORGE—Annette Hamilton, 492 McInnis Ave., Prince George, BC V2N 1Y7 Ph. (604) 563-5583

PRINCE RUPERT—Anthea & Tony Lewis, 606 Ritchie St., Prince Rupert, BC V8J 3N5 Ph. (604) 624-2983

RIDGE-MEADOWS—Lynn Mtichell, 19680-116 B Ave., Pitt Meadows, BC V0M 1P0 Ph. (604) 465-4488

TRAIL AREA—Linda & Howard Stanley, Box 415, Montrose, BC V0G 1P0 Ph. (604) 367-7982

VANCOUVER—Nancy & Bill Edmonds, 5829 Hudson St., Vancouver, BC V6M 2Z2 Ph. (604) 263-2174

David & Beverly Niederauer, 4590 West 13th. Ave., Vancouver, BC V6R 2V4 Ph. (604) 224-6732

AB   CALGARY—Jane & Stuart Grant, 332 Wildwood Dr., S.W.,Calgary, AB T3C 3E3 Ph. (403) 240-1467

EDMONTON—Corry & Gene Roach, 4858-32nd. Ave., Edmonton, AB T6L 4H9 Ph. (403) 463-8695

GRANDE PRAIRIE—Jane Littleton (Prof.), 10202-110 Ave., Grande Prairie, AB T8V 1S7 Ph. (403) 532-2506 (Contact)

LETHBRIDGE—Vi Armstrong, 47 Laval Blvd., Lethbridge, AB T1K 4E1 Ph. (403) 381-1361

MEDICINE HAT—Jean Rogers, 201-2nd. Ave., N.E., Apt. 3, Medicine Hat, AB T1A 5Z9 Ph. (403) 526-9060

SK   REGINA—Trevor & Audrey Roadhouse, 101 Cameron Cr., Regina, SK S4S 2X3 Ph. (306) 586-0900

Herb & Adaline Leir, 79 Milford Cr., Regina, SK S4N 1K6 Ph. (306) 757-5383

SASKATOON—Norm & Sheila Williams, 1637 Grieg Ave., Saskatoon, SK S7N 2R1 Ph. (306) 373-7149

Lynne Allin, Box 537, Elrose, SK S0L 0Z0 Ph. (306) 378-2714

YORKTON—Alice Light, 282-2ndAve. N., Yorkton, SK S3N 3H3 Ph. (306) 783-9288

MB   BRANDON—Karen Elves (Prof.) 3313 RosserAve., Brandon, MB R78 0H1 Ph. (204) 726-0647 or 727-5170 (Contact)

PORTAGE PLAINS—Sandra Wallace, 8 Wilson St., Portage La Prairie, MB R1N 3A6 Ph. (204) 857-9819

SOUTH CENTRAL (Manitou)—Jim & Emily Lovell, RR #1, La Riviere, MB R0G 1A0 Ph. (204) 242-2694

WINNIPEG—Pat & Ken Pinch, 73 Kingsway Ave., Winnipeg, MB R3M 0G2 Ph. (204) 475-9527

Gwen Brown, 73 Kingsway (or 4496 Ontario St., Vancouver, BC V5V 3H1 Ph. (604) 873-6030

Mary James, 1814 Assiniboine Ave., Winnipeg, MB R3J 0A1 Ph. (204) 832-3130 (Sub. Atlantic Rep.)

ON   KINGSTON—Sue & David Borrowman, Box 198, Syndenham, ON K0H 2T0 Ph. (613) 376-3632

MARATHON—Susan & Marcel Trudel, Box 1012, Marathon, ON P0T 2E0 Ph. (807) 229-0943

Carol & Larry Vien, Box 354, Marathon, ON P0T 2E0 Ph. (807) 229-0123

NEWMARKET—Elizabeth (Liz) Cross,Box 62, Aurora, ON L4G 3H1 Ph. (416) 727-2236

Angela Ambrozaitis, 1033 Wildwood Dr., Newmarket, ON L3Y 2B6 Ph. (416) 895-8157

NIAGARA—Stan & Emily Vaughan, 220 Niagara Falls Rd., Thorold, ON L2V 1J2 Ph. (416) 227-6796

SAULT STE. MARIE—Rev. Frank & Peggy Coyle, 380 Shannon Rd., Apt. 1, Sault Ste. Marie, ON P6A 4K5 Ph. (705) 942-8273

Jackie Bain, 14 Cedarwood Dr., Sault Ste. Marie P6B 5G4 Ph. (705) 949-2879

ST. THOMAS—David Thwaites, 34 Stokes Rd., St. Thomas, ON N5R 5V7 Ph. (519) 631-8432

PQ   MONTREAL—Rejeanne & <u>Jean-Paul Blais</u>, 257 Sherbrooke, Beaconsfield, PQ H9W 5S4 Ph. (514) 694-3464 (French)
Sandy Schwartz, 5614 Alpine, Montreal, PQ H4V 2X5 Ph. (514) 485-2199 (English language)

NS   ANTIGONISH—Jean Bacon-MacIntyre, R.R. 3, Malignant Cove, Antigonish, NS B2G 2L1 (Contact)
HALIFAX—Rev. Don & Norma Lawton, 4 Bedford St., Bedford, NS B4A 1W4 (Contacts)

NF   STEPHENVILLE—Cavell Hines, 19 Valley Rd., Stephenville, NF A2N 2R3 Ph. (709) 643-3678 (Contact)

PE   CORNWALL—Larry & Mary Peters, Site 5, Box 8, R.R. 4, Cornwall, PE C0A 1H0 (Contact)

YT   WHITEHORSE—Betsy Stinson, 612 Alexander St., Whitehorse, YT Y1A 2M3 Ph. (403) 667-4874 (Contact)

For additional information, write to the Canadian national office at:

The Compassionate Friends of Canada
685 William Avenue
Winnipeg, Manitoba R3E 0Z2
Telephone: (204) 787-2460

L.I.F.T.
Living is for Today

L.I.F.T., an open-ended self-help suppport group, is sponsored by Bereavement Services & Community Education, a division of the Humphrey Funeral Home—A.W. Miles Chapel. It is the first of its kind in Canada. Weekly meetings open to the community, offer the grieving sibling support, encouragement, and a "common language." Experiences and concerns shared provide the opportunity for all to discover new strengths and insights. Each group is facilitated by a professionally-trained person with the format and areas of interest chosen by the participants. There are no attendance or financial requirements.

Diana McKendree, a consultant/therapist, is Director of the program who also volunteers as a child therapist with Bereaved Families of Ontario, where she works with six to twelve-year-old grieving siblings. Using clay and art materials to aid in the expression of their feeling surrounding the loss, children draw and mold "their stories." Although children cannot clearly articulate the abstract concepts of death and separation, this permits healing and therapeutic results.

Diana McKendree, Director
Bereavement Services & Community Education
1403 Bayview Avenue
Toronto, Ontario, Canada M4G 3A8
Telephone: (416) 485-6415

M.A.D.D. *(Mothers Against Drunk Drivers)*

This group was begun by Candy Lightner after her thirteen-year-old daughter was killed by a repeat-offender drunk driver. The title of the organization was derived from her status as a single mother, but members include fathers, sons, daughters, siblings and others. "Today, MADD not only has members who are victims of this murder on the highway, but concerned citizens who wish to share in prevention," advises a chapter leader. "We are not 'fanatics' or 'the grief-stricken.' We are there so that other people do not have to go through what we have been through. While our arms are open to anyone who is a victim of a drunk driver, our main goal is to *prevent* it from happening on the road, and to clean the streets of these impaired drivers. Our national aim is to enforce legislation to take the drunk driver off the road, to provide victim support, and education to stimulate public awareness. As a result of the efforts of this group, new laws were put into effect in California." There are local chapters throughout the U.S.A.

For additional information, write to:
Norma Phillips, President, MADD
Mothers Against Drunk Driving
669 Airport Freeway, Suite 310
Hurst, Texas 76053
Telephone: (817) 268-MADD

Parents of Murdered Children

To families so cruelly bereaved, Parents of Murdered Children (POMC) provides help to any parent who has endured this tragedy. For those who have endured or are enduring such a loss, POMC offers help to parents troubled about any aspect of their child's murder. A self-help group, the parents affiliated with POMC believe strongly that "a person who has recovered from a problem can be far more helpful than a professional using only theoretical knowledge. Second, when an individual helps another without charge, they both benefit." Often siblings attend the group meetings and some chapters have had siblings develop groups as an offshoot.

Families of a homicide death have to bear an additional burden to the grief process—that of intrusions into their intense grief. The news media may focus on the victim and the grieving family. Police, lawyers, and others in the criminal justice system may require information, testimony, evidence, and so on. Whether a murder suspect is apprehended or not, there is further pain. There are trials, sentences pronounced, hearings, postponements—all taking their toll on the grieving family.

Should you wish information regarding chapter locations or any other details, contact:
Parents of Murdered Children, Inc.
1739 Bella Vista
Cincinnnati, Ohio 45237
Telephone: (513) 242-8025

Rothman-Cole Center for Sibling Loss

The Center provides individual and family counseling, focusing solely on sibling bereavement. Tom Cole, a lawyer, and Jerry Rothman, a psychotherapist, both lost a brother in childhood, and established the Rothman-Cole Center for Sibling Loss in 1985. At the Center, psychotherapist Rothman uses children's art to help them explore the feelings they may have suppressed about their bereavement. The goal: to help the surviving child grow intellectually, emotionally and socially.

For further information, contact:
Rothman-Cole Center For Sibling Loss
1456 West Montrose Avenue
Chicago, Illinois 60613
Telephone: (312) 769-0185

SHARE (Sources of Help in Airing and Resolving Experiences)

Until recently most hospitals were unprepared to deal with the despair of young parents who lose infants soon after birth. Today many new approaches have been initiated to help grief-stricken parents after miscarriages, stillborn children, and babies who die hours, days, and weeks after birth. This support group for parents whose infants have died was formed at St. John's Hospital in Springfield, Illinois, under the direction of Sister Jane Marie Lamb. The group is called SHARE, and that is its purpose—for young bereaved parents to be able to share their feelings. Subsequently, chapter after chapter of SHARE, and similar groups such as AMEND, HAND, UNITE, HOPING, CARE, BEREAVED PARENTS, CARETAKERS, CURE, ILAC, T.L.C., P.A.C.E.S., WEE CARE, PEND, SHARING HEART, KINDER-MOURN, HOPES, and others, continued to grow throughout the United States and in other countries.

Through the local SHARE meetings, members *can share* their experiences, thoughts, and feelings. Parents learn that the intensity and longevity of their feeings are normal. They gain a sense of wholeness when they realize their problems are not unique to them alone, but rather problems with which most bereaved parents are struggling. *These problems will often include discussions of sibling issues.* SHARE is not a therapy group, nor are these meetings "therapy" sessions. Yet healing is slowly and gently promoted as parents gain insight and understanding of their problems as well as those of surviving siblings.

Sister Jane Marie Lamb, SHARE's Program Facilitator, describes the group's concern for bereaved siblings: "Many of the SHARE families have a signifcant number of siblings, often very young children. Parents need support as they relate to the children. They question, 'Shall we tell the children?' 'Are they too young?' 'How do we tell them?' 'Can they understand?'

"We encourage parents to inform siblings in simple, concrete terms that can be understood at their age level; describe what 'dead' means relative to warmth, breathing, and movement; prepare the child as to what they might expect to see: size, how dressed, and so on, and offer them the option of seeing, touching, holding the baby, and of participating in rituals. Fears are allayed by assuring the child of the parental presence and support. They need to know that tears are acceptable and appropriate and that they can leave at any time during the ritual.

"Nancy Dodge, a SHARE volunteer, has developed *Thumpy's Story* as a means of modeling ways to talk with a child. *Thumpy's Story* portrays the surviving rabbit sibling telling of the death, burial and grief that followed the death of baby rabbit Bun. Reading the story opens communications between adults and children. Younger children, especially, will more easily respond to an animal than to an adult person. Thumpy's activity book becomes a tool to bring out feelings in the weeks and months to come.

"Our conviction is that death is a part of life and that children look to adults as role models. Unhealthy patterns of denial, protecting the child from involvement in painful life events, avoiding emotional conversation can affect the child for years to come. As adults we respond to life events in ways modeled in childhood. Developing healthy patterns of response in the child can prevent psychological difficulties as an adult.

SHARE is a philosophy of care and support for parents who have suffered the death of an infant through miscarriage, stillbirth, or early infant death. SHARE is there to provide comfort and support to these parents during the anticipatory time, as well as after the death of their child. We continue to reassure and give comfort beyond the hospital stay in the weeks and months to come through follow-up calls and correspondence, though a newsletter and a mutual-support group. We encourage the physical and emotional health of the parents and the siblings."

For additional information about SHARE, and Thumpy's Project, write to:
SHARE
St. Elizabeth's Hospital
211 South Third St.
Belleville, Illinois 62222
Telephone: (618) 234-2120

Sudden Infant Death Syndrome Groups

While medical research continues, SIDS also continues to claim the lives of thousands of babies each year. The aftermath of a SIDS death is overwhelming grief and guilt: grief because a loved one is gone; guilt because parents and siblings often blame themselves for the death of the infant. The parents' groups support the training and activities of health profession-als who help SIDS families understand that SIDS is neither preventable nor predictable. Volunteer SIDS families provide the sympathetic understanding desperately needed in a time of great personal loss. Chapter members stand by, ready to telephone, visit, or counsel grief-stricken parents at any time, even in the hospital emergency room.

For more information, contact:
The National Clearinghouse for SIDS
Suite 600
1555 Wilson Boulevard
Rosslyn, Virginia 22209
Telephone: (703) 522-0870
                    or
The National SIDS Foundation
2 Metro Plaza
Suite 205
8240 Professional Place
Landover, Maryland 20785
Telephone: (301) 459-3388

Survivors of Suicide

S.O.S is a self-help organization offering support and understanding to bereaved persons who have lost a loved one through suicide.

Survivors of Suicide maintains a listing of support groups in the United States and Canada for family and friends after a suicide death. For information about groups in your area, please send a self-addressed stamped envelope to Survivors of Suicide, P.O. Box 1393, Dayton, Ohio 45406.

T.I.G.E.R.S. (Teens In Grief: Educate, Rebuild, Support)

The focus of these grief support groups for teenage surviving siblings is to provide a safe, secure, comfortable atmosphere for young people to express their feelings about their loss, to educate them about the grieving process, and to assist them in feeling more comfortable about their own mortality, while comforting them in their loss.

For information about T.I.G.E.R.S., write:
Fr. Mike DiMaio, Grief Facilitator
521 Garden Ct.
Quincy, IL 62301
Telephone: (217) 223-4479
                              or
Ingrid Prunkl, RN, Therapist, and Group Facilitator
2811 Kingsridge
Quincy, IL 62301
Telephone: (217) 224-0733

Special Note:

If there are any groups or organizations that the reader believes should be included in this "Helping Hands" section, please contact the writer at the address below. We willl try to place these in future up-dated editions.

Katherine Fair Donnelly
c/o Dodd, Mead & Co., Publishers
71 Fifth Avenue
New York, N.Y. 10003

Suggested Readings

By
Froma Lippmann
Education/Resource Consultant
and Bereaved Sibling

For Adults:

Davidson, Glen W. *Understanding Mourning*, Minneapolis: Augsburg Publishing House, 1984.

Donnelly, Katherine Fair. *Recovering From the Loss of a Child*, New York: Macmillan Publishing Co., Inc., 1982.

Grollman, Earl (ed.). *Concerning Death*, Boston: Beacon Press, 1974.

Grollman, Earl A. *What Helped Me When My Loved One Died*, Boston: Beacon Press, 1981.

Hansen, J.C. and T.T. Frantz. *Death and Grief in the Family*, Rockville, MD: An Aspen Publication, 1984.

Kreis, Bernadine and Alice Pattie. *Up From Grief*, New York: The Seabury Press, 1969.

Kushner, Harold S. *When Bad Things Happen to Good People*, New York: Schocken Books, 1981.

Meagher, D.K. and R.D. Shapiro. *Death: The Experience*, Minneapolis, MN: Burgess Publishing Co., 1984.

Schweibert, Pat and Paul Kirk. *When Hello Means Goodbye*, Oregon: University of Oregon Health Sciences Center, 1981.

Temes, Roberta. *Living with an Empty Chair*, New York: Irvington Publishers, Inc., 1980.

Viorst, Judith. *Necessary Losses*, New York: Simon & Schuster, 1986.

Worden, William J. *Grief Counseling and Grief Therapy*, New York: Springer Publishing, 1982.

For Children:

*Clardy, Andrea Fleck. *Dusty Was My Friend*, New York: Human Sciences Press, 1984.

Caseley, Judith. *When Grandpa Came to Stay*, New York: Greenwillow Books, 1986.

dePaola, Tomie. *Nana Upstairs & Nana Downstairs*, New York: G.P. Putnam, 1973.

Fassler, Joan. *My Grandpa Died Today*, New York: Human Sciences Press, 1971.

Grollman, Earl A. *Talking About Death*, Boston: Beacon Press, 1970.

Hickman, Martha Whitmore. *Last Week My Brother Antony Died*, Nashville: Abingdon Press, 1984.

*LeShan, Eda. *Learning To Say Good-bye*, New York: Macmillan Publishing Company, Inc., 1976.

McLendon, Gloria Houston. *My Brother Joey Died*, New York: Julian Messner, 1982.

Murray, Gloria and Gerald G. Jampolsky, M.D. (ed.). *Another Look at the Rainbow: Straight from the Siblings*, Melbrae, Calif: Celestial Arts, 1982.

Pomerantz, Barbara. *Bubby, Me and Memories*, New York: Union of American Hebrew Congregations, 1983.

*Richter, Elizabeth. *Losing Someone You Love*, New York: G.P. Putnam, Inc., 1986.

*Rofes, Eric E. and The Unit At Fayerweather Street School. *The Kids' Book About Death and Dying*, Boston: Little, Brown and Company, 1985.

*Smith, Doris Buchanan. *A Taste of Blackberries*, New York: Harper & Row, 1973.

Varley , Susan. *Badger's Parting Gifts*, New York: Lothrop, Lee & Shepard, 1984.

Viorst, Judith. *The Tenth Good Thing About Barney*, New York: Atheneum, 1971.

Zolotow, Charlotte. *My Grandson Lew*, New York: Harper & Row, 1974.

* Books for children in the elementary and/or intermediate grades in school.

Note: Froma Lippmann is Parent Education/Resource Consultant, Arlington, Virginia. She teaches class for parents and works on programs with civic, educational and religious groups. She holds degrees from Teachers College, Columbia University. She is also Assistant Manager, Books Unlimited, Arlington, Virginia.

Index

Absence, sibling's awareness of, 45
Adolescents
  communication with, 220, 224–25
  and school, 157–61, 163, 165–66,
    167, 220–21
  See also. Teenagers.
Affection, sought from parents/
    relatives, 9, 118–19, 122
Akerland, Chuck, 187–94, 232–33
Akerland, Trey, 187–94, 233
Alcoholism, 122–23
ALERT, THE (newsletter), 94
Altman, Elaine Kraf, 14–15, 36, 47–48,
    76, 80, 141, 169–70
  See also. Kraf, Michael.
Altman, Martin, 14, 15, 36, 141
American Cancer Society, 241
Amis Compatissants du Canada, Les
  See Compassionate Friends of
    Canada, The
Anger
  at circumstances of death, 45
  at clergy, 54–56
  at God, 28, 55–56, 108
  internalizing of, 166
  at parents, 6, 47–48, 51–53, 95–96
  at psychologist, 49–50
  at sibling, 54, 116, 131–32, 148
  of surviving siblings, 17, 45–56, 108,
    116, 134, 136, 148
Anniversary of death, coping with,
    77–84, 176, 185–86
Anxieties, in teenagers, 165–66, 222
Apology, open letter of, 153–56
Approval, seeking parents, 10
Assurance, surviving siblings' need for,
    4, 109, 110, 180, 199, 208
Attention seeking, following suicide,
    189, 190
Autopsy, 36, 109

Banschick, Leonard, 120

Banschick, Sheren, 120–22
Banschick, Sylvia, 120–21
Bar mitzvah, coping with, 79, 154, 155
Behavioral changes
  in parents, 5, 51, 120, 152
  in surviving siblings, 5, 65, 67, 71,
    98–99, 121, 162, 163, 188–89,
    204–5
Bellucci, Linda, 94–95, 234, 235
Bellucci, Ron, 94
Bereaved Families of Ontario,
    Canada, 239–40
Bernhard, Clay, 87–88
Bernhard, Reed, 87–88
Birthdays, coping with, 79–80, 81, 102,
    153–54, 185
  See also. Holidays.
Birth order, effect on siblings'
    responses, 159
Boden, David, 37–38, 63
Boden, Leslie, 37–38, 63, 231
Boden, Scott, 37–38, 63
Brauer, Kim, 102–4
Brauer, Michael, 102–4
Brauer, Nicky, 103–4
Brauer, Patricia, 103–4
Brauer, Sandra, 103–4
Bridges, Allan, 108

Campbell, Florence, 23–25, 57–59, 81
Campbell, Jesse Ray, 23–25, 57–59
Campbell, Linwood, 57
Campbell, Trevor, 81
Candlelighters, 240–41
Candlelighters Foundation, 240
Capriotti, Barbara, 98–100, 147
Capriotti, Cathy, 98, 99, 147
Capriotti, Debbie, 98–100
Capriotti, Edward, 98–99
Capriotti, Edward Scott, 98
Carrion, Tony, 222–23
Carrion, Wanda, 222–23, 225

Cemetery, 120, 195
  fear of, 102, 124
  memories at, 176
  ride to, 73
  toast at, 133
  visiting, 74, 113, 131, 136, 223, 229
Center for Attitudinal Research,
    241–42
Channing, Diane Randazza, 19–20, 43,
    51–52, 152, 170
  See also. Randazza, Russell.
Christmas, coping with, 77, 80, 81, 82,
    120, 176, 211, 215
  See also. Holidays.
Churilla, Lenny, 177, 182, 184–85
Churilla, Michaela, 177, 186
Classmates
  reactions of, 4, 88, 160-61, 189
  sharing grief with, 16, 85, 196–97
Clergy
  anger at, 54–56
  consolation from, 108, 113, 232
  support of, 55, 232
Clothing, saving articles of, 7
Colburn, Christopher, 164
Colburn, Jeanette, 65–66, 163–68
Cole, Tom, 251
Communication
  with adolescents, 220, 224–25
  importance of, 50–51, 86, 87, 112,
    113, 133, 163, 171, 172, 191, 233
  lack of, 112, 121, 130, 131, 228
  of pain, 10, 53–54, 112, 115, 129,
    155–56, 188, 189, 223–25
  with surviving siblings, 38, 50,
    149–52, 159, 197–99, 208, 231
  verbal and nonverbal, 172
Compassionate Friends, Inc., The,
    53, 61, 62, 74, 75, 83, 85, 100,
    110, 128, 129, 140, 149, 161, 191,
    196, 197, 228, 233, 242–47
  U.S.A. chapter locations, 243–47
Compassionate Friends of Canada, The
    (Les Amis Compatissants du
    Canada), Canadian chapter
    leaders & contacts, 247–49
Conroy, Christopher, 122–24
Conroy, Kevin, 122–24
Consolation
  from clergy, 108, 113, 232
  from God, 23
  parents' inability to give, 1, 115, 119
Counseling, 127, 183, 236–38
Co-workers, 169–74
  apprehension about, 172
  fear of reactions from, 172–74
  support from, 169–70
Crying
  cautioned against, 46, 138–39, 166
  children's reaction to, 31, 33, 117,
    120, 140–43
  difficulty in, 181
  reasons for, 210

support for, 109
  of surviving siblings, 39, 44, 69, 73,
    94, 95, 111, 113, 117, 150, 227
Cullen, Father, 28, 29

Davidson, Dr. Glen, 167
Davis, Mary Johnston, 134
Death
  anger at circumstances, 45
  anniversary of, 77–84, 176, 185–86
  anxieties about cause of, 2, 4, 61,
    94–95, 123
  appearance of dead sibling, 33, 34,
    39, 108, 112, 130
  of children before parents, 2–3
  children's concept of, 136, 158, 165
  coping with, 88–93
  euphoria as reaction to, 190
  fear of, 2, 7, 104
  on learning of, 4–30
  life after, 69, 76, 212
  neonatal, 164
  nonacceptance of, 24
  as part of life, 253
  physical reaction to, 164, 194, 218
  physical shock of, 36
  premonitions of, 25–26, 109
  questions about, 159
  self-blame at, 94–95, 124
  shock of, 15–18, 29, 31–36, 40–41
  See also. Denial.
"Death: A Fact of Life" (course), 228
Denial, 31–44, 46, 72, 78, 108, 253
  and belief in mistake, 33–34
  fantasies, 3, 40–41
  and rituals, 3, 133–34
  of seriousness of illness, 25, 58
  and suicide, 188
  and surviving siblings, 3, 31–36, 115
Depression, 67, 119, 147, 174, 223, 230
  and suicide, 41–43, 130, 190, 199,
    220
"Did You Hear About Those Two Dumb
    Kids?" (Jakey Allayne Haimes),
    178
Divorce, 136
  following child's death, 139, 141,
    148–50
Dodge, Nancy, 253
Dohrenwend, David, 209–15
Dreams, traumatic events viewed as,
    40–41, 130
Drewes, Athena, 158–60, 238
Drugs, 70, 123–24, 132, 219

Easter Sunday, hopes for, 80
Eisen, Jonathan, 229–30
Eisen, Karen Schlesier, 32–33, 53–54,
    59–60, 138–41, 171, 228–30
Encouragement, messages of, 226–35
Eulogizing of dead child, 4, 53–56,
    153–56, 178–86
Euphoria, as reaction to death, 190

Famiano, Mike, 71–76
Famiano, Wendy, 71-76
Families, 217
  grief of, 183–84
  members of, 138–56, 175–86
  and suicide, 239
Fear
  of being left alone, 5, 85, 158
  of causing sibling's death, 5, 94–95, 99
  of cemetery, 102, 124
  of God, 99
  of leaving home, 157
  of own death, 2
  of parent's death, 2, 7, 104
Friends, need for, 48, 88, 147
Frogel, Alan David, 41–42, 52, 68
  See also. Kaner, Karen.
Funeral, 40, 54, 120, 203–4
  appearance at, 33, 215
  grief after, 111
  insensitivity of people at, 53
  open-casket viewing, 39, 76
  parents at, 142–43, 144, 159
  reactions at, 108
  teenagers at, 219
  See also. Cemetery.
Funeral directors, 33, 39
Funeral home, thoughts at, 34

Gardner, Carolyn, 210, 213–14
Gardner, Cathy, 213–14
Gardner, Jim, 213–14
Gardner, Linda, 213–14, 215
Gardner, Lisa, 213–14
Gardner, Lynn, 9, 209–15
Gardner, Mark, 213–14
Gardner, Michael, 213–14
God, 213, 214
  anger at, 28, 55–56, 108
  consolation from, 23
  fear of, 99
  justifying death, 55, 56
  mixed feelings about, 55–56
  as not responsible for death, 179
Goldstein, Jay, 25, 60–62, 79, 86, 228
Goldstein, Joshua, 61, 79, 85–87
Goldstein, Philip, 25, 61, 79, 85–86
Grandparents, 182–83
Grief
  counseling for, 136–38
  of families, 183–84
  after funeral, 111
  intensity of, 128–29
  normal reactions to, 113, 218
  of parents, 31–32, 73
  physical symptoms of, 66–71, 73–76, 164, 218–20
  selfish reaction of, 145–57
  sharing of, 16, 85, 126, 196–97, 219
  surviving with, 134
  symptoms of, 65–76
  at workplace, 173–74

Grieving process, 44, 110, 113–14
  length of, 86, 173–74
  surviving siblings included in, 92–93, 149, 159–60
  understanding of, 75–76
Griffith, Annie, 102
Griffith, Johana, 101–2
Griffith, Katharine, 101–2
Griffith, Maria, 101–2
Griffith, Robby, 101–2
Grigsby, Jonathan, 178
Griswold, Ashley, 97
Griswold, Gordon, 95
Griswold, Gregory, 95–98
Griswold, Jessica, 95–98
Griswold, Teri, 95–98
Guilt
  of parents, 53, 62, 199
  of surviving siblings, 2, 4, 57–64, 95, 113–14, 121, 123, 124, 130, 159, 175, 190–91, 222, 234
  unconscious, 166

Haimes, Dr. Allen, 63–64, 179, 182–84
Haimes, Bobby, 180–81
Haimes, Ian, 175, 176, 180
Haimes, Jakey Allayne, 154, 175–78
Haimes, Joshua, 175, 176, 178–80
Haimes, Judith, 63–64, 153–56, 177–86, 237
Haimes, Lorrie, 177, 181–82, 183–86
Haimes, Michael, 153–56, 175–86
  See also. Churilla, Lenny; Churilla, Michaela.
Halloween, coping with, 80
Heitner, Allison, 11–14, 34–36, 49–50, 59, 68–71, 145–47, 230–31
Heitner, Leslie, 11–14, 34–36, 49, 59, 69–71, 145–47, 230–31
Holidays, 77–84, 104, 120
  discussion of with surviving children, 82, 199–200, 211–13
  parental reminders during, 7–8, 185–86, 197
  and physical illness, 65
  refusal to acknowledge, 5
Home life, changes in, 115, 118, 131, 147, 198–99
Hope, mesages of, 226–35

Identity, loss of, 116
Illness, catastrophic, 241
Insensitivity of others, 12, 48–49
  at funeral, 53
Isolation, desire for, 49–50

Jampolsky, Dr. Gerald, 241
Jordan, Debbie, 132–34
Jordan, Jim, 132–34
Jordan, Jimmy, 134
Jordan, Jo Lynn, 132
Jordan, Rosemary (pseudonym), 134
Jordan, Van, 132–34

Journal of the American Medical Association, The, 89–93

Kaner, Karen, 41–43, 52, 68–69
    See also. Frogel, Alan David.
Keats, Carolyn, 18–19, 39, 145, 171
Keats, Susan, 18–19, 38–39, 48, 79,
    144–45, 171, 227
Kessler, Lori, 135
Kessler, Robyn, 135
Kessler, Scott, 135–37
Kessler, Vivian, 238
Kraf, Michael, 14–15, 36, 47–48, 76,
    79–80, 141, 169–70
Kreindler, Mitchell, 26–27, 28, 40,
    62–63
Kreindler, Simon, 26–28, 40, 62, 68
Kübler-Ross, Elisabeth, 76

Labor Day, coping with, 79
Lamb, Earline, 111–14
Lamb, Melvin, 113–14
Lamb, Sister Jane Marie, 66, 111–14,
    252–53
LeShan, Dr. Lawrence, 50–51
Levy, Marlene, 114–17, 147–48
Levy, Sandra, 114–15, 147
Life after death, 69, 76, 212
Lightner, Candy, 250
Lippmann, Charles, 45–47, 231–32
Lippmann, Froma, 45–47, 231–32, 239
Lippmann, John, 47
Living Is for Today (L.I.F.T.), 249–50

McKendree, Diana, 249–50
Malawski, Abe, 195–200
Malawski, Harvey, 195–98
Malawski, Judy, 197, 200
Malawski, Steven, 195–200
March, Corey, 88–93
March, Dr. Daniel M.S., 88–93
March, Elisabeth Herriott, 89–93
    See also. Scrimshaw, Dr. Susan C.M.
Meagher, Dr. David, 172
Memento, saving, 7, 83
Memories
    at cemetery, 176
    shared with parents, 8, 76, 100, 181,
        196, 197
Moran, Jennifer, 109
Moran, Molly, 109–10
Moran, Nadine, 108–10
Moran, Timothy, 108–10
Mothers Against Drunk Drivers
    (M.A.D.D.), 227, 250
Mother's Day, coping with, 77

"Naming A Surviving Sibling's Child"
    (Allen/Judith Haimes), 182–84
Neonatal death, 164
Niemela, Ann Witty, 201–8
Niemela, Brian, 201–4, 208

Niemela, Darren, 201–8
Niemela, Rusty, 201–4, 208
Niemela, Tamara Lynn, 203

O'Dell, Gwen, 14, 15, 36, 80
Okst, Barbara, 228
Olssen, Dr., 207, 208
Open Letter of Apology (Judith
    Haimes), 153–56
Organizations (alphabetical listing),
    239–55
Overprotection, by parents, 3–4, 6, 83,
    126, 135, 143–44, 149

Pain
    cessation of, 8–9, 46, 63, 64, 238
    communication of, 10, 53–54, 112,
        115, 129, 155–56, 188, 189,
        223–25
    not wanting to lose, 63
    of parents, 5, 111, 129, 191
    sharing others', 46, 54, 55, 193
    varying expressions of, 53, 150, 181
Panic, 71–76
Parents
    advice to, 157, 158–60
    affection sought from, 9, 118–19, 122
    alcoholism of, 122–23
    anger at, 6, 47–48, 51–53, 95–96
    arguments with, 51–52
    behavioral changes in, 5, 51, 120,
        152
    child's assumption of role of, 5–6,
        52, 138, 141, 175
    crying children's reaction to, 31, 140
    death of children before, 2–3
    deterioration of, 199
    difficulties faced by, 1, 101
    divorce following child's death, 139,
        141, 148–50
    eulogizing of lost child, 4, 153–56,
        182–84
    function of, 200
    at funeral, 142–43, 144, 159
    grief of, 31–32, 73
    guilt of, 53, 62, 199
    and holidays, 7–8, 185–86, 197
    inability to talk to, 112, 121, 131, 228
    memories shared with, 8, 100, 181,
        196, 197
    needs of, 40, 100, 138–39
    overprotection by, 3–4, 6, 83, 126,
        135, 143–44, 149
    overreactions of, 204
    physical illness of, 8
    premonition of death by, 25–26
    protection of, 112, 140–41, 166, 198
    questions to, 3, 98, 159
    reminders of dead child, 8
Parents of Murdered Children
    (POMC), 251
Peterson, Art, 127–29

Peterson, Elizabeth, 127
Peterson, Ronnie, 128, 129–30
Peterson, Tony, 127
Petrou, Karim Said, 177–78
Pfister, Billy, 17–18, 33–34, 78–79, 143,
    162, 170, 232
Pfister, John, 17–18, 162, 170
Pflaumbaum, Erik, 28, 56, 67
Pflaumbaum, Jeffrey, 56
Pflaumbaum, Madeleine Toomey,
    28–30, 39–40, 55–56, 66–68,
    80, 141–42, 226–27
Physical illness
    on holidays, 65
    of parents, 8
    of surviving siblings, 8, 65, 66, 68,
        74, 218
Physical reaction, to death, 164, 194,
    218
Professionalism, at workplace, 170,
    173–74
Psychological testing, 168
Psychologists, 42
    anger at, 49–50
    consultations with, 50–51, 130,
        204–7, 236–37
    need for, 115–17
    shopping around for, 50–51
Purpura, Angela, 148–50
Purpura, Cara, 149–50
Purpura, Cassandra, 149–50
Pustay, Andrew, 125–27
Pustay, George, 125–26
Pustay, Jessica, 126
Pustay, Katie, 126–27
Pustay, Monica, 126–27
Pustay, Suzanne, 126–27

Radtke, Carl, 150
    See also. Teague, Marie.
Randazza, Charles, 152
Randazza, Diane, See. Channing,
    Diane.
Randazza, Russell, 19–20, 43, 51–52,
    152, 170
Recovering from the Loss of a Child
    (Allen and Judith Haimes),
    63–64
Religion, struggle with, 119–20
Resentment, See. Anger.
Rituals, 3, 111, 133–34
Rosberger, Dr. Anne, 174
Rothman, Jerry, 251
Rothman-Cole Center for Sibling Loss,
    251–52
Ruiz, Nelson, 223–25
Ruiz, Lenny, 223–24

Saulisberry, Chuck, 22, 145
Saulisberry, Dan, 20–23, 45, 79, 145,
    232

Saulisberry, Jo, 21–23, 145
Saulisberry, Kathy, 22, 79, 145
Saulisberry, Tracy, 20–23, 45, 145
Schlesier, Billy, 32–33, 54, 60, 138, 139,
    229–30
    See also. Eisen, Karen Schlesier.
School, 16, 70, 157–68
    adolescents at, 157–61, 163, 165–66,
        167, 220–21
    advice to parents, 157, 158–60
    classmates at, 4, 16, 85, 88, 160–61,
        189, 196–97
    disruptive behavior at, 96, 121,
        206–8
    effect of death on work, 4, 62–63,
        162–63, 166–67
    insensitive comments at, 160–61
    leaving, 119
    as solution, 189–90
    students at risk, 216–17
    support sought from teachers, 157
Schwaegler, Gregory, 104–6
Schwaegler, Mary Rose, 104–5
Schwaegler, Steve, 104
Schwaegler, Susan, 104–6
Scrimshaw, Dr. Susan C.M., 88–93
SHARE (Sources of Help in Airing and
    Resolving Experiences), 105,
    114, 164, 252–54
Shaw, Holly, 216–25
Shields, Eloise, 157–58
SIDS (Sudden Infant Death Syndrome)
    groups, 135–37, 147, 164, 254
Spector, Ellen, 19, 80–81, 143–44,
    233–34
Spector, Philip, 19
Spiotto, Dorothy, 117–20
Spiotto, Helma, 117
Spiotto, Richard, 117–20
Students at risk, 216–17
Sudden Infant Death Syndrome
    Foundation, 94, 135
Suicide, 41–43, 127–33, 187–94, 233
    and anger at parents, 52
    attempts at, 220
    attention seeking after, 189, 190
    and denial, 188
    and families, 239
    proving existence by, 199
    thoughts of, 69–70, 75, 205
Sundland, Christopher, 15–17, 43–44,
    81–82, 151
Sundland, Joe, 15–16, 43–44, 81–84
Sundland, Richard, 15–17, 43–44,
    81–83
Sundland, Sherry, 15–17, 43–44,
    81–84, 151–52
Sundland, Tom, 15–16, 43–44, 81–82,
    151
Surviving siblings
    affection sought from parents/
        relatives, 9, 118–19, 122

Surviving siblings *(cont.)*
  anger of, 17, 45–56, 108, 116, 134, 136, 148
  assumption of parent's role by, 5–6, 52, 138, 141, 175
  assurance needed by, 4, 109, 110, 180, 199, 208
  behavioral changes in, 5, 65, 67, 71, 98–99, 121, 162, 163, 188–89, 204–5
  communication with, 38, 50, 149–52, 159, 197–99, 208, 231
  and denial, 3, 31–36, 115
  expectations of, 46–47, 86–87
  fears of, 2, 5, 7, 85, 94–95, 99, 102, 104, 124, 157, 158
  guilt of, 2, 4, 57–64, 95, 113–14, 121, 123, 124, 130, 159, 175, 190–91, 222, 234
  inability to mention name, 130, 197–99
  inadequacy feelings of, 180
  included in grieving process, 92–93, 149, 159–60
  lack of understanding of, 100–101
  memories shared with parents, 8, 76, 100, 181, 196, 197
  mental symptoms of, 66–67, 70
  naming child of, 182–84
  overprotection of, 3–4, 6, 83, 126, 135, 143–44, 149
  pain of, 8–9, 10, 53–55
  as parental afterthought, 47, 53
  and parental reminders of dead child, 8
  physical illness of, 8, 65, 66, 68, 74, 218
  problems/needs of, 4, 8, 10, 86, 158, 219
  reaction to parent behavior changes, 4–5, 52
  reaction to parents' grief, 31–32, 73
  retention of sibling's possessions, 7, 83
  school problems of, 4, 96, 119, 121, 190, 206–8
  secret thoughts of dead sibling, 9–10, 136
  and self-blame, at death, 94–95, 124
  sibling rivalry, 10, 116–17, 159
  statistics on, 2–3
Survivors of Suicide (S.O.S.), 233, 254–55

Tart, Cathy, 40, 80, 106–8
Tart, Cindy, 40–41, 48–49, 80, 106–7, 142–43, 161–62
Tart, Dennis, 40–41, 49, 80, 106–8, 142–43, 161–62
Teachers, 4
  advice to, 165–67

handling grieving siblings, 167
inspiration from, 232–33
special needs, 207–8
support sought from, 157
sympathy shown by, 85, 87–88, 220–21
Teague, Brian, 150–51
Teague, Don, 151
Teague, Lenny, 25–26, 150
Teague, Marie, 25–26, 150–51
Teague, Mike, 150–51
Teenagers
  anxieties in, 165–66, 222
  at funeral, 219
  phases of, 218
  problems faced by, 217
  at risk, 216–217
  view of death/grief, 177–78
  See also. Adolescents.
Temes, Dr. Roberts, 160, 162–63, 165
THANATOS (article), 182–84
Thanksgiving, coping with, 78, 80–81, 211, 213
  See also. Holidays.
Therapists, *See.* Psychologists.
Thumpy's Story, 253
T.I.G.E.R.S. (Teens In Grief: Educate, Rebuild, Support), 255
Time, healing power of, 226, 227, 228
Toomey, Kathleen, 28–30, 39, 55–56, 66–67, 80, 142
Toomey, Larry, 29–30, 39–40, 56, 67
Trip/vacation, helpfulness of, 44
Tucker, Betty, 26–28, 40, 54–55, 62–63, 68, 78, 231
  See also. Kreindler, Mitchell; Kreindler, Simon.
Tucker, Hank, 78
Tucker, Lenny, 27
Tucker, Michael, 78
Tucker, Tanya, 78

Waxstein, Dr., 206, 207, 208
What Is a Psychologist?, 116
"What We Can Teach the World Around Us" (workshop), 75
Wilson, Mark, 130–32
Wilson, Roberta, 130–32
Workplace, 169–74
  apprehension about return to, 172–74
  burying oneself in, 73–74
  fear of co-worker's reactions, 172–74
  grief at, 173–74
  healing at, 173–74
  overreactions at, 173
  physical symptoms at, 173
  problems at, 169, 173
  professionalism at, 170, 173–74
  support from co-workers at, 169–70
Workshops, need for, 167–68

EMMAUS PUBLIC LIBRARY
EMMAUS, PA. 18049